KB054192

직독직해로 읽는

피노키오

The Adventures of Pinocchio

직독직해로 읽는

피노키오

The Adventures of Pinocchio

개정판 2쇄 발행 2020년 12월 20일
초판 1쇄 발행   2010년 10월 20일

원작	카를로 콜로디		
역주	더 콜링(김정희, 박윤수, 조문경)		
디자인	DX		
일러스트	정은수		
발행인	조경아		
발행처	랭귀지북스		
주소	서울시 마포구 포은로2나길 31 벨라비스타 208호		
전화	02.406.0047	**팩스**	02.406.0042
이메일	languagebooks@hanmail.net		
MP3 다운로드	blog.naver.com/languagebook		
등록번호	101-90-85278	**등록일자**	2008년 7월 10일
ISBN	979-11-5635-031-6 (13740)		
가격	12,000원		

ⓒ LanguageBooks 2010

이 도서의 국립중앙도서관 출판예정도서목록(CIP)은 서지정보유통지원시스템 홈페이지(http://seoji.nl.go.kr)와
국가자료공동목록시스템(http://www.nl.go.kr/kolisnet)에서 이용하실 수 있습니다. (CIP제어번호 : CIP2015029022)

직독직해로 읽는

피노키오
The Adventures of Pinocchio

카를로 콜로디 원작
더 콜링 역주

Language Books

머리말

"어렸을 때 누구나 갖고 있던 세계명작 한 질.
그리고 TV에서 하던 세계명작 만화에 대한 추억이 있습니다."

"친숙한 이야기를 영어 원문으로 읽어 봐야겠다고 마음먹고 샀던 원서들은
이제 애물단지가 되어 버렸습니다."

"재미있는 세계명작 하나 읽어 보려고 따져 보는 어려운 영문법,
모르는 단어 찾느라 이리저리 뒤져 봐야 하는 사전,
몇 장 넘겨 보기도 전에 지칩니다."

　영어 독해력을 기르려면 술술 읽어가며 내용을 파악하는 것이 중요합니다. 현재 수능 시험에도 대세인 '직독직해' 스타일을 접목시킨 〈직독직해로 읽는 세계명작 시리즈〉는 세계명작을 영어 원작으로 쉽게 읽어갈 수 있도록 안내해 드릴 것입니다.

　'직독직해' 스타일로 읽다 보면, 영문법을 들먹이며 따질 필요가 없으니 쉽고, 끊어 읽다 보니 독해 속도도 빨라집니다. 이 습관이 들여지면 어떤 글을 만나도 두렵지 않을 것입니다.

　명작의 재미를 즐기며 영어 독해력을 키우는 두 마리의 토끼를 잡으세요!

　　〈직독직해로 읽는 세계명작 시리즈〉 영원한 파트너 윤수와 든든한 번역자 문경 씨, 빠듯한 스케줄임에도 불구하고 제시간에 마무리해 준 일러스트레이터 은수 씨, 늘 여러모로 도닥여 주시는 디자인 DX, 이 책이 출판될 수 있도록 늘 든든하게 지원해 주시는 랭귀지북스에 감사의 마음을 전합니다.

　　마지막으로 내 삶의 소망되시는 하나님께 영광을 올려 드립니다.

더 콜링 김정희

목차

How it happened / that Mastro Cherry, carpenter, / found
어쩌다 일어났을까   목수인 체리 노인이,   나무 토막

a piece of wood / that wept and laughed / like a child.
하나를 발견한 일이   울기도 하고 웃기도 하는   어린 아이처럼.

Centuries ago / there lived ——
옛날 옛적에   살았어요 —

"A king!" / my little readers will say / immediately. No,
"왕이!"   라고 여러분들은 말하겠지요   곧바로.   아니에요,

children, / you are mistaken. Once upon a time / there
어린이 여러분,   틀렸답니다.   옛날 옛적에

was a piece of wood. It was not / an expensive piece of
나무 토막 하나가 있었어요.   그것은 아니었다   값비싼 나무는.

wood. Far from it. Just a common block of firewood, /
            오히려 그 반대였다.   단지 땔감용의 흔한 조각이었다,

one of those thick, solid logs / that are put on the fire / in
두껍고 튼튼한 목재들 중 하나로,   불을 붙일 때 쓰는

winter / to make cold rooms / cozy and warm.
겨울에   추운 방을 만들기 위해   편하고 따뜻하게.

I do not know / how this really happened, / yet the fact
잘 모른다   어떻게 이런 일이 정말로 일어났는지,   하지만 사실이다

remains / that one fine day / this piece of wood / found
            어느 화창한 날   이 나무 토막이   있었다는 것은

itself / in the shop of an old carpenter. His real name
            늙은 목수의 가게 안에.   그의 진짜 이름은 안토니오였지만,

was Mastro Antonio, / but everyone called him / Mastro
                        모두들 그를 불렀다   '체리 노인'이라고,

Cherry, / for the tip of his nose / was so round / and red
                왜냐하면 그의 코 끝이   아주 동그랗고   빨갛고 반질거려서

and shiny / that it looked like a ripe cherry.
                잘 익은 체리처럼 보였기 때문에.

---

far from it 전혀 (그렇지 않다)[오히려 그 반대이다] | firewood 장작 | cozy 편안한 | carpenter 목수 | Mastro
거장, 노인 | | shiny 빛나는, 반짝거리는 | ripe 익은, 숙성한

As soon as he saw / that piece of wood, / Mastro Cherry
보자 마자　　　　그 나무 토막을,　　　　체리 노인은 가득찼다

was filled / with joy.
기쁨으로.

Rubbing his hands together / happily, / he mumbled half
두 손을 비비며　　　　행복하게,　　그는 중얼거리듯 말했다:
to himself:

"This has come / in the nick of time. I shall use it / to
"이게 굴러 들어왔네　　때마침.　　　　사용해야겠군

make the leg of a table."
탁자 다리를 만드는데."

He grasped the hatchet / quickly / to peel off the bark /
그는 손도끼를 잡았다　　재빨리　　나무 껍질을 벗기고

and shape the wood.
나무를 다듬으려고.

But / as he was about to give it / the first blow, / he stood
하지만　막 하려는 순간　　　　　첫 도끼질을,　　　노인은 멈추었다

still / with arm uplifted, / for he had heard / a wee, little
팔을 공중에 든 채로,　　들었기 때문에　　아주 작고,

voice say / in a beseeching tone:
약한 목소리를　애원조로 말하는:

"Please be careful! Do not hit me / so hard!"
"제발 조심해 주세요!　　때리지 말아주세요　너무 세게!"

What a look of surprise / shone on Mastro Cherry's
놀라움이 얼마나 컸을까요　　　　체리 노인의 얼굴에 나타난!

face! His funny face became / still funnier.
노인의 재미있게 생긴 얼굴은 변했다　　더욱 웃기게.

rub 문지르다, 비비다 | mumble to oneself 중얼[웅얼]거리(듯 말하)다 | in the nick of time 아슬아슬하게
때를 맞춰 | grasp 꽉 잡다, 움켜잡다 | hatchet (한 손으로 잡을 수 있는 작은) 손도끼 | peel off 벗겨지다 | bark
나무껍질 | blow 세게 때림, 강타 | uplifted 위로 올려진 | wee (크기가) 아주 작은 | beseeching 눈빛·어조 등이
애원조의, 애원하는 듯

He turned frightened eyes / about the room / to find out /
그는 놀란 눈으로 두리번거렸다   방 안을   알아내기 위해

where that wee, little voice / had come from / and he saw
어디에서 그 작고, 약한 목소리가   오는 건지   그런데 아무도 보이지

no one! He looked under the bench —— / no one! He peeped
않았다!   작업대 아래를 살펴봤지만 —   아무도 없었다! 벽장 안을 기웃

inside the closet —— / no one! He searched among the
거렸지만 —   아무도 없었다! 대팻밥 속을 찾아보았지만 —

shavings —— / no one! He opened the door / to look up and
아무도 없었다! 문을 열어   거리를 위 아래로 살펴보

down the street —— / and still no one!
았지만 —   여전히 아무도 없었다!

"Oh, I see!" / he then said, / laughing and scratching his
"오호, 아무렴!"   그는 말했다,   웃으며 가발을 긁적이면서.

Wig. "It can easily be seen / that I only thought / I heard
"틀림없이   내가 착각한 것 뿐이야   작은 목소리를

the tiny voice / say the words! Well, well —— / to work once
들었다고   말하는!   자, 자 —   다시 일하자고."

more."

He struck a most solemn blow / upon the piece of wood.
노인은 아주 강한 타격을 가했다   나무 토막 위에.

"Oh, oh! You hurt!" / cried the same / far-away little voice.
"아, 아야!   아프잖아요!"   똑같은 소리가 들렸다   저 멀리 어디선가 작은 목소리가.

Mastro Cherry grew dumb, / his eyes popped out of his
체리 노인은 말문이 막혔다,   그의 눈은 얼굴에서 튀어나올 듯했고,

head, / his mouth opened wide, / and his tongue hung down
입을 크게 벌린 채,   혀는 늘어졌다

/ on his chin.
턱까지.

---

bench (=workbench, a carpenter's bench) 목수의 작업대 | peep 훔쳐보다, 살짝 보다 | shavings (대패 등으로)
깎아 낸 부스러기, 대팻밥 | wig 가발 | solemn 엄숙한 | dumb 벙어리의, 말을 못 하는 | pop 눈이 휘둥그레지다 |
chin 턱 | regain 되찾다 | tremble 몸을 떨다 | stutter 말을 더듬다 | might it be that …일지도 모른다 | weep
울다, 눈물을 흘리다 | fix 손보다, 혼내 주다 | grab 붙잡다 | unmercifully 무자비하게, 잔인하게 | moan 신음하다 |
bravely 용감하게 | ruffling (up) (반반한 표면을) 헝클다

As soon as he regained / the use of his senses, / he said, /
겨우 가다듬고 나서　　　　정신을,　　　　　그는 말했다,

trembling and stuttering from fright:
공포로 몸을 떨고 말을 더듬으며:

"Where did that voice come from, / when there is no one
"어디에서 그 목소리가 들린 거지,　　　여기는 아무도 없는데?

around? Might it be / that this piece of wood has learned to
아마도 했을까　　이 나무 토막이 배우기라도

/ weep and cry / like a child? I can hardly believe it. Here it
울고 투정부리는 걸　어린 아이처럼?　믿을 수 없군.　　　어디 보자

is/ —— a piece of common firewood, / good only to burn / in
— 평범한 땔감인데,　　　　　잘 탈 것 같은

the stove, / the same as any other. Yet / —— might someone
난로에서,　다른 것과 마찬가지로.　　그런데　— 누가 숨어 있기라도 한 걸까

be hidden / in it? If so, / the worse for him. I'll fix him!"
그 안에? 그렇다면,　더 나쁜 일이지.　　내가 손 좀 봐 주겠어!"

With these words, / he grabbed the log / with both hands /
이렇게 말하면서,　　　그는 나무 토막을 집어　두 손으로

and started to knock it about / unmercifully. He threw it /
후려치기 시작했다　　　　　인정사정 없이.　그는 그걸 던졌다

to the floor, / against the walls of the room, / and even up to
바닥에,　벽에,　　　　　그리고 천장에까지.

the ceiling.

He listened for the tiny voice / to moan and cry. He waited
노인은 작은 목소리가 들리는지 귀를 기울였다　신음하고 울고 있는지.　2분을 기다렸지만

two minutes / —— nothing; / five minutes / —— nothing; / ten
— 아무 소리도 들리지 않았다; 5분이 흘러도　— 조용했다;

minutes / —— nothing.
10분이 지났지만　— 아무 소리도 없었다.

"Oh, I see," / he said, / trying bravely to laugh / and ruffling
"그럼, 그렇지,"　그는 말했다,　호탕하게 웃으려 애쓰며

up his wig / with his hand. "It can easily be seen / I only
가발을 헝클면서　손으로.　　　"틀림없군

imagined / I heard the tiny voice! Well, well —— / to work
내가 상상한 것이　작은 목소리를 들었다고!　자, 자 —

once more!"
다시 일하자고!"

The poor fellow was scared / half to death, / so he tried to
가여운 노인은 겁에 질려   거의 죽을 것 같았기에,   애써 불렀다

sing / a gay song / in order to gain courage.
즐거운 노래를   용기를 내려고.

He set aside the hatchet / and picked up the plane / to make
손도끼를 옆에 내려 놓고   대패를 집어   나무를 다듬으

the wood / smooth and even, / but as he drew it / to and fro,
려고 했다   부드럽고 평평하게,   그러나 대패질을 하자   앞뒤로,

/ he heard the same tiny voice.
또 다시 작은 목소리가 들렸다.

This time / it giggled / as it spoke:
이번에는   낄낄대며   말했다:

"Stop it! Oh, stop it! Ha, ha, ha! You tickle my stomach."
"그만하세요! 앗, 그만!   하,하,하!   배가 간지러워요."

This time / poor Mastro Cherry fell / as if shot. When he
이번에는   가여운 체리 노인은 쓰러졌다   마치 번개라도 맞은 것처럼.

opened his eyes, / he found himself / sitting on the floor.
눈을 떴을 때,   그는 발견했다   마루바닥에 앉아 있는 자신을.

His face had changed; / fright had turned / even the tip of
그의 얼굴은 변해버렸다;   공포로 인해 바뀌었다   코 끝마저

his nose / from red to deepest purple.
빨간색에서 진한 보라색으로.

Key Expression

as soon as ~ : ~ 하자 마자

as soon as는 '~하자마자'의 뜻으로 쓰이는 접속사입니다. as soon as는 the moment, the instant로 바꾸어 쓸 수 있으며 on~ing의 동명사 구문도 같은 의미를 가지고 있어요.

특히 유의할점은 as soon as와 같은 시간의 접속사가 쓰이는 부사절 구문은 현재시제가 미래시제를 대신한다는 것입니다. 단, 과거를 나타낼 때는 신경 쓰지 않아도 됩니다.

ex) As soon as he saw that piece of wood, Mastro Cherry was filled with joy.
(=on seeing that piece of wood, ~)
나무토막을 보자마자, 체리 노인의 마음은 기쁨으로 가득 찼다.

---

fellow (남자나 소년을 가리켜) 녀석[친구] | gay 명랑한, 즐거운 | plane 대패 | to and fro 앞뒤로 | giggle 피식
웃다, 킥킥거리다 | tickle (장난을 치느라고 손가락으로) 간지럼을 태우다[간지럽히다] | fright (섬뜩하게) 놀람, 두려움

2

Mastro Cherry gives / the piece of wood / to his friend
체리 노인은 준다   그 나무 토막을   그의 친구 제페토에게.

Geppetto, / who takes it / to make himself a Marionette /
그는 그것을 가지고   꼭두각시를 만들었다

that will dance, fence, / and turn somersaults.
춤을 추고, 칼 싸움도 하고,   공중곡예도 할 수 있는.

In that very instant, / a loud knock sounded / on the door.
바로 그 순간,   큰 노크 소리가 들렸다   문에서.

"Come in," / said the carpenter, / not having an atom of
"들어오세요,"   목수가 말했다,   힘조차 남지 않은 채로

strength left / with which to stand up.
                똑바로 일어설.

At the words, / the door opened / and a dapper little old
말이 끝나자 마자,   문이 열리고   말쑥한 작은 노인이

man / came in.
        들어왔다.

His name was Geppetto, / but / to the boys of the
그의 이름은 제페토였다,   하지만   이웃 아이들에게

neighborhood / he was Polendina,*(Cornmeal mush) / on
                그는 '폴랜디나'*(옥수수 스프)라고 불리었다

account of the wig / he always wore / which was just the
가발 때문에   항상 쓰고 다니는   노란 옥수수 색깔과 똑같은.

color of yellow corn.

Geppetto had a very bad temper. Woe to the one / who
제페토는 성질이 고약했다.   재앙이 있으리

called him Polendina! He became as wild / as a beast / and
그를 폴랜디나라고 부르는!   그는 괴팍해져서   짐승처럼

no one could soothe him.
아무도 그를 달랠 수 없었다.

marionette (팔·다리·머리에 줄을 매달아 움직이는) 인형, 꼭두각시 | fence 펜싱(fencing)을 하다 | somersaults
공중제비 | atom 원자 | dapper 남자가 (키가 작고) 말쑥한 | cornmeal 옥수수 가루 | mush 곤죽 (같은 덩어리·반죽)
(美) 옥수수 죽 | temper (걸핏하면 화를 내는) 성질[성미] | woe (be) to…! …에게 재난이 있으라!, 화가 미칠진저! |
soothe 달래다, 진정시키다

"Good day, Mastro Antonio," / said Geppetto. "What are
"안녕, 안토니오," 제페토가 말했다.

you doing / on the floor?"
"뭐하고 있나 바닥에서?"

"I am teaching / the ants / their A B C's."
"가르치는 중이야 개미들에게 글씨를."

"Good luck to you!"
"잘해 보시게!"

"What brought you here, / friend Geppetto?"
"여긴 어떻게 왔는가, 제페토?"

"My legs. And it may flatter / you to know, / Mastro
"두 다리로 왔지. 그런데 실은 자네에게, 안토니오,

Antonio, / that I have come to you / to beg for a favor."
자네한테 온 거라네 부탁이 있어서."

"Here I am, / at your service," / answered the carpenter, /
"내가 여기 있으니, 마음대로 말해 보게." 목수가 답했다,

raising himself on to his knees.
무릎을 짚고 일어서며.

"This morning / a fine idea came to me."
"오늘 아침에 좋은 아이디어가 떠올랐어."

"Let's hear it."
"한 번 들어보세."

"I thought of / making myself / a beautiful wooden
"생각했네 만들어 볼까 하고 멋진 나무 꼭두각시를.

Marionette. It must be wonderful, / one that will be able to
진짜 근사할 거야, 춤도 추고, 칼싸움도 할 수 있는

dance, fence, / and turn somersaults. With it / I intend to
놈이면, 공중곡예도 할 수 있는. 그 꼭두각시를 데리고

go around the world, / to earn my crust of bread / and cup
세계를 돌아다닐 계획이야, 밥벌이도 하고 와인도 마실 수

of wine. What do you think of it?"
있고. 어떻게 생각하나?"

"Bravo, Polendina!" / cried the same tiny voice / which
"멋진데, 폴렌디나!" 아까 그 작은 목소리가 외쳤다 들려오는

came from / no one knew where.
아무도 모르는 곳에서.

On hearing himself called Polendina, / Mastro Geppetto
자신을 폴렌디나라고 부르는 걸 듣는 순간,   제페토 노인은 잘 익은 고추처럼

turned the color of a red pepper / and, / facing the
빨갛게 변했다   그리고,   목수를 향해,

carpenter, / said to him angrily:
화를 내며 말했다.

"Why do you insult me?"
"어찌 나를 놀리나?"

"Who is insulting you?"
"누가 놀렸다는 겐가?"

"You called me Polendina."
"자네가 나더러 폴렌디나라고 그랬잖아!"

"I did not."
"난 안 그랬어."

"I suppose / you think I did! Yet I KNOW / it was you."
"그럼   자네는 내가 그랬다 생각하는군! 하지만 내가 알지 그건 자네였어."

"No!"
"아냐!"

"Yes!"
"맞아!"

"No!"
"아냐!"

"Yes!"
"맞아!"

And growing angrier each moment, / they went / from
점점 더 흥분함에 따라,   변해 갔다

words to blows, / and / finally began / to scratch and bite /
말싸움이 몸싸움으로,   그리고   마침내 시작했다   할퀴고 물고

and slap each other.
서로 때리기를.

---

flatter 아첨하다, 알랑거리다 | beg 간청하다 | earn one's crust 밥벌이를 하다 | slap (손바닥으로) 철썩 때리다[치다]
| insult 모욕하다

When the fight was over, / Mastro Antonio had /
싸움이 끝나자,   안토니오 노인은 갖고 있었다

Geppetto's yellow wig / in his hands / and Geppetto found
제페토 노인의 노란 가발을   그의 손에   그리고 제페토는 발견했다

/ the carpenter's curly wig / in his mouth.
목수의 곱슬곱슬한 가발을   그의 입에서.

"Give me back / my wig!" / shouted Mastro Antonio / in a
"돌려주게   내 가발을!"   안토니오 노인이 소리쳤다

surly voice.
흥분한 목소리로.

"You return mine / and we'll be friends."
"내 가발을 주게   그리고 이만 화해하세."

The two little old men, / each with his own wig back / on
두 노인은,   서로 가발을 돌려받아

his own head, / shook hands / and swore to be good friends
각자 머리에 쓰고,   악수를 나눈 후   좋은 친구로 지내자고 맹세했다

/ for the rest of their lives.
남은 여생 동안.

"Well then, / Mastro Geppetto," / said the carpenter, / to
"자, 그러면,   제페토,"   목수가 말했다,   보여

show / he bore him no ill will, "what is it / you want?"
주기 위해 그에게 악의가 없음을,   "무엇인가   자네가 원하는 게?"

"I want / a piece of wood / to make a Marionette. Will you
"필요하네   나무 토막이   꼭두각시를 만들.   하나 줄 수

give it / to me?"
있겠어   내게?"

Mastro Antonio, / very glad indeed, / went immediately
안토니오 노인은,   아주 기뻐하면서,   즉시 달려가

/ to his bench / to get the piece of wood / which had
그의 작업대로   바로 그 나무 토막을 가지러   그를 겁에 질리게 만든

frightened him / so much. But / as he was about to give it
너무나.   그러나 그걸 막 건네 주려는 순간

/ to his friend, / with a violent jerk / it slipped / out of his
친구에게,   거세게 흔들리더니   미끄러져서   그의 손에서 떨어져

hands / and hit against poor Geppetto's thin legs.
불쌍한 제페토의 마른 정강이에 부딪쳤다.

curly 곱슬곱슬한: 동그랗게 말린 | surly 성질 못된, 무례한 | jerk 홱 움직이다(갑자기 날카롭게 움직이거나 무엇을 움직이게 하는 동작을 나타냄)

"Ah! Is this the gentle way, / Mastro Antonio, / in which
"아이쿠! 이게 친절한 방법인가,   안토니오,   친구에게 선물을

you make your gifts? You have made me / almost lame!"
주는?   나를 만들 뻔했네   하마터면 절름발이로!"

"I swear to you / I did not do it!"
"맹세컨대   내가 그런 게 아니야!"

"It was I, / of course!"
"그럼 나였군,   물론!"

"It's the fault / of this piece of wood."
"그건 잘못이야   이 나무 토막의"

"You're right; / but remember / you were the one / to throw
"그래;   하지만 기억해 둬   자네가 바로 그 사람인 걸   그것을 던진

it / at my legs."
    내 다리에."

"I did not throw it!"
"난 던지지 않았어!"

"Liar!"
"거짓말쟁이!"

"Geppetto, / do not insult me / or I shall call you
"제페토,   날 욕하지 말게   안 그러면 자네를 폴렌디나라고 부를 거야!"

Polendina."

"Idiot."
"바보!"

"Polendina!"
"폴렌디나!"

"Donkey!"
"멍청이!"

"Polendina!"
"폴렌디나!"

"Ugly monkey!"
"얼간이!"

"Polendina!"
"폴렌디나!"

lame 절름발이의 | liar 거짓말쟁이 | donkey 당나귀 | rage 격렬한 분노, 격노 | then and there 그 자리에서
바로, 즉석에서 | thrashing 매질, 몽둥이질 | scratch 긁힌[할퀸] 자국[상처], 찰과상 | settle[square]
accounts[an account] with ~와의 거래를 청산하다; ~에게 원한을 풀다 | limp 기운이 없는, 축 처진

On hearing himself / called Polendina / for the third time,
듣는 순간　자신을 폴렌디나라고 부르는 걸　세 번씩이나,

/ Geppetto lost his head / with rage / and threw himself /
제페토는 이성을 잃었다　화를 내며　달려들었다

upon the carpenter. Then and there / they gave each other /
목수에게로.　그 자리에서 바로　그들은 서로에게 주었다

a sound thrashing.
심한 매질을.

After this fight, / Mastro Antonio had / two more scratches
싸움이 끝나자,　안토니오 노인에게는 생겼다　할퀸 자국이 두 개 더

/ on his nose, / and Geppetto had two buttons / missing
코에,　그리고 제페토는 단추 두 개가 없어졌다

from his coat. Thus having settled their accounts, / they
코트에서 떨어져서.　이렇게 싸움이 무승부로 끝나자,　그들은

shook hands / and swore to be good friends / for the rest of
악수를 나누고　좋은 친구로 지내자고 맹세했다　남은 여생 동안.

their lives.

Then Geppetto took / the fine piece of wood, / thanked
그리고 나서 제페토는 가져갔다　나무 토막을,　안토니오 노인에게

Mastro Antonio, / and limped away / toward home.
고맙다는 인사를 하고,　절뚝거리며　집으로.

Key Expression 🎵

as~as… : …만큼 ~한

'as + …(형용사/부사 원급) +as ~'는 '…만큼 ~한'이란 의미입니다. 'A = B'의
이러한 비교 표현을 원급비교 혹은 동등비교라고 부릅니다.
참고로 첫번째 as 앞에 not을 붙여 not as[so] + ~ +as …가 되면 '…만큼 ~
하지 않은'이라 해석하여 'A < B'의 의미를 가지게 된다는 점에 유의하세요.

ex) He became as wild as a beast and no one could soothe him.
그는 야수처럼 괴팍해져서 누구도 그를 달랠 수 없었다.

3

As soon as he gets home, / Geppetto *fashions* **the Marionette**
집으로 돌아오자 마자,　　　　　　　제페토 노인은 꼭두각시를 만들고

/ and calls it Pinocchio. The first *pranks* **of the Marionette.**
피노키오라 부른다.　　　　　　꼭두각시의 첫 번째 장난이 시작된다.

Little as Geppetto's house was, / it was neat **and**
제페토의 집은 작지만,　　　　　　　　　　깨끗하고 편안했다.

comfortable. It was a small room / on the ground floor, /
　　　　　　그의 집은 작은 방이었다　　1층에 있는,

with a tiny window / under the stairway.
작은 창문을 가진　　　　　계단 아래.

The furniture could not have been much simpler: / a very
가구는 더할 수 없이 소박했다:　　　　　　　　　매우 낡은 의자,

old chair, / a rickety **old bed, / and a** tumble-down **table.**
곧 부서질 듯한 오래된 침대,　　금방 넘어질 듯한 탁자.

A fireplace full of burning logs **/ was painted on the wall /**
활활 타오르는 장작으로 가득 찬 벽난로는　　벽에 그려진 것이었다

opposite the door. Over the fire, / there was painted a pot /
문 맞은편에 있는.　　　　　불 옆에는,　　　　　　냄비가 그려져 있었다

full of something / which kept boiling happily away / and
뭔가로 가득 찬 채　　　　기분 좋게 계속 끓고 있는

sending up clouds / of what looked like real steam.
김을 내뿜으면서　　　　진짜 수증기처럼 보이는.

As soon as he reached home, / Geppetto took his tools / and
집에 도착하자마자,　　　　　제페토는 연장을 꺼내서

began to cut and shape the wood / into a Marionette.
나무를 자르고 나무를 조각하기 시작했다　　　꼭두각시 모양으로.

"What shall I call him?" / he said to himself. "I think / I'll
"이름을 뭐라고 짓지?"　　　　노인은 중얼거렸다.　　　　"그래,

call him PINOCCHIO. This name will make **his** fortune. **I**
'피노키오'라고 불러야겠다.　　이 이름은 이 녀석에게 행운을 가져다 줄 거야.

knew / a whole family of Pinocchi / once / —— Pinocchio
나는 알고 있었지   피노키오 가족을   예전에   — 아버지는 '피노키

the father, / Pinocchia the mother, / and Pinocchi the
오'였고,   어머니는 '피노키아',   아이들은 모두 '피노키'였어 —

children —— / and they were all lucky. The richest of
children   그리고 그들 모두 운이 좋았어.   그들 중 가장 잘 사는 사람도

them / begged for his living."
구걸로 생계를 꾸렸지만 말이야."

After choosing the name / for his Marionette, / Geppetto
이름을 짓고 난 후   꼭두각시를 위한,   제페토는 열심히

set seriously / to work to make / the hair, the forehead,
시작했다   만드는 일을   머리카락, 이마, 눈을.

the eyes. Fancy his surprise / when he noticed / that
노인이 얼마나 놀랐는지 상상해 보세요   깨달았을 때

these eyes moved / and then stared fixedly / at him.
이 눈들이 움직이며   뚫어져라 쳐다보고 있는 것을   그를.

Geppetto, / seeing this, / felt insulted / and said / in a
제페토는,   이것을 보고,   기분이 나빠져서   말했다

grieved tone:
슬픈 목소리로:

"Ugly wooden eyes, / why do you stare so?"
"못생긴 나무 눈아,   왜 나를 쏘아보는 거지?"

There was no answer.
대답은 없었다.

After the eyes, / Geppetto made the nose, / which
눈 다음으로,   제페토는 코를 만들었는데,

began to stretch / as soon as finished. It stretched / and
쑥쑥 자라기 시작했다   완성되자 마자.   코는 자라고,

stretched / and stretched / till it became so long, / it
또 자라고   또 자랐다   너무 길어져서,

seemed endless.
끝이 없는 듯 보였다.

fashion (손으로) 만들다 | pranks (농담으로 하는) 장난 | neat 정돈된, 말쑥한 | ground floor 1층 | stairway
계단 | rickety (제대로 만들어지지 않아) 곧 무너질[부서질] 듯한 | tumble-down (건물이) 황폐한, 금방 넘어질 듯한
| log 통나무 | pot 냄비, 솥 | steam 김, 증기 | make (a) fortune 부자가 되다, 재산을 모으다 | living 생활비;
생계 수단 | forehead 이마 | fancy 생각[상상]하다 | fixedly (시선을) 박고[고정시키고] | grieve 비통해 하다

23

Poor Geppetto kept cutting it / and cutting it, / but the
불쌍한 제페토는 계속 잘라냈고   또 잘라냈다.   하지만 깎아 내면

more he cut, / the longer grew that impertinent nose. In
깎아 낼수록,   그 건방진 코는 계속 자라기만 했다.

despair / he let it alone.
그는 절망하여 그냥 내버려두기로 했다.

Next / he made the mouth.
다음으로는 입을 만들었다.

No sooner was it finished / than it began to laugh / and
입이 완성되자 마자   그 입이 웃기 시작했고

poke fun at him.
그를 조롱했다.

"Stop laughing!" / said Geppetto angrily; / but he might
"웃지 마!"   제페토가 화를 내며 말했다;   하지만 말하는 편이

as well have spoken / to the wall.
나았을 것이다   벽에 대고.

"Stop laughing, I say!" / he roared / in a voice of thunder.
"웃지 말라고 했지!"   그는 소리를 질렀다 천둥치는 듯한 소리로.

The mouth stopped laughing, / but it stuck out / a long
그 입은 웃음을 멈추었지만,   쑥 내밀었다

tongue.
긴 혀를.

Not wishing to start an argument, / Geppetto made
시비를 걸고 싶지 않았기 때문에,   제페토는 믿는 척 했다

believe / he saw nothing / and went on with his work.
아무것도 못 보았다고   그리고 일을 계속했다.

After the mouth, / he made the chin, / then the neck, the
입을 만든 후에,   턱을 만들었다,   다음은 목, 어깨, 몸통, 팔,

shoulders, the stomach, the arms, / and the hands.
그리고 손을.

As he was about to / put the last touches / on the finger
막 하려고 할 때   마지막 손질을   손가락 끝에,

tips, / Geppetto felt / his wig being pulled off. He
제페토는 느꼈다   그의 가발이 벗겨지는 것을.

impertinent 무례한, 버릇없는 | despair 절망 | poke fun at ~을 조롱하다[웃음거리로 삼다] | might as well
…하는 편이 낫다 | roar 고함치다 | stick out ~을 내밀다 | start an argument 시비를 걸다 | make believe
(…인) 체[척]하다

glanced up / and what did he see? His yellow wig was /
위를 올려다 보았을 때   제페토는 무엇을 보았을까요?   그의 노란 가발이 있었다

in the Marionette's hand. "Pinocchio, give me my wig!"
꼭두각시의 손에.   "피노키오야, 그 가발을 돌려줘!"

But instead of giving it back, / Pinocchio put it / on his
하지만 가발을 돌려주는 대신,   피노키오는 그것을 놓았다

own head, / which was half swallowed up / in it.
자기 머리 위에,   그러자 얼굴의 반이 가려진 채로   가발에.

At that unexpected trick, / Geppetto became very sad /
피노키오의 예기치 않은 장난에,   제페토는 너무 슬펐고,

and downcast, / more so / than he had ever been before.
우울했다.   훨씬 더   지금까지 그 어느 순간보다.

"Pinocchio, you wicked boy!" / he cried out. "You are
"피노키오, 이 말썽꾸러기야!"   그는 외쳤다.

not yet finished, / and you start out / by being impudent /
"아직 완성되지도 않았는데,   벌써 시작하다니   무례하게 구는 것을

to your poor old father. Very bad, my son, / very bad!"
불쌍한 늙은 아빠에게.   그러면 못쓴다, 애야,   나쁜 짓이야!"

And he wiped away a tear.
그리고는 눈물을 닦았다.

The legs and feet / still had to be made. As soon as they
다리와 발은   아직 만들어져야 했다.   다리와 발을 만들자 마자,

were done, / Geppetto felt a sharp kick / on the tip of his
제페토는 날카로운 발길질을 느꼈다   그의 콧잔등을 차는.

nose.

Key Expression 🎵

the 비교급~, the 비교급… : ~하면 할수록 더욱 더 …하다
'the 비교급 + (주어 + 동사), the 비교급 + (주어 + 동사)' 의 형태로 사용하며 '~
하면 할수록 더욱 더 …하다'라는 의미를 가지고 있어요.

ex) The more he cut, the longer grew that impertinent nose.
                    (강조를 위한 '주어+동사'의 도치)
    그가 깎아내면 깎아낼수록, 그 건방진 코는 더욱 더 길어졌다.

glance 흘깃 보다 | swallow 삼키다 | unexpected 뜻밖의, 예기치 않은 | trick 속임수; (골탕을 먹이기 위한) 장난
[농담] | downcast 풀이 죽은 | wicked 못된, 사악한 | cry out ~을 외치다 | impudent 무례한 | wipe (먼지나
물기를 없애기 위해) 닦다

"I deserve it!" / he said to himself. "I should have thought
"이런 일을 당해도 싸!"   그는 혼잣말로 중얼거렸다.   "미리 생각을 했어야 했는데

of this / before I made him. Now it's too late!"
          만들기 전에.   이젠 너무 늦었어!"

He took hold of the Marionette / under the arms / and put
그는 꼭두각시를 안아   두 팔로

him on the floor / to teach him to walk.
바닥에 내려놓았다   걷는 것을 가르치기 위해.

Pinocchio's legs were so stiff / that he could not move
피노키오의 다리는 너무 뻣뻣해서   움직일 수 없었다,

them, / and Geppetto held his hand / and showed him /
         그래서 제페토는 그의 손을 잡고   보여 주었다

how to put out / one foot after the other.
발을 내딛는 방법을   한 발씩.

When his legs were limbered up, / Pinocchio started
다리가 부드러워지자,   피노키오는 걷기 시작했고

walking / by himself / and ran / all around the room. He
          혼자서   뛰어다녔다   온 방안 곳곳을.

came to the open door, / and with one leap / he was out
그는 열려진 문으로 가더니   껑충 뛰어서   거리로 나갔다.

into the street. Away he flew!
                달아난 것이었다!

Poor Geppetto ran after him / but was unable to catch
불쌍한 제페토는 그를 뒤쫓았지만,   그를 잡을 수 없었다,

him, / for Pinocchio ran / in leaps and bounds, / his two
          피노키오가 뛰었기 때문에   너무 빨리,

wooden feet, / as they beat on the stones / of the street, /
그의 두 나무 다리로,   마치 돌을 두드리는 것처럼   거리의,

making as much noise / as twenty peasants / in wooden
엄청난 소음을 만들면서   20명의 농부처럼   나막신을 신은.

shoes.

---

deserve it 자업자득이다 | take hold of 〈유형·무형의 것을〉 잡다, 쥐다, 제어[조종]하다 | stiff 뻣뻣한 | limber up
(운동·시합 전에) 몸을 풀다[준비 운동을 하다] | in leaps and bounds 급속히; 대폭 | peasant 소작농 | by sheer
luck 정말 운이 좋아서 | happen along 우연히 오다[지나치다] | Carabineer 기총병, 근위 스코틀랜드 용기병 연대
| runaway 달아난, 가출한 | colt (4~5세 된) 수망아지 | resolve 다짐하다

26   The Adventures of Pinocchio

"Catch him! Catch him!" / Geppetto kept shouting. But the
"저 놈 잡아라! 저 놈 잡아라!" 제페토가 계속 외쳤다.

people in the street, / seeing a wooden Marionette running
그러나 거리의 사람들은, 나무로 만든 꼭두각시가 달리는 것을 보면서

/ like the wind, / stood still / to stare and to laugh / until
바람처럼, 그냥 서 있었다 쳐다보고 웃으면서

they cried.
눈물이 날 때까지.

At last, / by sheer luck, / a Carabineer*(A military
마침내, 다행히도, 경찰관이 우연히 나타났다.

policeman) happened along, / who, hearing all that noise, /
그는 시끄러운 소리를 듣고,

thought that it might be a runaway colt, / and stood bravely
도망친 망아지라고 생각해서, 용감하게 섰다

/ in the middle of the street, / with legs wide apart, / firmly
길 한가운데, 두 다리를 넓게 벌리고,

resolved to stop it / and prevent any trouble.
멈추려는 의지를 확고히 한 채 소란을 멈추기 위해.

Pinocchio saw the Carabineer / from afar / and tried his
피노키오는 경찰관을 보았고 저 멀리서 달아나기 위해 최선을

best to escape / between the legs of the big fellow, / but
다했다 그 큰 사람의 두 다리 사이로.

without success.
하지만 실패로 돌아갔다.

The Carabineer grabbed him / by the nose / (it was an
경찰관은 피노키오를 잡았다 그의 코를

extremely long one / and seemed made on purpose / for
(그것은 매우 긴 코였으며 목적으로 만들어진 듯 보였다

that very thing) / and returned him / to Mastro Geppetto.
바로 그런 용도로) 그리고 피노키오를 돌려줬다 제페토 노인에게.

The little old man / wanted to pull Pinocchio's ears. Think
작은 노인은 피노키오의 귀를 잡아당기려고 했다. 제페토가

how he felt / when, / upon searching for them, / he
어떻게 느꼈을지 생각해 보세요 그때, 귀를 찾으려다가,

discovered / that he had forgotten / to make them!
깨달았을 때 잊었다는 사실을 귀를 만드는 것을!

All he could do / was to seize Pinocchio by the back of
그가 할 수 있는 일이라고는   피노키오의 뒷덜미를 잡아서

the neck / and take him home. As he was doing so, / he
집으로 데려가는 것이었다.   그렇게 하는 중에,

shook him two or three times / and said to him angrily:
피노키오를 두세 번 흔들고   화를 내며 말했다:

"We're going home now. When we get home, / then we'll
"당장 집으로 가자.   집에 가서,

settle this matter!"
두고 보자꾸나!"

Pinocchio, / on hearing this, / threw himself on the
피노키오는,   이 말을 듣자,   바닥에 드러눕더니

ground / and refused to take another step. One person
한 발짝도 떼려 하지 않았다.   사람들이 차례대로

after another / gathered around the two.
둘의 주위로 몰려들었다.

Some said one thing, / some another.
누군가 한 마디를 했다,   다른 사람들도 이러쿵저러쿵 말했다.

"Poor Marionette," / called out a man. "I am not
"불쌍한 꼭두각시군,"   한 사람이 소리쳤다.   "놀랄 일도 아니지

surprised / he doesn't want to go home. Geppetto, / no
집에 돌아가기 싫어하는 것도.   제페토는,

doubt, / will beat him unmercifully, / he is so mean /
틀림없이,   저 애를 무자비하게 때릴 거야,   그는 너무 못되고

and cruel!"
잔인하거든!"

"Geppetto looks like a good man," / added another, /
"제페토는 좋은 사람처럼 보이지,"   누군가 거들었다,

"but / with boys / he's a real tyrant. If we leave that poor
"하지만   아이들한텐   그는 완전 폭군이라니까.   불쌍한 꼭두각시를 남겨두었다간

Marionette / in his hands / he may tear him / to pieces!"
그의 손에   찢어 버리고 말거야   산산조각 내서!"

---

seize 와락 붙잡다 | no doubt 틀림없이 | unmercifully 무자비하게 | mean 못된, 심술궂은 | cruel 잔혹한,
잔인한 | tyrant 폭군, 독재자 | at liberty 풀려난 | defend 옹호하다, 변호하다 | wail (슬픔·통증 때문에) 울부짖다,
통곡하다, 흐느끼다 | sob 흐느껴 울기[우는 소리], 흐느낌 | ungrateful 감사할 줄 모르는, 은혜를 모르는, 배은망덕한

They said so much / that, finally, / the Carabineer ended
어찌나 말이 많던지,   마침내,   경찰관은 결정했다

matters / by setting Pinocchio at liberty / and dragging
         피노키오를 놓아주고   제페토를 감옥에 끌고 가는

Geppetto to prison. The poor old fellow did not know /
것으로.   불쌍한 노인은 몰랐다

how to defend himself, / but wept and wailed / like a child
자신을 변호하는 방법을,   울고 통곡하는 것 밖에는   어린 아이처럼

/ and said between his sobs:
      그래서 흐느끼며 말했다:

"Ungrateful boy! To think / I tried so hard / to make you a
"은혜도 모르는 놈!   생각해 보니   내가 얼마나 애를 썼는데

well-behaved Marionette! I deserve it, / however! I should
널 멋진 꼭두각시로 만들려고!   당해도 싸지,   하지만!

have given the matter more thought."
이 문제를 좀 더 생각했어야 했는데."

What happened after this / is an almost unbelievable
그 후에 일어난 일도   믿기 힘든 이야기죠,

story, / but you may read it, / dear children, / in the
     읽어 보세요,   어린이 여러분,

chapters that follow.
다음 장에서.

Key Expression

신체 접촉의 표현 : ~의 …을 잡다/치다/보다

신체 접촉을 표현할 때는 '동사 + 사람 + 전치사 + the + 신체부위'의 형식으로 쓰고, '~의 …을 잡다/치다/보다'라는 의미를 나타냅니다. 이때 전치사는 동사의 종류에 따라 달라져요.

▶ [잡다] take/catch/seize/hold/grasp + 사람 + by + the + 신체부위
▶ [치다] strike/hit/pat/tap/touch + 사람 + on + the + 신체부위
▶ [보다] look/gaze/stare + 사람 + in + the + 신체부위

ex) All he could do was to seize Pinocchio by the back of the neck and take him home.
그가 할 수 있는 일이라고는 피노키오의 뒷덜미를 잡아서 집에 데리고 가는 게 다였다.

mini test 1

A. 다음 문장을 해석해 보세요.

(1) His real name was Mastro Antonio, / but everyone called him / Mastro Cherry, / for the tip of his nose was / so round and red and shiny / that it looked like a ripe cherry.
→

(2) The poor fellow was scared / half to death, / so he tried to sing / a gay song / in order to gain courage.
→

(3) When the fight was over, / Mastro Antonio had / Geppetto's yellow wig / in his hands / and Geppetto found / the carpenter's curly wig / in his mouth.
→

(4) Over the fire, / there was painted a pot / full of something / which kept boiling happily away / and sending up clouds / of what looked like real steam..
→

B. 다음 주어진 문장이 되도록 빈칸에 써 넣으세요.

(1) 그는 정신을 다시 차리자마자, 공포로 몸을 떨고 말을 더듬으며 말했다.

_____, he said, trembling and stuttering from fright.

(2) 그는 짐승처럼 거칠어져서 아무도 그를 달랠 수 없었다.

_____ and no one could soothe him.

(3) 제페토의 집은 작았지만, 깔끔하고 편안했다.

_____, it was neat and comfortable.

A. (1) 그의 진짜 이름은 안토니오였지만, 모든 사람들은 그를 체리 노인이라고 불렀다. 그의 코 끝이 너무 둥글고 빨갛고 반짝거려서 잘 익은 체리처럼 보였기 때문이다. (2) 그 불쌍한 사람은 겁에 질려 거의 죽을 것 같았기에, 용기를 얻기 위해 즐거운 노래를 부르려고 애썼다. (3) 싸움이 끝나자, 안토니오의 손에는

30   The Adventures of Pinocchio

(4) 그가 할 수 있는 일이라고는 <u>피노키오의 뒷덜미를 잡고</u> 집으로 데려가는 것이 다였다.

All he could do was _____ and take him home.

C. 다음 주어진 문구가 알맞은 문장이 되도록 순서를 맞춰 보세요.

(1) 이번에는 불쌍한 체리 노인은 총을 맞은 것처럼 쓰러졌다.
[fell / This time / shot / Mastro Cherry / poor / as if]
→

(2) 여긴 어떻게 왔나, 제페토 친구여?
[here, / brought / friend Geppetto? / you / What]
→

(3) 가구는 더할 나위 없이 소박했다.
[could / have / not / The furniture / much / simpler / been]
→

(4) 그를 만들기 전에 이것을 생각했어야만 했는데.
[should / before / thought of / made / I / this / I / him. / have]
→

D. 다음 단어에 대한 맞는 설명과 연결해 보세요.

(1) mumble ▶ ◀ ① move your fingers lightly over a sensitive part of their body

(2) tickle ▶ ◀ ② make long, loud, high-pitched cries

(3) surly ▶ ◀ ③ speak to oneself very quietly

(4) wail ▶ ◀ ④ behaves in a rude way

제페토의 노란 가발이 들려 있었고, 제페토는 목수의 곱슬머리 가발을 입에 물고 있었다. (4) 불 위에는 무 연기로 가득 차 행복하게 끓고 있는 냄비가 그려져 있었으며 진짜 수증기처럼 보이는 연기를 내뿜고 있었 다. | B. (1) As soon as he regained the use of his senses (2) He became as wild as a beast (3) Little as Geppetto's house was (4) to seize Pinocchio by the back of the neck | C. (1) This time poor Mastro Cherry fell as if shot. (2) What brought you here, friend Geppetto? (3) The furniture could not have been much simpler. (4) I should have thought of this before I made him. | D. (1) ③ (2) ① (3) ④ (4) ②

4

Pinocchio falls asleep / with his feet on a foot warmer, /
피노키오는 잠이 들었다　　　　　　　　다리를 난로 위에 둔 채,

and awakens the next day / with his feet all burned off.
그리고 다음 날 깨어보니　　　　　　　두 다리가 모두 타버렸다.

Pinocchio hated the dark street, / but he was so hungry
피노키오는 어두운 거리가 싫었다.　　　　　　하지만 너무 배가 고파서,

that, / in spite of it, / he ran out of the house. The night was
　　　그럼에도 불구하고,　　집 밖으로 뛰어나갔다.　　　　밤은 칠흑같이 어두웠다.

pitch black. It thundered, / and bright flashes of lightning / .
칠흑같이.　　　　　천둥이 울었고,　　　번갯불이

now and again shot / across the sky, / turning it into a sea
이따금 번쩍이면서　　　　하늘을 가로질러,　　　불바다로 만들었다.

of fire. An angry wind blew cold / and raised dense clouds
성난 바람이 차갑게 불었고　　　　　시커먼 먼지 구름을 일으켰으며,

of dust, / while the trees shook and moaned / in a weird
　　　나무들이 흔들리면서 신음 소리를 냈다　　　　　섬뜩하게.

way.

Pinocchio was greatly afraid / of thunder and lightning, /
피노키오는 너무나 무서워했다　　　　천둥과 번개를,

but the hunger he felt / was far greater / than his fear. In
그러나 그가 느낀 배고픔이　　　훨씬 컸다　　　그의 두려움보다.

a dozen leaps and bounds, / he came to the village, / tired
힘껏 달려서,　　　　　그는 마을에 도착했다,　　　완전히 지쳐서,

out, / puffing like a whale, / and with tongue hanging.
　　고래처럼 숨을 헐떡거리며,　　혀를 쑥 내민 채.

The whole village was dark / and deserted. The stores were
마을 전체가 어둡고　　　　　황량했다.　　　가게들은 닫혀 있었고,

---

in spite of 에도 불구하고 | pitch-black 칠흑같이 새까만[어두운] | flash 섬광, 번쩍임 | lightning 번개, 번갯불 |
now and again 이따금, 때때로 | dense 짙은[자욱한] | moan 신음소리 같은 소리를 내다 | weird 기괴한, 섬뜩한
| thunder 천둥, 우레 | tired out 몸이 몹시 고달프다 | puff (특히 달리기를 한 뒤에) 숨을 헉헉[헐떡]거리다 |
whale 고래 | desert 사람이 없는 | desperation 자포자기, 필사적임 | doorway 출입구 | wildly 미친 듯이

closed, / the doors, the windows. In the streets, / not even
문도, 창문도 닫혀 있었다.   거리에는,   개 한 마리도

a dog / could be seen. It seemed / the Village of the Dead.
보이지 않았다.   마치 보였다   '죽음의 마을'처럼.

Pinocchio, / in desperation, / ran up to a doorway, / threw
피노키오는,   자포자기 하여,   어느 대문을 향해 달려가,

himself upon the bell, / and pulled it wildly, / saying to
초인종에 돌진하여,   황급하게 벨을 눌렀다,   중얼거리며:

himself: / "Someone will surely answer that!"
            "누군가는 분명 대답하겠지!"라고.

He was right. An old man in a nightcap / opened the
그의 말대로였다.   취침용 모자를 쓴 한 노인이   창문을 열고

window / and looked out.
밖을 내다보았다.

He called down angrily:
그는 화를 내면서 소리쳤다:

"What do you want / at this hour of night?"
"무슨 일이야   이렇게 늦은 밤 시간에?"

"Will you be good / enough to give me / a bit of bread? I
"죄송하지만   주실 수 있나요   빵을 좀?

am hungry."
배가 고파요."

"Wait a minute / and I'll come right back," / answered
"잠시만 기다려   곧 돌아올 테니."   노인은 대답했다,

the old fellow, / thinking / he had to deal with / one of
                생각하면서   혼내줘야겠다고

those boys / who love to roam around / at night / ringing
아이들 중 하나를   떠돌아다니기를 좋아하는   밤에

people's bells / while they are peacefully asleep.
초인종을 울리며   사람들이 평화롭게 잠든 동안.

After a minute or two, / the same voice cried:
잠시 후,   노인의 목소리가 다시 들렸다:

"Get under the window / and hold out your hat!"
"창문 밑에 서서   모자를 내밀어라!"

Pinocchio had no hat, / but he managed to get / under
피노키오는 모자가 없었지만,   겨우 도착했고

the window / just in time / to feel / a shower of ice-cold
창문 아래   바로 그때   느꼈다   얼음처럼 차가운 물세례가

water / pour down / on his poor wooden head, / his
            쏟아지는 것을   그의 나무 머리 위로,

shoulders, and over his whole body.
어깨로, 그리고 온몸으로.

He returned home / as wet as a rag, / and tired out / from
그는 집으로 돌아왔다   걸레처럼 흠뻑 젖어서,   그리고 지쳐버렸다

weariness and hunger.
피곤과 배고픔으로.

As he no longer had any strength left / with which to
더 이상 힘이 남아 있지 않았기 때문에   서 있을,

stand, / he sat down on a little stool / and put his two feet
그는 작은 의자에 앉아   두 다리를 난로 위에 올려 놓았다

on the stove / to dry them.
                  말리기 위해.

There he fell asleep, / and while he slept, / his wooden feet
거기에서 잠이 들었고,   잠이 든 동안에,   나무로 만들어진 발은

/ began to burn.
  타기 시작했다.

Slowly, very slowly, / they blackened / and turned to ashes.
천천히, 매우 천천히,   다리는 까맣게 되었고   결국 재로 변했다.

Pinocchio snored away happily / as if his feet were not
피노키오는 행복하게 코를 골았다   마치 두 다리가 자기 것이 아닌 것처럼.

his own. At dawn / he opened his eyes / just as a loud
        새벽에 되어   그는 눈을 떴다   큰 노크 소리 때문에

knocking / sounded at the door.
                문에서 들리는.

"Who is it?" / he called, / yawning and rubbing his eyes.
"누구세요?"   그가 물었다,   하품을 하고 눈을 비비며.

"It is I," / answered a voice.
"나다,"   목소리가 답했다.

It was the voice of Geppetto.
그것은 바로 제페토의 목소리였다.

Key Expression

as if 가정법 : 마치 ~인 것처럼

as if는 가정법의 특수한 형태로 '마치 ~인 것처럼'이란 의미로 쓰여요.
특히 as if절에 be동사가 쓰일 때에는 주어에 관계없이 항상 were가 온다는
점을 잊지 마세요.

▶ as if 가정법 과거 : 주절 현재시제, as if + 주어 + 과거동사 (마치 ~인 것처럼)
▶ as if 가정법 과거완료 : 주절 과거/현재완료 시제, as if + 주어 + had pp (마치
~였던 것처럼)

ex) Pinocchio snored away happily as if his feet were not his own.
    피노키오는 마치 그의 발이 자신의 것이 아닌 것처럼 행복하게 코를 골았다.

nightcap 취침용 모자 | deal with ~를 (상)대하다 | manage to 간신히[용케] 해내다, (어떻게든) …하다[해내다] |
rag (특히 걸레·행주 등으로 쓰는) 해진 천[누더기] | weariness 피곤 | no longer 더 이상 ~아니다 | stool (등받이와
팔걸이가 없는) 의자 | blacken 검게 만들다; 검어지다 | ash 재 | snore 코를 골다 | yawn 하품하다

5

Geppetto returns home / and gives his own breakfast / to
제페토는 집으로 돌아와서   자신이 먹으려는 아침을 줬다

the Marionette.
꼭두각시에게.

The poor Marionette, / who was still half asleep, / had
불쌍한 꼭두각시는,   반쯤은 잠에 취해서,

not yet found out / that his two feet were burned / and
아직 모르고 있었다   두 다리가 타버려서   사라진 것을.

gone. As soon as he heard / his Father's voice, / he
듣자마자   아빠 목소리를,

jumped up from his seat / to open the door, / but, / as he
자리에서 뛰어내렸다   문을 열기 위해,   하지만, 그렇게

did so, / he staggered / and fell headlong to the floor.
했을 때,   그는 비틀거리며   바닥에 거꾸로 엎어지고 말았다.

In falling, / he made as much noise / as a sack of wood /
쓰러질 때,   엄청난 소리가 났다   나무 자루처럼

falling from the fifth story of a house.
5층 집에서 떨어지는.

"Open the door for me!" / Geppetto shouted / from the
"문 열어라!"   제페토가 소리쳤다   밖에서.

street.

"Father, dear Father, / I can't," / answered the Marionette
"아빠, 아빠,   열 수 없어요," 꼭두각시가 대답했다

/ in despair, / crying and rolling on the floor.
절망하여,   울면서 바닥에 몸을 구르며.

"Why can't you?"
"왜 그러니?"

---

staggered 비틀[휘청]거리다, 비틀[휘청]거리며 가다 | headlong (머리부터) 거꾸로, 곤두박질쳐서 | sack 부대, 자루
| whipping (벌로 가하는) 채찍질 | shavings 깎아 낸 부스러기, 대팻밥 | sound (체벌이) 심한[모진] | sorrowful
(아주) 슬픈 | fondle 애무하다 | caress 애무하다, 어루만지다

"Because someone has eaten / my feet."
누가 먹어 버렸어요   내 발을.'

"And who has eaten them?"
"그럼 누가 네 발을 먹었니?"

"The cat," / answered Pinocchio, / seeing that little animal
"고양이가요,"   피노키오는 대답했다,   작은 동물을 보며

/ busily playing with some shavings / in the corner of the
바쁘게 대팻밥을 가지고 놀던   방 한구석에서.

room.

"Open! I say," / repeated Geppetto, / "or I'll give you a
"문 열라고 했다!"   제페토가 반복했다,   "안 그러면 채찍으로 혼내 줄테다

sound whipping / when I get in."
                들어가서."

"Father, believe me, / I can't stand up. Oh, dear! Oh, dear!
"아빠, 믿어 주세요,   일어설 수 없어요.   오, 맙소사!   오, 맙소사!

I shall have to walk / on my knees / all my life."
난 이제 걸어야 할 거야   무릎으로   평생 동안."

Geppetto, / thinking / that all these tears and cries / were
제페토는,   생각하면서   이 모든 눈물과 울음 소리가

only other pranks of the Marionette, / climbed up the side
꼭두각시의 또 다른 장난이라고,   집 옆을 기어올라

of the house / and went in / through the window.
             안으로 들어갔다   창문을 통해.

At first / he was very angry, / but on seeing / Pinocchio
처음에   그는 매우 화가 났었다,   하지만 보는 순간   피노키오가 뻗어 있는

stretched out / on the floor / and really without feet, / he
것을   바닥에   그리고 정말로 다리가 없는 것을,

felt very sad and sorrowful. Picking him up from the
그는 매우 슬펐고 애절함을 느꼈다.   그를 바닥에서 들어올려,

floor, / he fondled and caressed him, / talking to him /
        쓰다듬고 어루만졌다,   그에게 말하며

while the tears ran down / his cheeks:
눈물을 흘리면서   두 뺨에:

"My little Pinocchio, / my dear little Pinocchio! How did
"나의 피노키오,　　　사랑하는 피노키오야!　　　어쩌다 타버렸니

you burn / your feet?"
네 두 다리가?"

"I don't know, Father, / but believe me, / the night has been
"모르겠어요, 아빠,　　　하지만 믿어 주세요,　　　그 날 밤은 너무 끔찍했어요

a terrible one / and I shall remember it / as long as I live.
절대로 못 잊을 거예요　　　내가 살아있는 한.

The thunder was so noisy / and the lightning so bright ——
천둥은 너무 시끄럽고　　　번개는 번쩍이고 —

/ and I was hungry. And then / the Talking Cricket said
그리고 배가 고팠어요.　　　그리고 그때　　말하는 귀뚜라미가 내게 말했어요,

to me, / 'You deserve it; / you were bad;' / and I said to
'넌 그래도 싸　　　넌 나쁜 애야'라고　　　그래서 내가 말했죠,

him, / 'Careful, Cricket;' / and he said to me, 'You are a
'말 조심해, 귀뚜라미야,'　　　그런데 그가 말하는 거예요,　　'넌 꼭두각시이고

Marionette / and you have a wooden head;' / and I threw
나무로 만든 머리를 가졌지;'　　　그래서 난 망치를 던져서

the hammer / at him / and killed him. It was his own fault,
그에게　　　그를 죽였어요.　　　그건 귀뚜라미 잘못이에요,

/ for I didn't want to kill him. And I put the pan / on the
왜냐하면 전 죽일 생각이 없었으니까요.　　　그래서 프라이팬을 놓는데　　석탄 위에,

coals, / but the Chick flew away / and said, 'I'll see you
병아리가 도망치면서　　　말했어요,　　'또 보자!

again! Remember me / to the family.' And my hunger grew,
안부 전해 줘　　　식구들한테.'라고　　　배고픔이 심해져서,

/ and I went out, / and the old man with a nightcap / looked
밖으로 나갔는데,　　　취침용 모자를 쓴 노인이

out of the window / and threw water on me, / and I came
창 밖을 내다보더니　　　내게 물을 퍼부었어요,　　　그래서 집에 돌아와서

home / and put my feet on the stove / to dry them / because
난로 위에 다리를 올려 놓았어요　　　말리려고

cricket 귀뚜라미 | pan (손잡이가 달린 얕은) 냄비 | coals (특히 타고 있는) 석탄 조각 | remember me to ~에게
안부 전해 주세요 | jumbled 무질서한(chaotic) | pear (과일) 배

I was still hungry, / and I fell asleep / and now my feet are
왜냐하면 여전히 배고팠으니까요, 그리고 잠이 들었는데   지금 내 발은 사라져 버렸지는데

gone / but my hunger isn't!
배고픔은 사라지지 않았어요!

"Oh! —— Oh! —— Oh!" And poor Pinocchio began to
"엉!   — 엉!   — 엉!"   그리고 나서 불쌍한 피노키오는 소리를 지르기 시작했고

scream / and cry so loudly / that he could be heard / for
너무 크게 울어서   들릴 정도였다

miles around.
수마일 떨어진 곳에서도.

Geppetto, / who had understood nothing of / all that
제페토는,   아무것도 이해할 수 없었던   그 모든 두서 없는

jumbled talk, / except that the Marionette was hungry, / felt
이야기에 대해,   꼭두각시가 배고프다는 사실을 제외하고는,

sorry for him, / and pulling three pears / out of his pocket, /
그를 불쌍히 여겨,   배 세 개를 꺼내   주머니에서,

offered them to him, / saying:
그에게 주었다,   말하면서:

"These three pears were / for my breakfast, / but I give
"이 세 개의 배는   내 아침 식사란다,   하지만 네게 줄게

them to you / gladly. Eat them / and stop weeping."
기꺼이.   어서 먹어라   그리고 그만 울어."

Key Expression 🔔

so~that… : 너무 ~ 해서 …하다

'so + 형용사/부사 + that…'은 '너무 ~해서 …하다'라는 의미로 결과를 나타내는 구문이에요. so 대신 much를 사용할 수도 있으며, 형용사/부사 자리에 명사가 올 경우에는 so가 아닌 such를 사용합니다.

ex) Poor Pinocchio began to scream and cry so loudly that he could be heard for miles around.
불쌍한 피노키오는 너무 크게 소리지르며 울기 시작해서 수마일 밖에서도 들릴 정도였다.

39

"If you want / me to eat them, / please peel them / for me."
"만약 원한다면　　내게 그것을 먹이기를,　　껍질을 깎아 주세요　　　나를 위해."

"Peel them?" / asked Geppetto, / very much surprised. "I
"껍질을 깎아 달라고?"　제페토가 물었다.　　매우 놀라면서.

should never have thought, / dear boy of mine, / that you
"전혀 몰랐구나.　　　　사랑하는 내 아들아,　　네가 아주 조심스

were so dainty and fussy / about your food. Bad, very
럽고 까다롭다는 걸　　음식에 대해.　　그건 아주 나쁜 짓이란다!

bad! In this world, / even as children, / we must accustom
　이 세상에는,　　　아이들조차도,　　　익숙해져야 해

ourselves / to eat of everything, / for we never know / what
무엇이든 먹을 수 있도록,　　왜냐하면 알 수 없는 법이니까

life may hold in store / for us!"
인생에서 어떤 일이 생길지　　우리 앞에!"

"You may be right," / answered Pinocchio, / "but I will not
"아빠 말씀이 맞아요."　피노키오가 대답했다,　　　"하지만 이 배를 먹지

eat the pears / if they are not peeled. I don't like them."
않겠어요　　껍질을 깎아주지 않으면.　　껍질은 싫어요."

And good old Geppetto / took out a knife, / peeled the
그러자 착한 제페토 노인은　　칼을 꺼내 와서,　　　배 세 개의 껍질을

three pears, / and put the skins / in a row on the table.
깎았고,　　　그 껍질을 놓았다　　탁자 위에 일렬로.

Pinocchio ate one pear / in a twinkling / and started to
피노키오는 배 하나를 먹었다　　눈 깜짝할 사이에　　그리고 던지려고 했다

throw / the core away, / but Geppetto held his arm.
속씨를 멀리,　　　　그러나 제페토가 그의 팔을 잡았다.

"Oh, no, / don't throw it away! Everything in this world /
"오, 안 돼,　버리지 마라!　　이 세상에 모든 것은

may be of some use!"
어딘가 쓸모가 있거든!"

"But the core / I will not eat!" / cried Pinocchio / in an
"하지만 속씨는　　난 먹지 않을 거예요!"　피노키오가 소리쳤다

angry tone.
화난 말투로.

dainty 조심스러운, 얌전한 | fussy (특히 별 중요하지 않은 것에) 안달복달하는, 까다로운 | in a row (여러 번을)
잇달아(연이어) | accustom oneself to ~에 익숙해지다 | in a twinkling 눈 깜짝할 사이에 | core (과일의) 속 |
devour 걸신들린 듯 먹다 | wry 찡그린 | wail 울부짖다, 통곡하다 | one after another 연달아 | observe ~을 보다
[(보고) 알다 | in store (~에게) 닥쳐올

"Who knows?" / repeated Geppetto calmly.
"누가 알겠니?" 제페토가 차분하게 대꾸했다.

And later / the three cores were placed / on the table / next
그리하여 세 개의 속씨가 놓여졌다 탁자 위

to the skins.
껍질 옆에.

Pinocchio had eaten the three pears, / or rather devoured
피노키오는 배 세 개를 먹었다, 아니 그보다는 게걸스럽게 삼키듯

them. Then he yawned deeply, / and wailed:
해치웠다. 그러고 나서 길게 하품을 했고, 흐느꼈다.

"I'm still hungry."
"아직도 배가 고파요."

"But I have no more / to give you."
"하지만 더 이상 없구나 네게 줄 것이."

"Really, nothing / —— nothing?"
"정말, 아무것도 — 아무것도요?"

"I have only these three cores / and these skins."
"이 세 개의 속씨뿐이다 이 껍질하고."

"Very well, then," / said Pinocchio, / "if there is nothing
"좋아요, 그럼." 피노키오가 말했다. "아무것도 없다면

else / I'll eat them."
그거라도 먹어야죠."

At first / he made a wry face, / but, one after another, / the
처음엔, 찡그린 얼굴을 했지만, 그러나, 차례차례로,

skins and the cores / disappeared.
껍질과 속씨가 사라졌다.

"Ah! Now I feel fine!" / he said / after eating the last one.
"와! 이제 기분이 나아졌어요!" 그는 말했다 마지막까지 다 먹은 후에.

"You see," / observed Geppetto, / "that I was right / when
"봐라," 제페토가 말했다, "내 말이 맞지

I told you / that one must not be too fussy / and too dainty
말했잖아 사람은 너무 까다로워서도 안 되고 너무 조심스러워도 안 된다고

/ about food. My dear, we never know / what life may have
음식에 대해. 내 아들아, 알 수 없는 법이란다 인생에서 어떤 일이 생길지

in store / for us!"
우리 앞에!"

41

🎩 6 🎩

Geppetto makes Pinocchio / a new pair of feet, / and sells
제페토는 피노키오에게 만들어 준다   새로운 두 다리를,   그리고 그의 코

his coat / to buy him an A-B-C book.
트를 판다   영어 책을 사 주기 위해.

The Marionette, / as soon as his hunger was appeased, /
꼭두각시는,   배고픔이 가시자 마자.

started to grumble and cry / that he wanted a new pair of
툴툴거리며 울기 시작했다   새 발을 만들어 달라며.

feet.

But Mastro Geppetto, / in order to punish him for his
하지만 제페토 노인은,   피노키오가 저지른 잘못에 대해 벌을 주려고.

mischief, / let him alone the whole morning. After dinner
아침 내내 내버려 두었다.   저녁을 먹은 후

/ he said to him:
그에게 말했다:

"Why should I make your feet / over again? To see you
"내가 왜 네 다리를 만들어줘야 하지   다시?   도망치는 걸 보려고

run away / from home / once more?"
집에서   또 다시?"

Key Expression 🔑

부정의 동의 표현 neither do I

부정적인 말에 대해 '또한 ~하지 않다'라는 뜻을 표현할 때 neither를 사용합니다. 'neither + 조동사(일반동사는 do) + 주어'의 형태로 사용합니다. 반대로 긍정적인 말에 대한 동의에는 so를 사용합니다.

ex) A : I have none. 난 없어요.
    B : Neither have I. 나도 없어.

---

appease 달래다 | grumble 투덜[툴툴]거리다 | mischief 나쁜 짓[장난] | will (바라는) 뜻 | learn a trade 일
[기술]을 배우다 | comfort 위안을 주는[위로가 되는] 사람[것] | staff 직원 | stern 엄중한, 근엄한 | diligently
부지런히 | slender 가느다란 | nimble 빠른, 날렵한 | model (조각품 등의 형체를) 만들다[빚다]

"I promise you," / answered the Marionette, / sobbing, /
"약속할게요," 꼭두각시가 말했다, 훌쩍이며,

"that from now on / I'll be good —— "
"이제부터는 착한 아이가 될게요 — "

"Boys always promise that / when they want something,"
"아이들이란 늘 그렇게 약속하지 뭔가 원하는게 있을 때면,"

/ said Geppetto.
제페토가 말했다.

"I promise / to go to school / every day, / to study, / and
"약속할게요 학교에 가겠다고 매일, 공부하겠다고, 그리고

to succeed ——"
성공하겠다고 — "

"Boys always sing that song / when they want their own
"아이들이란 늘 그런 노래를 부르지 바라는 게 있을 때면,"

will."

"But I am not like other boys! I am better than all of them
"하지만 전 다른 아이들과 달라요! 어떤 아이보다 착해요

/ and I always tell the truth. I promise you, Father, / that
그리고 항상 진실만 말해요. 약속해요, 아빠,

I'll learn a trade, / and I'll be the comfort and staff / of
일을 배울 거예요, 그리고 편하게 모실게요

your old age."
아빠가 나이 들면,

Geppetto, / though trying to look very stern, / felt his
제페토는, 매우 엄한 표정을 지으려 했지만,

eyes fill with tears / and his heart soften / when he saw
그의 눈은 눈물로 가득찼고 마음이 누그러졌다 피노키오가 보이자

Pinocchio / so unhappy. He said no more, / but taking his
너무 불행하게. 그는 더 이상 아무 말 없었지만, 연장을 가져와,

tools / and two pieces of wood, / he set to work diligently.
그리고 두 나무 조각도, 부지런히 일을 하기 시작했다.

In less than an hour / the feet were finished, / two slender,
한 시간도 채 안 돼 발이 완성되었다, 두 개의 가느다랗고,

/ nimble little feet, / strong and quick, / modeled / as if by
날렵한 다리였다, 강하고 빠른, 조각된 것처럼 마치

an artist's hands.
마치 조각가의 손에 의해.

43

"Close your eyes and sleep!" / Geppetto then said to the
"눈을 감고 자거라!"
제페토는 꼭두각시에게 말했다.

Marionette.

Pinocchio closed his eyes / and pretended to be asleep, /
피노키오는 눈을 감고
자는 척 했다,

while Geppetto stuck on the two feet / with a bit of glue /
제페토가 두 다리를 붙이는 동안
접착제로

melted in an eggshell, / doing his work so well / that the
달걀 껍질에서 녹인,
너무 잘 붙여서

joint could hardly be seen.
자국이 전혀 보이지 않았다.

As soon as the Marionette felt his new feet, / he gave one
꼭두각시는 두 다리가 생긴 걸 느끼자마자,
냉큼 뛰어내렸고

leap / from the table / and started to skip and jump around,
탁자에서
뛰어다니기 시작했다,

/ as if he had lost his head / from very joy.
마치 미친 사람처럼
아주 기뻐서.

"To show you / how grateful I am / to you, Father, / I'll
"보여 주기 위해
내가 얼마나 감사하는지
아빠께,

go to school / now. But / to go to school / I need a suit of
학교에 가겠어요
당장.
하지만 학교에 가려면
옷이 필요해요."

clothes."

Geppetto did not have a penny / in his pocket, / so he
제페토는 한 푼도 없었다
주머니에,
그래서 아들에게

made his son / a little suit of flowered paper, / a pair of
만들어 주었다
꽃무늬 종이로 된 옷과,
신발 한 켤레를

shoes / from the bark of a tree, / and a tiny cap / from a bit
나무 껍질로 만든,
그리고 작은 모자도

of dough.
빵 조각으로 만든.

Pinocchio ran / to look at himself / in a bowl of water, /
피노키오는 달려갔다
자신의 모습을 보기 위해
물이 든 대야에,

and he felt so happy / that he said proudly:
그리고 너무 행복해서
빼기듯 말했다:

"Now I look like a gentleman."
"이제 꼭 신사처럼 보여요."

"Truly," / answered Geppetto. "But remember / that fine
"정말 그렇구나," 제페토가 대답했다. "하지만 기억하렴

clothes do not make the man / unless they be neat and
좋은 옷이 사람을 만드는 게 아니란 걸 단정하고 깨끗한 옷이 아니라면."

clean."

"Very true," / answered Pinocchio, / "but, in order to go to
"맞아요," 피노키오가 대답했다, "하지만, 학교에 가려면,

school, / I still need something / very important."
여전히 뭔가 필요해요 아주 중요한."

"What is it?"
"그게 뭐지?"

"An A-B-C book."
"영어책이요."

"To be sure! But how shall we get it?"
"그렇구나! 그런데 어떻게 구하지?"

"That's easy. We'll go to a bookstore / and buy it."
"그야 쉽죠. 서점에 가서 사요."

"And the money?"
"그럼 돈은?"

"I have none."
"전 없어요."

"Neither have I," / said the old man / sadly.
"나도 없는데." 노인이 말했다 슬프게.

Pinocchio, / although a happy boy always, / became sad
피노키오는, 항상 명랑한 소년이었지만, 슬프고 풀이 죽었다

and downcast / at these words. When poverty shows itself,
이 말을 듣고. 가난이 그 모습을 드러내면,

/ even mischievous boys understand / what it means.
말썽꾸러기 아이들조차 알게 되는 법이다 그 의미를.

---

pretend to 시늉을 하다 | glue 접착제 | melt 녹다, 녹이다 | eggshell 달걀 껍질 | joint 연결 부위 | lose one's head 흥분하다 | grateful 고마워하는, 감사하는 | dough 밀가루 반죽 | bowl (우묵한) 그릇, 통 | to be sure 틀림없다[분명하다] | downcast 풀이 죽은 | poverty 가난, 빈곤 | mischievous 짓궂은, 말썽꾸러기의

"What does it matter, / after all?" / cried Geppetto / all at
"뭐가 문제니, 　　　　　　결국?" 　　　　제페토가 외쳤다

once, / as he jumped up / from his chair. Putting on his
갑자기, 　일어서면서 　의자에서. 　　　낡은 외투를 걸치고,

old coat, / full of darns and patches, / he ran out of the
꿰맨 자리와 덧댄 옷감으로 가득 찬, 　　집 밖으로 나갔다

house / without another word.
아무 말 없이.

After a while / he returned. In his hands / he had the
잠시 후 　　　그가 돌아왔다. 　그의 손에는 　　영어책이 있었다

A-B-C book / for his son, / but the old coat was gone.
아들에게 줄, 　　하지만 낡은 외투는 사라졌다.

The poor fellow was in his shirt sleeves / and the day
불쌍한 노인은 셔츠 차림이었고 　　　　　날은 추웠다.

was cold.

"Where's your coat, Father?"
"외투는 어디 있어요, 아빠?"

"I have sold it."
"팔았단다."

"Why did you sell your coat?"
"왜 외투를 팔았어요?"

"It was too warm."
"너무 더워서."

Pinocchio understood the answer / in a twinkling, / and,
피노키오는 그 대답의 의미를 알아차렸다 　　눈 깜짝할 사이에, 　그리고,

/ unable to restrain his tears, / he jumped on his father's
눈물을 참지 못하고, 　　　　아빠의 목을 끌어안고

neck / and kissed him / over and over.
입맞췄다 　　수없이.

---

darn (옷의) 꿰맨[기운] 자리 | patch (구멍 난 데를 때우거나 장식용으로 덧대는 데 쓰이는) 조각 | after a while
잠시 후 | restrain (감정 등을) 억누르다[참다] | over and over 여러 번 되풀이하여[거듭거듭] | castle in the air
터무니없는 공상, 환상, 백일몽 | arithmetic 산수

7

Pinocchio sells his A-B-C book / to pay his way into the
피노키오는 그의 영어책을 판다　　　　　　꼭두각시 연극을 보기 위해.

Marionette Theater.

See Pinocchio / hurrying off to school / with his new
피노키오가 보인다　　　학교로 서둘러 향하는　　　　　새 영어책을

A-B-C book / under his arm! As he walked along, /
　　　　　팔에 끼고!　　　　가는 동안,

his brain was busy / planning hundreds / of wonderful
머리속은 바빴다　　　　수백 가지 계획하느라　　　멋진 일들을 ,

things, / building hundreds / of castles in the air. Talking
　　　수백 가지 공상을 하느라　　터무니없는.　　　　중얼거리며,

to himself, / he said:
그가 말했다:

"In school / today, / I'll learn to read, / tomorrow to write,
"학교에서　　오늘은,　　읽기를 배우고,　　　내일은 쓰기를,

/ and the day after tomorrow / I'll do arithmetic. Then, /
　그리고 모레는　　　　　　셈하는 것을 배워야지.　　그러면,

clever as I am, / I can earn a lot of money. With the very
똑똑해져서,　　　돈을 많이 벌 수 있을 거야.　　처음 번 돈으로,

first pennies / I make, / I'll buy Father a new cloth coat.
　　　　내가 번,　　아빠께 새 외투를 사 드려야지.

Cloth, did I say? No, it shall be of gold and silver / with
옷감이라고 말했나?　　아니지, 금과 은으로 만들어져야지

diamond buttons. That poor man certainly deserves it;
다이아몬드 단추가 달린.　가여운 그 분은 그럴 자격이 있어;

for, / after all, / isn't he in his shirt sleeves / because he
왜냐하면,　결국,　　아빠가 셔츠 차림이 되었잖아　　　충분히 좋으시니까

was good enough / to buy a book / for me? On this cold
　　　　　　　책을 사 줄 정도로　　내게?　　이렇게 추운 날씨에,

day, / too! Fathers are indeed good / to their children!"
그것도!　아버지들은 정말로 착한 분들이야　　아이들에게는!"

47

As he talked to himself, / he thought / he heard sounds of
혼잣말을 하면서,　　　　　　그는 생각했다　　피리 소리와 북 소리가 들린다고

pipes and drums / coming from a distance: / pi-pi-pi, pi-
　　　　　　　　　멀리서부터 오는:　　　　　삐-삐-삐, 삐-삐-삐 …

pi-pi… / zum, zum, zum, zum.
　　　　　둥, 둥, 둥, 둥.

He stopped / to listen. Those sounds came / from a little
그는 걸음을 멈추고　귀 기울였다.　소리는 들렸다　　　　좁은 거리로부터

street / that led to a small village / along the shore.
　　　작은 마을로 향한　　　　　　　　해변을 따라.

"What can that noise be? What a nuisance / that I have to
"이 소리는 뭐지?　　　　　　　　귀찮구나　　　　　학교에 가야 하다니!

go to school! Otherwise…"
그렇지 않다면…"

There he stopped, / very much puzzled. He felt / he had to
그 자리에 멈춰 서서,　　아주 많이 망설였다.　　　그는 생각했다

make up his mind / for either one thing or another. Should
결심을 해야 한다고　　이럴까 저럴까.

he go to school, / or should he follow the pipes?
학교에 가야 할까,　　아니면 피리 소리를 따라 갈까?

"Today / I'll follow the pipes, / and tomorrow / I'll go to
"오늘은　　피리 소리를 따라 가고,　　　　내일은　　　　학교에 가는 거야.

school. There's always plenty of time / to go to school," /
　　　　　시간은 항상 많으니까　　　　　　학교에 갈."

decided the little rascal / at last, / shrugging his shoulders.
어린 악동은 결정했다　　　　결국,　　어깨를 으쓱이며.

No sooner said / than done. He started down the street,
말 떨어지기 무섭게　　실행에 옮겼다.　그는 거리를 따라 가기 시작했다,

/ going like the wind. On he ran, / and louder grew / the
　바람같이 뛰면서.　　　　　　달리면 달릴수록,　　커졌다

sounds of pipe and drum: / pi-pi-pi, pi-pi-pi, pi-pi-pi… /
피리와 북 소리가:　　　　　삐-삐-삐, 삐-삐-삐, 삐-삐-삐 …

shore 기슭, 해안[해변], 호숫가 | nuisance 성가신 사람 | otherwise 그렇지 않으면 | puzzle 어리둥절하게 만들다
| make up one's mind 결심하다 | pipe 피리 | rascal 악동 | shrug one's shoulders 어깨를 움츠리다[으쓱해
하다](불쾌·절망·놀람·의심·냉소 따위의 몸짓) | square 광장 | brilliant 훌륭한, 멋진 | somehow 왜 그런지 (
모르겠지만), 왠지 | letter 글자, 문자

zum, zum, zum, zum.
둥, 둥, 둥, 둥.

Suddenly, / he found himself / in a large square, / full of
갑자기   그는 발견했다   자신이 큰 광장에 있음을,   서 있는 사람들

people standing / in front of a little wooden building /
로 가득 찬   작은 나무로 만든 건물 앞에

painted in brilliant colors.
화려한 색으로 칠해진.

"What is that house?" / Pinocchio asked a little boy near
"저 집은 뭐니?"   피노키오가 옆에 있는 아이에게 물었다.

him.

"Read the sign / and you'll know."
"포스터를 읽으면   알 수 있지."

"I'd like to read, / but somehow I can't / today."
"나도 읽고 싶어.   하지만 왠지 글을 못 읽겠어   오늘은."

"Oh, really? Then / I'll read it / to you. Know, then, /
"이런, 정말이니?   그럼   내가 읽어 줄게 네게.   그럼, 자,

that written in letters of fire / I see the words: / GREAT
빨간 글씨로 적혀 있는데   글씨가 보여:

MARIONETTE THEATER.
'꼭두각시 인형극 대공연'이라고.

"When did the show start?"
"공연은 언제 시작했니?"

"It is starting now."
"지금 막 시작했어."

"And how much does one pay / to get in?"
"얼마를 내야 하는데   안에 들어가려면?"

"Four pennies."
"4페니야."

Pinocchio, / who was wild / with curiosity / to know what
피노키오는,   미칠 지경이었다   호기심 때문에   안에서 어떤 일이 있었나

was going on inside, / lost all his pride / and said to the boy
는지 알고 싶어서,   자존심을 버리고   아이에게 말했다

/ shamelessly:
부끄러움도 잊은 채:

"Will you give me four pennies / until tomorrow?"
"4페니 좀 빌려줄 수 있니   내일까지?"

"I'd give them to you / gladly," answered the other, / poking
"나도 주고 싶지만   기꺼이,"   아이가 대답했다,

fun at him, / "but just now / I can't give them / to you."
비웃으며,   "하지만 마침   줄 돈이 없어   네게는."

"For the price of four pennies, / I'll sell you my coat."
"4페니 값으로,   내 외투를 팔게."

"If it rains, / what shall I do with a coat / of flowered paper?
"비가 오면,   외투로 무엇을 할 수 있는데   꽃무늬 종이로 된?

I could not take it off / again."
벗지도 못할 텐데   다시."

"Do you want to buy my shoes?"
"신발은 어때?"

"They are only good enough / to light a fire with."
"그건 좋겠다   불을 지필 때나."

"What about my hat?"
"내 모자는 어때?"

"Fine bargain, / indeed! A cap of dough! The mice might
"그거 좋네,   정말로! 빵으로 만든 모자라니! 쥐들이 와서

come / and eat it / from my head!"
먹겠는데   내 머리에서부터!"

Pinocchio was almost in tears. He was just about to / make
피노키오는 눈물이 나려 했다.   막 하려 했지만,

shamelessly 몰염치하게도 | poke fun ~을 조롱하다 | bargain 합의, 흥정 | mice 쥐(mouse의 복수형)
| lack ~이 부족하다 | hesitate 망설이다, 주저하다 | common sense 상식 | ragpicker 넝마주이 | shiver (추위
등으로 가볍게) (몸을) 떨다

one last offer, / but he lacked the courage / to do so. He
마지막 제안을,　　　　　용기가 나지 않았다　　　　　　그렇게 할.

hesitated, / he wondered, / he could not make up his mind.
그는 망설였고,　　궁금했다,　　　　마음의 결정을 내릴 수 없었다.

At last / he said:
마침내　　그가 말했다:

"Will you give me four pennies / for the book?"
"4페니를 줄 수 있니　　　　　　이 책이면?"

"I am a boy / and I buy nothing from boys," / said the little
"난 어린이고　　어린이한테 아무것도 사지 않아,"　　　　어린 친구가 말했다

fellow / with far more common sense / than the Marionette.
　　　　좀 더 상식이 있는　　　　꼭두각시보다는.

"I'll give you four pennies / for your A-B-C book," / said a
"내가 4페니를 주마　　　　네 영어책을 주면,"　　　　넝마주이가

ragpicker / who stood by.
말했다　　옆에 서 있던.

Then and there, / the book changed hands. **And to think /**
그렇게 거기서,　　　책은 다른 손에 넘어갔다.　　　생각해 보세요

that poor old Geppetto sat at home / in his shirt sleeves,
불쌍하고 늙은 제페토가 집에 앉아 있다고　　　셔츠 차림으로,

/ shivering with cold, / having sold his coat / to buy that
　추위에 떨면서,　　　　외투를 팔았기 때문에　　　　그 작은 책을 사려고

little book / for his son!
　　　아들을 위해!

비교급 강조 : 훨씬 더 ~한
형용사나 부사를 강조할 때에는 so나 very를 사용하는데요, 비교급의 형용사
와 부사를 강조하여 '훨씬 더 ~한'이란 의미를 나타낼 때에는 아래의 5개 부사
가 사용됩니다.

even, much, far, a lot, still + 비교급 (첫 글자를 따서 'emfas'로 외워보세요!)
much, by far, the very + 최상급

ex) "I am a boy and I buy nothing from boys," said the little fellow with far more
    common sense than the Marionette.
    "나는 어린 아이이고 아이에게서 아무것도 하지 않아"라고 꼭두각시보다 훨씬 상
    식이 있는 어린 친구가 말했다.

mini test 2

A. 다음 문장을 해석해 보세요.

(1) Pinocchio hated the dark street, / but he was so hungry that, / in spite of it, / he ran out of the house.
→

(2) As soon as he heard / his Father's voice, / he jumped up from his seat / to open the door, / but, / as he did so, / he staggered / and fell headlong to the floor.
→

(3) Pinocchio began to scream / and cry so loudly / that he could be heard / for miles around.
→

(4) In this world, / even as children, / we must accustom ourselves / to eat of everything, / for we never know / what life may hold in store / for us!
→

B. 다음 주어진 문구가 알맞은 문장이 되도록 순서를 맞춰보세요.

(1) 거리에는, 개 한 마리도 보이지 않았다.
(not / a dog / the streets, / even / seen / In / be / could)
→

(2) 피노키오는 그의 발이 <u>자신의 것이 아닌 것처럼</u> 행복하게 코를 골았다.
(were / his / as / his feet / not / own / if)
→ Pinocchio snored away happily _____.

(3) 내가 살아있는 한 그것을 잊지 않겠어요.
(long / shall / I / as / it / I / as / remember / live)
→

A. (1) 피노키오는 밤 거리를 싫어했지만, 그럼에도 불구하고 너무 배가 고파서 집을 나섰다. (2) 아버지의 목소리를 듣자 마자, 그는 문을 열기 위해 의자에서 벌떡 일어났다. 하지만 그렇게 하자, 그는 비틀거리며 바닥으로 떨어져 버렸다. (3) 피노키오는 소리지르기 시작했고 너무 크게 울어서 수 마일 밖에서도 들

52   The Adventures of Pinocchio

(4) 학교에 가야 한다니 정말 귀찮구나!
(go to / nuisance / have to / What / I / a / school! / that)
→

C. 다음 주어진 문장이 본문의 내용과 맞으면 T, 틀리면 F에 동그라미 하세요.

(1) Pinocchio went out to get some food, but he failed.
(T / F)

(2) Pinocchio burned his legs while he was sleeping.
(T / F)

(3) After all, Pinocchio didn't eat the skins and cores of the pears.
(T / F)

(4) Geppetto sold his hat to buy Pinocchio an A-B-C book.
(T / F)

D. 의미가 서로 비슷한 것끼리 연결해 보세요.

(1) weird   ▶   ◀ ① soothe

(2) jumbled   ▶   ◀ ② naughty

(3) appease   ▶   ◀ ③ odd

(4) mischievous   ▶   ◀ ④ chaotic

8

The Marionettes recognize / their brother Pinocchio, / and
꼭두각시들은 알아보고   그들의 형제인 피노키오에게,

greet him / with loud cheers; / but the Director, Fire Eater,
인사한다   크게 환영하면서;   하지만 단장인, 불 먹는 사나이가,

/ happens along / and poor Pinocchio almost loses his life.
갑자기 나타나   불쌍한 피노키오는 거의 죽을 뻔 한다.

Quick as a flash, / Pinocchio disappeared / into the
불꽃처럼 재빨리,   피노키오는 사라졌다

Marionette Theater. And then / something happened /
꼭두각시 극장 속으로.   그리고 나자   뭔가가 일어났다

which almost caused a riot.
거의 폭동을 일으킬 만한.

The curtain was up / and the performance had started.
커튼이 올라 갔고   공연이 시작되었다.

Harlequin and Pulcinella were reciting / on the stage / and,
할리퀸와 폴치넬라가 연기를 하고 있었다   무대 위에서   그리고,

/ as usual, / they were threatening each other / with sticks
평소처럼,   서로를 위협했다

and blows.
막대기와 주먹으로.

The theater was full of people, / enjoying the spectacle
극장은 사람들로 가득 찼다.   그 광경을 즐거워 하며

/ and laughing / till they cried / at the antics / of the two
웃고 있는   눈물이 날 때까지   익살스러운 짓을 보고

Marionettes.
두 꼭두각시의.

The play continued / for a few minutes, / and then
연극은 계속 되었다   몇 분 간,   그리고 나서 갑자기,

suddenly, / without any warning, / Harlequin stopped
어떤 경고도 없이,   할리퀸이 말을 멈추었다.

talking. Turning toward the audience, / he pointed to the
관객들을 향해 돌아서더니,   그는 오케스트라 뒤 쪽을 가리키며,

rear of the orchestra, / yelling wildly / at the same time:
크게 소리쳤다   동시에:

"Look, look! Am I asleep or awake? Or do I really see
"저기 봐 봐!   꿈이야 생시야?   내가 정말 피노키오를 본 거야

Pinocchio / there?"
저기 있는?"

"Yes, yes! It is Pinocchio!" / screamed Pulcinella.
"맞아, 맞아!   피노키오야!   폴치넬라가 소리쳤다.

"It is! It is!" / shrieked Signora Rosaura, / peeking in/ from
"정말! 정말!"   로사우라 부인이 소리쳤다,   안쪽을 엿보던

the side of the stage.
무대 한쪽에서.

"It is Pinocchio! It is Pinocchio!" / yelled all the
"피노키오야!   피노키오야!"   꼭두각시들이 모두 소리쳤다,

Marionettes, / pouring out of the wings. "It is Pinocchio. It
무대 양쪽에서 뛰쳐나오며.   "피노키오야.

is our brother Pinocchio! Hurrah for Pinocchio!"
우리의 형제 피노키오야!   피노키오 만세!"

"Pinocchio, come up to me!" / shouted Harlequin. "Come
"피노키오, 이리 와!"   할리퀸이 소리쳤다.

to the arms / of your wooden brothers!"
"품으로 어서 와   나무로 만든 형제들의!"

Key Expression

Harlequin과 Pulcinella

Harlequin(할리퀸)과 Pulcinella(폴치넬라)는 commedia dell 'arte(코메디아 델라르테)라고 불리는 16~18세기 이탈리아의 희극에 등장하는 인물들이에요.
이 외에도 할리퀸과 사랑에 빠지는 명랑하고 영리한 하녀 역의 Colombina(콜롬비나), 교활하고 탐욕스럽지만 종종 속임수에 속는 베네치아(판탈로네) 등이 있습니다.

▶ Harlequin(할리퀸) : 극의 주역으로 다이아몬드 무늬의 알록달록한 옷을 입고 등장하는 소박하지만 교활하고 재치있는 재치있는 하인입니다. 그 어원은 라틴어 Herculinus로 그 의미는 작은 헤라클레스란 뜻이에요.
▶ Pulcinella(폴치넬라) : 비열하고 사악하며 교묘한 재주를 가진 역할로 항상 새부리처럼 기다란 코가 있는 가면을 쓰고 등장합니다. 주로 모든 것을 다 알면서도 멍청한 역할을 하는 음흉한 모습과 물리적 폭력을 통해 웃음을 유발하는 역할을 맡아요.

greet 맞다, 환영하다 | cheer 환호(성), 응원의 함성 | riot 폭동 | recite 암송하다 | antics 익살스러운 짓 | yell 소리 지르다 | Signora 부인, 여사, 마님(영어의 Madam, Mrs.에 해당, 특히 (이탈리아의) 귀부인, 마님) | peek (재빨리) 훔쳐보다 | pour 쏟아져 나오다 | wings (연극 무대의 양쪽) 끝[옆] | hurrah 만세

At such a loving invitation, / Pinocchio, / with one leap
너무나 따뜻한 환영에,　　　　피노키오는,　　경충 뛰어

/ from the back of the orchestra, / found himself / in the
오케스트라 뒤쪽에서부터,

front rows. With another leap, / he was on the orchestra
맨 앞줄에 섰다.　또 한 번 뛰어오르자,　그는 오케스트라 지휘자 머리 위에 있었다.

leader's head. With a third, / he landed on the stage.
　　　　세 번째 뛰어오르자,　무대 위에 착지했다.

It is impossible / to describe / the shrieks of joy, / the warm
불가능하다　　　설명하기는　　기쁨의 환호와,　　따뜻한 포옹과,

embraces, / the knocks, / and the friendly greetings / with
　　　토닥이던 손길,　그리고 다정한 인사들을

which / that strange company / of dramatic actors and
이것은　낯선 무리들이　　연극 배우들로 구성된

actresses / received Pinocchio.
　　피노키오를 맞이하는 태도였다.

It was a heart-rending spectacle, / but the audience, /
가슴이 미어지는 광경이었지만,　　관객들은,

seeing that the play had stopped, / became angry / and
연극이 멈춘 걸 보고,　　화가 나서

began to yell:
소리치기 시작했다:

"The play, the play, / we want the play!"
"공연을 해, 공연을,　우리는 공연을 원한다!"

The yelling was of no use, / for the Marionettes, / instead
외침은 아무 소용이 없었다,　꼭두각시들에게,

of going on with their act, / made twice as much racket /
공연을 계속하기는 커녕,　두 배 더 소란을 피웠다,

as before, / and, / lifting up Pinocchio on their shoulders, /
이전보다,　그리고는, 피노키오를 어깨 위로 들어 올려

carried him / around the stage / in triumph.
데려갔다　무대 주위로　의기 양양하게.

---

land 착륙하다 | embrace 포옹하다 | heart-rending 가슴이 미어지는 | racket 시끄러운 소리, 소음 | in
triumph 의기양양하여

At that very moment, / the Director came out of his room.
바로 그 순간,　　　　　　　단장이 방에서 나왔다.

He had such a fearful appearance / that one look at him
그는 너무나 무서운 외모를 가져서　　　　　　그를 보는 사람이면 누구나

/ would fill you / with horror. His beard was as black as
가득 찼다　　　공포로.　　그의 수염은 칠흑같이 까맣고,

pitch, / and so long / that it reached / from his chin down
　　　　너무 길어서　　　뻗어 있었다　　턱에서부터 내려와

/ to his feet. His mouth was as wide as an oven, / his teeth
발까지.　　　입은 오븐만큼 크고,　　　　　　이는 짐승의

like yellow fangs, / and his eyes, / two glowing red coals.
노란 송곳니처럼 생겼으며,　눈은,　두 개의 불타는 빨간 석탄 조각 같았다.

In his huge, / hairy hands, / a long whip, / made of green
그의 크고,　　털이 많은 손에는,　긴 채찍이　　초록색 뱀과 검은 고양이의

snakes and black cats' tails / twisted together, / swished /
꼬리로 만든,　　　　　　함께 꼬아서,　　　획 하고 움직였다

through the air / in a dangerous way.
공중에서　　매우 위험하게.

At the unexpected apparition, / no one dared / even to
느닷없이 나타난 유령을 보자,　　아무도 감히　　숨조차 쉴 수 없었다.

breathe. One could almost hear / a fly go by. Those poor
　　　거의 들릴 정도였다　　　파리가 나는 소리까지.

Marionettes, / one and all, / trembled / like leaves / in a
불쌍한 꼭두각시들은,　모두,　　떨었다　　나뭇잎처럼

storm.
폭풍 속의.

---

fearful 걱정하는 | as black as pitch 칠흑같이 새까만 | fangs (뱀·개 등의) 송곳니 | glowing 타는 듯한, 새빨간
| coals (특히 타고 있는) 석탄 조각 | swish 휙[쌩] 소리를 내며 움직이다 | apparition 유령 | one and all 모두
[모든 사람들] | ogre (이야기 속에 나오는) 사람을 잡아먹는 거인 | spit (꼬치 요리에 쓰이는) 쇠꼬챙이 | well-
seasoned 잘 마른 | wriggle (몸이나 몸의 일부를) 꿈틀거리다 | squirm (초조하거나 불편하거나 하여 몸을) 꿈틀[
꼼지락]대다 | eel 장어 | pitifully 측은하게, 가련하게

"Why have you brought such excitement / into my
"왜 소란을 피우는 게냐   내 극장에 와서,"

theater;" / the huge fellow asked Pinocchio / with the voice
거인이 피노키오에게 물었다   괴물의 목소리로

of an ògre / suffering with a cold.
감기에 걸린.

"Believe me, / your Honor, / the fault was not mine."
"믿어 주세요,   나리,   제 잘못이 아니에요."

"Enough! Be quiet! I'll take care of you / later."
"듣기 싫다!   조용히 해!   내가 처리하마   나중에."

As soon as the play was over, / the Director went to the
연극이 끝나자 마자,   단장은 부엌으로 갔다,

kitchen, / where a fine big lamb was slowly turning / on
거기에는 멋지고 큰 양고기가 천천히 돌아가고 있었다

the spit. More wood was needed / to finish cooking it. He
쇠꼬챙이에 꽂혀. 더 많은 땔감이 필요했다   요리를 마치려면.

called Harlequin and Pulcinella / and said to them:
그는 할리퀸과 폴치넬라를 불러서   말했다:

"Bring that Marionette / to me! He looks / as if he were
"그 꼭두각시를 데려와라   나에게! 그 놈은 보여   마치 만들어진 것처럼

made / of well-seasoned wood. He'll make a fine fire / for
잘 마른 나무로.   그 놈은 불이 잘 붙겠어

this spit."
꼬치구이 하기에."

Harlequin and Pulcinella hesitated / a bit. Then, frightened
할리퀸과 폴치넬라는 망설였다   약간. 하지만, 공포에 질려

/ by a look from their master, / they left the kitchen / to
극단 주인이 노려보자,   부엌을 떠났다   그의 말을

obey him. A few minutes later / they returned, / carrying
따르기 위해. 몇 분 후에   그들이 돌아왔다,

poor Pinocchio, / who was wriggling and squirming / like
불쌍한 피노키오를 데리고,   몸을 꼼지락거리고 비틀며

an eel / and crying pitifully:
장어처럼   불쌍하게 소리지르는:

"Father, save me! I don't want to die! I don't want to die!"
"아빠, 구해 주세요!   저 죽기 싫어요!   저 죽기 싫다고요!"

Fire Eater gives Pinocchio / five gold pieces / for his
불 먹는 사나이는 피노키오에게 준다   다섯 닢의 금화를,

father, Geppetto; / but the Marionette meets a Fox and a
그의 아버지, 제페토를 위해;   하지만 꼭두각시는 여우와 고양이를 만나

Cat / and follows them.
고양이   그들을 따라간다.

The next day / Fire Eater called Pinocchio / aside / and
다음 날   불 먹는 사나이는 피노키오를 불러서   따로

asked him:
물었다:

"What is your father's name?"
"네 아버지 이름이 뭐냐?"

"Geppetto."
"제페토예요."

"And what is his trade?"
"무슨 일을 하시지?"

"He's a wood carver."
"나무를 깎는 일이요."

"Does he earn much?"
"돈은 많이 버시니?"

"He earns so much / that he never has a penny in his
"너무 많이 벌어서   주머니에 동전은 한 닢도 없을 정도예요.

pockets. Just think that, / in order to buy me / an A-B-C
생각해 보세요,   내게 사 주기 위해   영어책을

book / for school, / he had to sell the only coat / he owned,
학교에 가라고,   유일한 외투를 팔아야 했으니까요,   아버지가 가진,

/ a coat so full of darns and patches / that it was a pity."
꿰맨 자리와 덧댄 옷감으로 너무나 가득 차 있는 외투를   정말 안 됐어요.'

trade 직업, 일(특히 손을 사용하고, 특별한 훈련과 기술이 필요한 종류) | wood carver 목각사 | darn 꿰매다 |
regard 안부(의 말) | in turn 차례차례 | beside oneself (with something) (감정이 북받쳐) 어쩔 줄을 모르는[
제정신이 아닌] | set out 출발하다[(여행을) 시작하다] | barely 간신히, 가까스로, 빠듯하게 | courteously 공손하게

"Poor fellow! I feel sorry for him. Here, / take these five
"불쌍한 양반!   정말 안 됐구나.   여기,   금화 다섯 닢을 가져가라.

gold pieces. Go, / give them to him / with my kindest
          가서,   아빠께 드려라   내 안부도 전하고."

regards."

Pinocchio, / as may easily be imagined, / thanked him /
피노키오는,   상상하는 대로,   그에게 감사의 말을 전했다

a thousand times. He kissed / each Marionette / in turn, /
수천 번씩.   그는 입맞췄다   모든 꼭두각시에게   차례차례,

even the officers, / and, / beside himself with joy, / set out
심지어 경관들까지,   그리고,   기뻐서 어쩔 줄 모르며,

on his homeward journey.
집으로 향했다.

He had gone barely half a mile / when he met a lame Fox
반 마일도 채 못 가서   그는 절름발이 여우와 장님고양이를 만났다,

and a blind Cat, / walking together / like two good friends.
                          함께 걷고 있는   둘이 좋은 친구처럼.

The lame Fox leaned / on the Cat, / and the blind Cat let /
절름발이 여우는 기대었다   고양이에게,   장님고양이는 따라 갔다

the Fox lead him along.
여우가 이끄는 대로.

"Good morning, Pinocchio," / said the Fox, / greeting him
"안녕, 피노키오,"   여우가 말했다,

courteously.
공손하게 인사하면서.

Key Expression

지각동사의 목적보어

지각동사란 감각을 통해 보고 듣고 느끼는 것을 표현하는 동사입니다. 지각동사는
5형식 문장에서 쓰이는 동사로 목적보어 자리에는 동사원형이나 현재분사가 오
며 '~(목적어)가 …하는 것을 보다/듣다/느끼다'라고 해석합니다.

▶ 보다(see, look at, watch),
▶ 듣다(hear, listen to),   + 목적어 + 동사원형/현재분사
▶ 느끼다(feel)

현재분사가 목적보어로 쓰이는 경우는 동작의 진행을 강조하고 싶을 때입니다.

ex) I saw him yesterday standing at the door of his house.
    나는 어제 그가 집의 문 앞에서 서 있는 것을 보았다.

"How do you know my name?" / asked the Marionette.
"내 이름을 어떻게 아니?"   꼭두각시가 물었다.

"I know your father well."
"너희 아빠를 잘 알거든."

"Where have you seen him?"
"우리 아빠를 어디에서 봤는데?"

"I saw him / yesterday / standing at the door of his house."
"그를 봤어   어제   집 문 앞에 서 있는."

"And what was he doing?"
"그럼 뭘 하고 계셨어?"

"He was in his shirt sleeves / trembling with cold."
"셔츠 바람으로   추위에 떨고 계셨어."

"Poor Father! But, after today, / God willing, / he will
"불쌍한 아빠!   하지만, 오늘부터,   신의 가호로,

suffer no longer."
더 이상 떨지 않을 거야."

"Why?"
"어째서?"

"Because I have become a rich man."
"내가 부자가 됐으니까."

"You, a rich man?" / said the Fox, / and he began to laugh
"네가, 부자라고?"   여우가 말했다,   그리고 웃기 시작했다

out / loud. The Cat was laughing also, / but tried to hide it /
크게.   고양이도 웃고 있었지만,   웃음을 숨기려고 애썼다

by stroking his long whiskers.
긴 수염을 쓰다듬으며.

"There is nothing to laugh at," / cried Pinocchio / angrily.
"웃을 일이 아니거든,"   피노키오가 소리쳤다   화가 나서.

"I am very sorry / to make your mouth water, / but these, /
"미안하지만   군침 돌게 해서,   여기,

as you know, / are five new gold pieces."
보다시피,   금화 다섯 닢이야."

And he pulled out the gold pieces / which Fire Eater had
그리고 그는 금화를 꺼냈다   불 먹는 사나이가 그에게 준.

given him.

At the cheerful tinkle / of the gold, / the Fox unconsciously
황홀한 짤랑거리는 소리를 듣자   금화의,   여우는 무의식적으로 내밀었다

held out / his paw / that was supposed to be lame, / and
그의 앞발을   절름발이여야 하는,

the Cat opened wide his two eyes / till they looked like
그리고 고양이는 두 눈을 번쩍 떠서   마치 등불이 켜진 것처럼 보였다,

live coals, / but he closed them / again / so quickly / that
하지만 눈을 감았다   다시   아주 재빨라서

Pinocchio did not notice.
피노키오가 눈치채지 못하게.

"And may I ask," / inquired the Fox, / "what you are going
"물어 봐도 되니?"   여우가 물었다.   "뭘 할 건데

to do / with all that money?"
그 돈을 가지고?"

"First of all," / answered the Marionette, / "I want to buy
"제일 먼저,"   꼭두각시가 대답했다,   "새 외투를 사 드릴 거야

a fine new coat / for my father, / a coat of gold and silver /
아빠께,   금과 은으로 만든 외투를,

with diamond buttons; / after that, / I'll buy an A-B-C book
다이아몬드 단추가 박힌;   그 후에,   영어책을 살 거야

/ for myself."
내 자신을 위해."

"For yourself?"
"네 자신을 위해?"

"For myself. I want to go to school / and study hard."
"나를 위해서.   나는 학교에 가고 싶어   공부도 열심히 하고."

"Look at me," / said the Fox. "For the silly reason / of
"날 봐,"   여우가 말했다.   "그런 바보 같은 이유 때문에

wanting to study, / I have lost a paw."
공부를 하고 싶다는,   나는 발을 잃었어."

"Look at me," / said the Cat. "For the same foolish reason, /
"날 봐,"   고양이가 말했다.   "바보 같은 똑같은 이유 때문에,

I have lost / the sight of both eyes."
나는 잃었어   두 눈의 시력을."

stroke (동물의 털을) 쓰다듬다 | tinkle 쨍그렁[짤랑/딸랑]하는 소리 | unconsciously 무의식적으로 | paw (동물의
발톱이 달린) 발

At that moment, / a Blackbird, / perched on the fence /
그 순간,　　　　　　찌르레기 한 마리가,　　울타리에 앉아

along the road, / called out / sharp and clear:
길 가에,　　　　　　소리쳤다　　　날카롭고 선명하게:

"Pinocchio, / do not listen to bad advice. If you do, / you'll
"피노키오,　　　나쁜 친구들의 충고는 듣지 마.　　그렇게 했다가는,

be sorry!"
후회하게 될 거야!"

Poor little Blackbird! If he had only kept his words / to
불쌍한 찌르레기!　　　그냥 잠자코 있었으면 있었으면 좋았을 걸!

himself! In the twinkling of an eyelid, / the Cat leaped on
　　　　　　　눈 깜짝 할 사이에,　　　　　고양이가 덮치더니,

him, and ate him, / feathers and all.
　　그 새를 잡아먹었다,　　깃털까지 모두.

After eating the bird, / he cleaned his whiskers, / closed
새를 먹어 치운 후,　　　　고양이는 수염을 닦고 나서,

his eyes, / and became blind / once more.
눈을 감고,　　장님이 되었다　　　다시 한 번.

"Poor Blackbird!" / said Pinocchio / to the Cat. "Why did
"불쌍한 찌르레기!"　　　피노키오가 말했다　　고양이에게.

you kill him?"
"찌르레기를 왜 죽였니?"

"I killed him / to teach him a lesson. He talks too much.
"새를 죽인 거야　　교훈을 가르쳐 주기 위해.　　그 새는 말이 너무 많아.

Next time / he will keep his words to himself."
다음 번엔　　조용히 있을 거야."

By this time / the three companions had walked / a long
여태까지　　　세 친구들은 걸어왔다　　　　　먼 거리를.

distance. Suddenly, / the Fox stopped / in his tracks / and,
갑자기,　　　　　　여우가 멈췄다　　가던 길을　　　그리고,

/ turning to the Marionette, / said to him:
　꼭두각시를 돌아보며,　　　　　말했다:

"Do you want to double your gold pieces?"
"금화를 두 배로 불리고 싶지 않니?"

"What do you mean?"
"무슨 말이야?"

"Do you want / one hundred, a thousand, two thousand
"원하지 않니   백 개, 천 개, 이천 개의 금화를

gold pieces / for your miserable five?"
            초라한 다섯 닢으로?"

"Yes, but how?"
"원하지, 그런데 어떻게?"

"The way is very easy. Instead of returning home, /
"방법은 아주 쉬워.   집으로 돌아가는 대신,

come with us."
우리랑 함께 가자."

"And where will you take me?"
"어디로 가는데?"

"To the City of Simple Simons."
"'얼간이들의 도시'로."

Pinocchio thought / a while / and then said / firmly:
피노키오는 생각했다   잠시   그리고 나서 말했다   단호하게:

"No, I don't want to go. Home is near, / and I'm going /
"싫어, 난 가고 싶지 않아.   집에 거의 다 왔고,   나는 가는 중이야

where Father is waiting / for me. How unhappy he must
아빠가 기다리는 곳으로   나를.   얼마나 슬퍼하시겠어

be / that I have not yet returned! I have been a bad son, /
      내가 아직도 안 돌아와서!   나는 나쁜 아들이었어,

and the Talking Cricket was right / when he said / that a
그리고 말하는 귀뚜라미가 옳았어   그가 말했을 때

disobedient boy cannot be happy / in this world. I have
말 안 듣는 아이는 행복해질 수 없다고   이 세상에서.   나는 이 교훈

learned this / at my own expense. Even last night / in the
을 배웠어   값비싼 비용을 들여서.   어젯밤에도

theater, / when Fire Eater…
극장에서,   불 먹는 사나이가…

Brrrr!!!!! … The shivers run / up and down / my back / at
부르르!!!!! …   소름이 돋아   위 아래로   내 등에

the mere thought of it."
그 생각만 하면."

blackbird (북미산) 찌르레기 | perch 앉아 있다, 걸터앉다 | fence 울타리 | eyelid 한쪽 눈꺼풀 | whisker (고양이
·쥐 등의) 수염 | company 함께 있는 사람 | double 두 배[갑절]로 되다[만들다] | Simple Simons 얼뜨기 사이먼
(영국 전래 동요의 주인공); 얼간이 | firmly 단호히, 확고히 | disobedient 반항하는, 거역하는 | shiver 몸서리 |
mere 겨우, 일개의

65

"Well, then," / said the Fox, / "if you really want to go
"음, 그렇다면," 여우가 말했다. "정말 집에 가고 싶다면,

home, / go ahead, / but you'll be sorry."
어서 가, 하지만 후회하게 될 거야."

"You'll be sorry," / repeated the Cat.
"후회하게 될 거야," 고양이가 따라 했다.

"Think well, Pinocchio, / you are turning your back / on
"잘 생각해, 피노키오, 넌 지금 등을 돌리고 있어

Dame Fortune."
'운명의 여신'에게서'.

"On Dame Fortune," / repeated the Cat.
"'운명의 여신'에게서," 고양이가 따라 했다.

"Tomorrow / your five gold pieces / will be two
"내일이면 네 금화 다섯 닢이 2천 개가 될 텐데!"

thousand!"

"Two thousand!" / repeated the Cat.
"2천 개!" 고양이가 따라 했다.

"But / how can they possibly become so many?" / asked
"하지만 어떻게 그렇게 많아질 수 있어?"

Pinocchio / wonderingly.
피노키오가 물었다 궁금해 하며.

"I'll explain," / said the Fox. "You must know that, / just
"설명해 주지," 여우가 말했다. "알아야 해,

outside the City of Simple Simons, / there is a blessed
'얼간이 의 도시' 밖에는, 축복 받은 땅이 있어

field / called the Field of Wonders.
'기적의 땅'이라고 불리우는.

In this field / you dig a hole / and in the hole / you bury a
이 땅에 구멍을 파고 그 구멍 안에

gold piece.
금화 한 닢을 묻는 거야.

Dame Fortune 운명의 여신 | wonderingly 경탄하며 | blessed 신성한, 복 받은 | sprinkle 뿌리다 | sprout
새싹, 싹이 나다 | blossom 꽃이 피다

After covering up the hole / with earth / you water it
구멍을 덮은 후에   흙으로   물을 잘 주고,

well, / sprinkle a bit of salt on it, / and go to bed. During
소금을 조금 뿌리고,   잠자리에 드는 거지.   밤새,

the night, / the gold piece sprouts, / grows, / blossoms, /
금화가 싹을 틔우고,   자라서,   꽃을 피우지,

and next morning / you find a beautiful tree, / that is
그리고 다음 날 아침이면   아름다운 나무를 보게 될 거야,

loaded with gold pieces."
금화가 주렁주렁 달려 있는."

"So that / if I were to bury my five gold pieces," / cried
"그럼   금화 다섯 닢을 묻으면,"   피노키오가

Pinocchio / with growing wonder, / "next morning / I
외쳤다   더욱 더 놀라며,   "다음 날 아침이면

should find / —— how many?"
볼 수 있는 거야   — 얼마나 많이?

"It is very simple / to figure out," / answered the Fox.
"그야 매우 간단하지   계산하는 건,"   여우가 말했다.

Key Expression 🍴

If I were to ~ : 실현 불가능한 일에 대한 가정

If절에 were to를 사용하는 가정법은 실현 가능성이 희박한 일을 가정할 때 쓰이는 구문으로 가정법 미래라고 표현하기도 합니다. 주절에는 조동사의 과거형을 사용하며 그 형태는 다음과 같습니다.

▶ If + 주어 + were to + 동사원형 ~, 주어 + would/should/could/might + 동사원형 ~ (만약 ~ 한다면, ~ 할텐데)

ex) So that if I were to bury my five gold pieces, next morning I should find — how many?
   그렇다면 만약 내가 금화 다섯 닢을 묻으면, 다음 날 아침 몇 개를 발견하게 되는 거지?

"Why, you can figure it / on your fingers! Granted that each
"자, 계산할 수 있어   네 손가락으로!   가열 한 닢당 500개라고 치면,

piece gives you five hundred, / multiply five hundred by
                                  5 곱하기 500을 하면 돼.

five. Next morning / you will find / twenty-five hundred
다음 날 아침   넌 발견할 거야   2,500개의 새롭고, 번쩍이는 금화를."

new, sparkling gold pieces."

"Fine! Fine!" / cried Pinocchio, / dancing about / with joy.
"멋져!   멋져!"   피노키오가 외쳤다,   춤추면서   기뻐서.

"And as soon as I have them, / I shall keep two thousand for
"그럼 그 금화들을 갖게 되면,   2천 개는 내가 갖고

myself / and the other five hundred / I'll give to you two."
내가   나머지 5백 개는   너희 둘에게 줄게."

"A gift for us?" / cried the Fox, / pretending to be insulted.
"우리에게 선물을?"   여우가 소리쳤다,   마치 모욕당한 듯.

"Why, of course not!"
"당치 않아!"

"Of course not!" / repeated the Cat.
"당치 않아!"   고양이가 따라 했다.

"We do not work / for gain," / answered the Fox. "We work
"우리는 일하는 게 아니야   대가를 바라고,"   여우가 대답했다.   "우린 일하는 거야

/ only to enrich others."
단지 사람들을 부자로 만들어 주려고."

"To enrich others!" / repeated the Cat.
"사람들을 부자로 만들려고!"   고양이가 따라 했다.

"What good people," / thought Pinocchio / to himself. And
"참 좋은 사람들이군,"   피노키오가 생각했다.

forgetting his father, / the new coat, / the A-B-C book, / and
그리고는 아빠를 잊어버린 채,   새 외투도,   영어책도,

all his good resolutions, / he said to the Fox and to the Cat:
그리고 모든 훌륭한 다짐들을,   여우와 고양이에게 말했다.

"Let us go. I am with you."
"가자.   너희랑 같이 갈게."

---

granted that 설사 ~이라 할지라도[하더라도] | gain 얻게 되다 | enrich 질을 높이다, 풍요롭게 하다 | resolution
해결, 다짐

10

Pinocchio, / not having listened to the good advice / of the
피노키오는,   좋은 충고를 듣지 않고

Talking Cricket, / falls into the hands of the Assassins.
말하는 귀뚜라미의,   강도의 손에 떨어지다.

"Dear, oh, dear! When I come to think of it," / said the
"맙소사, 오, 이런!   생각해 보니,"

Marionette to himself, / as he once more / set out on his
꼭두각시가 중얼거렸다,   한 번 더   여행을 떠나면서,

journey, / "we boys are really very unlucky. Everybody
"우리 어린이들은 정말 너무 불행해.   다들 우리를 꾸짖고,

scolds us, / everybody gives us advice, / everybody
충고하고,   우리에게 경고하지.

warns us. If we were to allow it, / everyone would try to
만일 허락된다면,   누구나 아빠와 엄마가 되려고 할 거야

be father and mother / to us; / everyone, / even the Talking
우리에게;   누구나,   말하는 귀뚜라미마저.

Cricket. Take me, / for example.
나를 봐,   그 예로.

Key Expression 🍴

granted that ~ : 가령 ~라 치고, 설사 ~라 하더라도

동사 grant는 if 없이 조건의 의미를 나타내는 표현에 사용할 수 있습니다.
granting that, granted that과 같이 사용해 주로 양보의 의미를 지닌
even if(설사 ~라 하더라도)를 대체하는 구문으로 사용됩니다.
grant처럼 if가 없이 조건절의 접속사 역할로 사용할 수 있는 동사로 suppose
와 provide도 자주 쓰입니다.

ex) Granted that each piece gives you five hundred, multiply five hundred by five.
Next morning you will find twenty-five hundred new, sparkling gold pieces.
가령 한 닢당 500개라고 치면, 5 곱하기 500을 해 봐. 다음 날 아침 넌 2,500개
의 번쩍이는 새 금화를 발견할 거야.

assassin 암살범

Just because I would not listen to / that bothersome Cricket,
듣지 않았다는 이유만으로 귀찮은 귀뚜라미 말을,

/ who knows / how many misfortunes may be awaiting
누가 알겠어 얼마나 많은 불행이 나를 기다리고 있을지!

me! Assassins indeed! At least / I have never believed in
강도라니 정말! 적어도 나는 강도를 믿은 적도 없었고,

them, / nor ever will. To speak sensibly, / I think / assassins
앞으로도 그럴 거야. 논리적으로 말해서, 나는 생각해

have been invented / by fathers and mothers / to frighten
강도는 만들어진 거라고 아빠와 엄마에 의해 아이들을 겁 주려고

children / who want to run away / at night. And then, / even
뛰어 나가고 싶어하는 밤에. 그러니,

if I were to meet them on the road, / what matter? I'll just
만약 길에서 강도를 만난다 해도, 뭐가 문제인데?

run up to them, / and say, / 'Well, signori, / what do you
그들에게 똑바로 달려가서, 말할 거야, '자, 나리, 뭘 원하세요?

want? Remember / that you can't fool with me! Run along
기억하세요 나를 놀릴 수 없다는 걸! 가서

/ and mind your business.' At such a speech, / I can almost
볼일이나 보세요.' 그렇게 말하면, 보게 되겠지

see / those poor fellows / running like the wind. But / in
그 불쌍한 강도들이 바람처럼 도망치는 것을. 하지만

case they don't run away, / I can always run myself…"
혹시 도망가지 않는다면, 내가 도망치면 되니까…"

Pinocchio was not given time / to argue any longer, / for he
피노키오는 시간이 없었다 더 이상 생각할,

thought he heard a slight rustle / among the leaves / behind
바스락거리는 소리를 들은 것 같았기 때문에 나뭇잎 속에서

him.
등 뒤에.

He turned to look and behold, / there in the darkness /
뒤돌아 보니, 어둠 속에

stood two big black shadows, / wrapped / from head to foot
두 개의 크고 검은 물체가 서 있었다, 뒤집어 쓴 머리부터 발 끝까지

bothersome 성가신 | misfortune 불운, 불행 | sensibly 현명하게, 분별 있게(reasonably) | mind your
business 참견 마라 | rustle 바스락거리는 소리 | behold 보다

/ in black sacks. The two figures leaped / toward him / as
검은 자루로.　　　　이 두 물체는 뛰어왔다　　　　그를 향해

softly / as if they were ghosts.
부드럽게　마치 유령처럼.

"Here they come!" / Pinocchio said to himself, / and, not
"강도가 왔잖아!"　　　피노키오가 중얼거렸다,　　　　그리고, 몰랐기

knowing / where to hide the gold pieces, / he stuck / all
때문에　　금화를 어디에 숨겨야 할지,　　　　붙여 넣었다　　모두를

four of them / under his tongue.
네 개 모두를　　혀 밑에.

He tried to run away, / but hardly / had he taken a step, /
그는 도망치려고 했으나,　　좀처럼　　　발이 떨어지지 않았다,

when he felt / his arms grasped / and heard / two horrible,
알았을 때　　팔이 잡힌 걸　　　그리고 들었다　두 개의 끔찍하고,

/ deep voices / say to him: / "Your money or your life!"
낮은 목소리가　그에게 말하는 것을:　"돈을 내 놓든지 목숨을 내 놓아라!"

On account of the gold pieces / in his mouth, / Pinocchio
금화들 때문에　　　　　　　　입 속에 있는,

could not say a word, / so he tried / with head and hands
피노키오는 한 마디도 할 수 없었고,　그래서 노력했다　머리와 손과 몸짓으로

and body / to show, / as best he could, / that he was only a
과 몸으로　보이기 위해,　최선을 다해,　　　　그는 가난한 꼭두각시일 뿐이

poor Marionette / without a penny / in his pocket.
라고　　　　　　한 푼도 없는　　　　주머니에.

"Come, come, / less nonsense, / and out with your money!"
"자, 자,　　　　　허튼 수작 부리지 말고,　　돈을 내 놔!"

/ cried the two thieves / in threatening voices.
두 강도가 외쳤다　　　　　위협적인 말투로.

Once more, / Pinocchio's head and hands said, / "I haven't
다시 한 번,　　　　피노키오의 머리와 손이 말했다,

a penny."
"돈이 없어요."

"Out with that money / or you're a dead man," / said the
"돈을 내놔라　　　　그렇지 않으면 넌 죽은 목숨이다,"

taller of the two Assassins.
둘 중 키 큰 강도가 말했다.

"Dead man," / repeated the other.
"넌 죽은 목숨이다,"　　다른 강도가 따라 했다.

"And after having killed you, / we will kill your father
"널 죽인 다음에,　　　　네 아버지도 죽일 테다."

also."

"Your father also!"
"네 아버지도!"

"No, no, no, not my Father!" / cried Pinocchio, / wild with
"안 돼, 안 돼, 안 돼, 아빠는 안 돼!"　　피노키오가 소리쳤다,　　공포에 질려;

terror; / but as he screamed, / the gold pieces tinkled /
하지만 그가 소리 지르자,　　　금화들이 짤랑거렸다

together / in his mouth.
모두　　　입 속에서.

"Ah, you rascal! So that's the game! You have the money
"아하, 요런 못된 놈!　　그렇게 된 거였군!　　　돈을 숨겼구나

hidden / under your tongue. Out with it!"
혀 밑에.　　　　이리 내놔!"

But / Pinocchio was as stubborn as ever.
하지만　피노키오는 꼼짝도 하지 않았다.

---

nonsense 허튼수작 | tinkle 쨍그렁[짤랑/딸랑]하는 소리 | rascal 악동 | stubborn 완고한 | nail 못으로 박다[
고정하다] | in desperation 절망하여, 자포자기하여 | pry open 비집어 열다 | hare 토끼 | spit out (입에 든 음식
등을) 뱉다 | assailer 공격자 | swiftly 신속히, 빨리

"Are you deaf? Wait, young man, / we'll get it from you /
"귀가 먹었나?   기다려라, 이 놈,   우리가 꺼내겠다

in a twinkling!"
당장!"

One of them / grabbed the Marionette / by the nose / and
그 중 하나가   꼭두각시의 코를 잡고   또 다른 하나가

the other by the chin, / and they pulled him / unmercifully
턱을 잡더니,   그를 잡아당겼다   인정사정없이

/ from side to side / in order to make him / open his mouth.
양 옆으로   그를 만들려고   입을 벌리게.

All was of no use. The Marionette's lips / might have been
모두 다 소용 없었다.   꼭두각시의 입술은   못으로 박아 고정된 듯 보였다

nailed / together. They would not open.
함께.   전혀 열리려 하지 않았다.

In desperation / the smaller of the two Assassins / pulled
의기소침하여   둘 중 키 작은 강도가

out a long knife / from his pocket, / and tried to pry
긴 칼을 꺼냈다   주머니에서,   그리고 피노키오의 입을 비집어 열려고

Pinocchio's mouth open / with it.
했다   그 칼로.

Quick as a flash, / the Marionette sank his teeth deep / into
번개처럼 빠르게,   피노키오는 이빨을 깊게 파묻고

the Assassin's hand, / bit it off / and spat it out. Fancy his
그 강도의 손에,   물어 뜯어서,   뱉어 버렸다.   얼마나 놀랐는지

surprise / when he saw / that it was not a hand, / but a
상상해 보세요   보았을 때   그것이 손이 아니라,

cat's paw.
고양이의 발이었다는 걸.

Encouraged by this first victory, / he freed himself /
첫 승리에 용기를 얻어,   그는 탈출했다,

from the claws / of his assailers / and, / leaping over the
발톱으로부터   공격자의   그리고,   숲을 뛰어넘어

bushes / along the road, / ran swiftly / across the fields.
길을 따라,   빠르게 달렸다   들판을 건너.

His pursuers were after him / at once, / like two dogs /
추적자들은 그를 따라왔다   즉시,   마치 두 마리 개처럼

chasing a hare.
토끼를 뒤쫓는.

After running / seven miles or so, / Pinocchio was well-
달리고 나자   7마일 정도,   피노키오는 거의 지쳤다.

nigh exhausted.

Seeing himself lost, / he climbed up / a giant pine tree /
길을 잃었음을 알고서,   그는 기어올라가   키 큰 소나무로

and sat there / to see what he could see. The Assassins
앉았다   볼 수 있는 걸 알아보려고.   강도들도 올라가려고 했지만,

tried to climb also, / but they slipped and fell.
                    미끄러져 떨어졌다.

Far from giving up the chase, / this only spurred them on.
추적을 포기하기는 커녕,   그들을 더 북돋을 뿐이었다.

They gathered / a bundle of wood, / piled it up / at the foot
그들은 모았고   나무 덤불을,   쌓아서

of the pine, / and set fire to it.
소나무 아래에,   그리고 불을 지폈다.

In a twinkling / the tree began to sputter / and burn / like
순간   나무는 탁탁 소리를 내며   타기 시작했다   촛불처럼

a candle / blown by the wind. Pinocchio saw the flames
          바람에 흔들리는.   피노키오는 불길이 올라오는 것을 보았다

climb / higher and higher. Not wishing to end his days / as
          점점 높게.   생을 마감하기 싫었으므로

a roasted Marionette, / he jumped / quickly / to the ground
구이가 된 꼭두각시로,   그는 뛰어내렸다   재빨리   땅으로

/ and off he went, / the Assassins close to him, / as before.
          그리고 자리를 떴는데,   강도들이 가까이 왔다,   이전처럼.

Dawn was breaking when, / without any warning /
날이 밝아 오자,   어떤 예고도 없이

whatsoever, / Pinocchio found his path / barred by a deep
어떻게든,   피노키오는 길을 발견했다   깊은 웅덩이로 가로 막힌

hare 토끼 | well-nigh 거의 | spur 자극하다, 박차를 가하다 | pile (물건을 차곡차곡) 쌓다 | pine 소나무 |
sputter (엔진·불길 등이) 펑펑 하는 소리를 내다 | roast 굽다 | go off 자리를 뜨다 | whatsoever (whatever의
강조형) 어떻게든 | bar (길을) 막다

pool / full of water / the color of muddy coffee.
물로 가득 찬　　　　　흙탕물 색의.

What was there to do? With a "One, two, three!" / he
할 수 있는 일이 뭘까?　　　　　"하나, 둘, 셋!"하고

jumped clear / across it. The Assassins jumped also, / but
완벽하게 뛰어넘었다　웅덩이를.　　　강도들도 뛰었지만,

not having measured their distance well / ——splash!!!——
거리를 잘 가늠하지 못해　　　　　　　　— 풍덩!!! —

/ they fell right / into the middle of the pool. Pinocchio
곧바로 빠졌다　　웅덩이 한가운데.　　　　　　피노키오는

/ who heard the splash / and felt it, too, / cried out, /
첨벙거리는 소리를 들은　　빠졌을 거라고 생각했고,　외쳤다,

laughing, / but never stopping / in his race:
웃으면서,　　하지만 멈추지 않으면서　달리는 걸:

"A pleasant bath to you, signori!"
"목욕 잘하세요, 나리!"

He thought / they must surely be drowned / and turned his
그는 생각했다　그들은 당연히 물에 빠져 죽었을 거라고　그리고 고개를 돌려보았다

head to see. But / there were the two somber figures / still
　　　　　그러나 두 명의 어두침침한 물체가 있었다

following him, / though their black sacks were drenched /
여전히 그를 뒤쫓는,　검은 자루가 흠뻑 젖었는데도 불구하고

and dripping with water.
물을 뚝뚝 흘리면서.

splash 첨벙하는 소리 | drown 익사하다 | somber 어둠침침한(dark), 검은, 거무스름한, 흐린 | drench 흠뻑 적시다
| drip 방울방울 흐르다

mini test 3

A. 다음 문장을 해석해 보세요.

(1) The yelling was of no use, / for the Marionettes, / instead of going on with their act, / made twice as much racket / as before.
   →

(2) His beard was as black as pitch, / and so long / that it reached / from his chin down / to his feet.
   →

(3) "So that / if I were to bury my five gold pieces," / cried Pinocchio / with growing wonder, / "next morning / I should find—how many?".
   →

(4) On account of the gold pieces / in his mouth, / Pinocchio could not say a word.
   →

B. 다음 주어진 문장이 되도록 빈칸에 써 넣으세요.

(1) 나는 어제 그가 그의 집 앞 문에 서 있는 것을 보았어.

   →

(2) 네가 한다면 넌 후회하게 될 거야.

   →

(3) 내가 길에서 그들을 만난다 해도, 뭐가 문제인데?

   →

(4) 그들 중 한 명은 <u>꼭두각시의 코를 잡았고</u> 다른 한 명은 턱을 잡았다.

   → One of them _____ and the other by the chin.

Answer

A. (1) 외쳐봤자 아무 소용이 없었다. 왜냐하면 꼭두각시들은 공연을 계속하기는 커녕 이전보다 두 배 더 소란을 피웠으니까. (2) 그의 턱수염은 칠흑같이 검었고, 너무 길어서 턱에서부터 발까지 뻗어있었다. (3) "그러면 내가 금화 다섯닢을 묻는다면", 피노키오가 더욱 의아해하며 소리쳤다. "내일 아침에 몇개를 발견하게

C. 다음 주어진 문구가 알맞은 문장이 되도록 순서를 맞춰 보세요.

(1) 가서 그에게 내 안부를 전하면서 그것들을 주렴.
    (give / Go, / my / to him / kindest regards / them / with)
    →

(2) 내가 아직 돌아가지 않았으니 그가 얼마나 슬퍼할까!
    (have not /he / How / that / I / yet / unhappy / must be /
    returned!)
    →

(3) 추적을 포기하기는 커녕, 이것이 그들을 더 북돋을 뿐이었다.
    (from / Far / giving up / only / this / them / the chase, /
    spurred / on)
    →

(4) 모든 것이 아무 소용 없었다.
    (no / All / use / was / of)
    →

D. 다음 단어에 대한 맞는 설명과 연결해 보세요.

(1) swish   ▶   ◀ ① make soft sounds while moving

(2) wriggle   ▶   ◀ ② twist and turn with quick
                                           movements

(3) rustle   ▶   ◀ ③ make them completely wet

(4) drench   ▶   ◀ ④ moves quickly through the air

11

The Assassins chase Pinocchio, / catch him, / and hang
강도들은 피노키오를 쫓아와,   붙잡은 다음,   매단다

him / to the branch / of a giant oak tree.
    가지에,   커다란 떡갈나무의

As he ran, / the Marionette felt / more and more certain /
달리면서,   그는 느꼈다   점점 더 강하고 확실하게

that he would have to give himself up / into the hands of
자신이 잡히고야 말 것이라고   추적자들의 손아귀에.

his pursuers. Suddenly / he saw a little cottage / gleaming
    갑자기   그는 작은 오두막을 보았다   하얗게 빛나는

white / as the snow / among the trees of the forest.
눈 같은   숲 속 나무들 가운데에서.

"If I have enough breath left / with which to reach / that
"숨쉴 힘이 남아있다면   도착할 때까지만

little house, / I may be saved," / he said to himself.
저 작은 집에,   난 살 수 있을 거야."   혼잣말을 했다.

Not waiting another moment, / he darted swiftly / through
지체하지 않고,   그는 전속력으로 달렸고

the woods, / the Assassins still after him.
숲을 가로질러,   강도들은 여전히 그를 쫓아왔다.

After a hard race / of almost an hour, / tired and out of
필사적으로 달린 후   거의 한 시간을,   지치고 숨이 찼지만,

breath, / Pinocchio finally reached / the door of the cottage
    피노키오는 마침내 도착하여   그 오두막의 문 앞에

/ and knocked. No one answered.
두드렸다.   아무 대답도 없었다.

He knocked again, / harder than before, / for behind him
그는 다시 두드렸다,   더 세게,   왜냐하면 그의 뒤에서

/ he heard the steps / and the labored breathing / of his
발소리가 들렸기 때문에   그리고 헐떡이는 숨소리를   박해자들의.

pursuer 추적자 | gleam 어슴푸레 빛나다 | cottage 오두막 | dart 쏜살같이 달리다 | out of breath 숨이 가쁜 | labor 노동하다, 힘쓰다 | persecutor 박해자 | bang 쾅 하고 치다 | maiden 처녀, 아가씨 | azure 하늘색의 | beseech 간청하다

persecutors. The same silence followed.
하지만 여전히 침묵이었다.

As knocking was of no use, / Pinocchio, / in despair,
두드려도 소용이 없다는 것을 알고, 피노키오는, 절망하여,

/ began to kick and bang / against the door, / as if he
발로 차고 머리로 두드리기 시작했다 문을 향해,

wanted to break it. At the noise, / a window opened /
마치 부수려는 듯. 그 소란에, 창문이 열렸고

and a lovely maiden / looked out. She had azure hair /
아름다운 소녀가 내다 보았다. 그녀는 하늘색 머리카락을 가졌다

and a face white / as wax. Her eyes were closed / and her
하얀 얼굴에 밀랍처럼. 그녀는 눈을 감은 채

hands crossed / on her breast.
손은 십자 모양으로 올렸다 가슴 위에.

With a voice so weak / that it hardly / could be heard, /
아주 작은 목소리로 좀처럼 들리지 않는,

she whispered:
그녀는 속삭였다:

"No one lives / in this house. Everyone is dead."
"아무도 살지 않아 이 집에는. 모두 죽었어."

"Won't you, / at least, / open the door / for me?" / cried
"해 줄 수 있죠, 적어도, 문을 여는 걸 나를 위해?"

Pinocchio / in a beseeching voice.
피노키오가 소리쳤다 애원하는 목소리로.

"I also am dead."
"나도 죽었어."

> ### Key Expression 🎯
>
> **more and more : 점점 더**
>
> more and more는 '점점 더'라는 의미입니다. 이와 같이 '비교급 + and
> + 비교급'은 '점점 더 ~한(하게)'이란 뜻을 가진 표현입니다.
> 특히 형용사의 '비교급 + and + 비교급'은 앞에 grow, become, get과 같은 상
> 태 변화를 나타내는 2형식 동사와 함께 쓰여 '점점 더 ~해지다'라는 의미로 쓰
> 이는 경우가 많아요.
>
> ex) As he ran, the Marionette felt more and more certain.
> 달리면서, 꼭두각시는 점점 더 확실하게 느꼈다.
> Death was creeping nearer and nearer.
> 죽음이 점점 더 가까이 다가오고 있었다.

"Dead? What are you doing / at the window, / then?"
"죽었다고? 뭘 하고 있죠 창문에서, 그럼?"

"I am waiting for / the coffin / to take me away."
"난 기다리고 있어 관을 나를 멀리 데려갈."

After these words, / the little girl disappeared / and the
이 말을 한 후, 그 소녀는 사라졌고

window closed / without a sound.
창문이 닫혔다 소리 없이.

"Oh, Lovely Maiden / with Azure Hair," / cried Pinocchio,
"오, 아름다운 소녀여 하늘색 머리를 가진," 피노키오가 외쳤다,

/ "open, / I beg of you. Take pity / on a poor boy / who is
"열어 주세요, 부탁해요. 불쌍히 여겨 주세요 불쌍한 아이를

being chased / by two Assass——"
쫓기고 있는 두 강도에게 — "

He did not finish, / for two powerful hands grasped him /
그는 말을 채 끝내지 못했다. 두 개의 강한 손이 잡았기 때문에

by the neck / and the same two horrible voices / growled /
그의 목을 그리고 똑같은 두 개의 끔찍한 목소리가 으르렁거렸다

threateningly: / "Now we have you!"
위협적으로: "이제 잡았다!"

The Marionette, / seeing death / dancing before him, /
꼭두각시는, 죽음을 보면서 그의 앞에서 춤추는,

trembled so hard / that the joints of his legs / rattled / and
몸을 너무 심하게 덜덜 떨어서 다리 관절들이 달가닥거렸고

the coins tinkled / under his tongue.
동전들이 쨍그랑 소리를 내었다 혀 밑에서.

"Well," / the Assassins asked, / "will you open your mouth
"자," 강도가 물었다, "입을 열거냐

/ now / or not? Ah! You do not answer? Very well, / this
지금 안 열거냐? 어라! 대답을 안 해? 좋아,

time / you shall open it."
이번엔 꼭 열게 해 주마."

coffin 관 | growl 으르렁거리다 | threateningly 위협적으로 | rattle 달가닥[덜거덕]거리다 | in dismay
당황하여, 깜짝 놀라 | noose 올가미 | limb (큰) 나무가지 | give a gasp 숨이 막히다[멎다]

Taking out / two long, sharp knives, / they struck two
꺼내서 두 개의 길고, 날카로운 칼을, 두 번 강하게 찔렀다

heavy blows / on the Marionette's back.
꼭두각시의 등을.

Happily for him, / Pinocchio was made / of very hard
하지만 다행히도, 피노키오는 만들어졌으므로 매우 강한 나무로

wood / and the knives broke / into a thousand pieces. The
칼은 부서졌다 산산조각으로.

Assassins looked / at each other / in dismay, / holding the
강도들은 쳐다봤다 서로를 당황하여, 칼자루를 든 채

handles of the knives / in their hands.
손에.

"I understand," / said one of them / to the other, / "there is
"이제 알겠다," 한 강도가 말했다 다른 놈에게, "할 수 있는

nothing left to do / now / but to hang him."
일은 아무 것도 없어 지금 저 놈을 매다는 것 밖에."

"To hang him," / repeated the other.
"저 놈을 매달자." 다른 하나가 따라 했다.

They tied Pinocchio's hands / behind his shoulders / and
그들은 피노키오의 손을 묶고 어깨 뒤로

slipped the noose / around his neck. Throwing the rope /
올가미를 둘렀다 목 주변에. 로프를 던져서

over the high limb / of a giant oak tree, / they pulled / till
높은 가지 위로 커다란 떡갈나무의, 잡아당겼다

the poor Marionette hung far up / in space.
불쌍한 꼭두각시가 매달릴 때까지 공중에.

Satisfied with their work, / they sat / on the grass / waiting
자신들이 한 일에 만족하면서, 그들은 앉았다 잔디 위에

for Pinocchio / to give his last gasp. But / after three hours
피노키오를 기다리면서 마지막 숨이 멎기를. 하지만 세 시간이 지나도

/ the Marionette's eyes were still open, / his mouth still
꼭두각시의 눈은 여전히 떠 있었고, 입은 계속 닫혀 있으며

shut / and his legs kicked / harder than ever.
다리는 버둥거렸다 더욱 세차게.

Tired of waiting, / the Assassins called to him / mockingly:
기다림에 지쳐서,　　　강도들은 말했다　　　　　조롱하며:

"Good-by / till tomorrow. When we return / in the
"안녕　　　내일까지.　　　우리가 돌아오면

morning, / we hope / you'll be polite / enough to let us find
아침에,　　　바란다　　　얌전히 있길　　　발견할 수 있게

you / dead and gone / and with your mouth wide open."
네가 죽어버려서　　　그리고 입도 크게 벌린 채로."

With these words / they went.
이 말을 남기고　　　그들은 떠났다.

A few minutes went by / and then / a wild wind / started to
몇 분이 지났고　　　그리고 나서　　　강한 바람이　　　불기 시작했다.

blow. As it shrieked and moaned, / the poor little sufferer
바람이 윙윙거리며 신음 소리를 내자,　　　불쌍한 피노키오는 바람에 흔들렸다

was blown / to and fro / like the hammer of a bell. The
앞 뒤로　　　마치 종을 두드리는 망치처럼.

rocking made him seasick / and the noose, / becoming
몸이 흔들리자 멀미가 났고　　　올가미는,　　　점점 더 세게,

tighter and tighter, / choked him. Little by little / a film
　　　그의 목을 졸랐다.　　　조금씩

covered his eyes.
그의 눈앞이 흐려졌다.

Death was creeping / nearer and nearer, / and the
죽음이 다가 오고 있었다　　　점점 더 가까이,

Marionette still hoped / for some good soul / to come to his
그래도 꼭두각시는 여전히 바랐다　　어떤 착한 영혼이　　　그를 구해 주러 올 거라고,

rescue, / but no one appeared. As he was about to die, / he
하지만 아무도 나타나지 않았다.　　거의 죽기 직전에,

thought of his poor old father, / and hardly conscious of /
그는 불쌍한 아빠를 생각했다,　　　그리고 전혀 의식하지 못하면서

what he was saying, / murmured to himself:
자신이 무엇을 말하고 있는지,　　　혼자 중얼거렸다:

mockingly 조롱하듯이, 희롱하여 | seasick 뱃멀미 | choke 숨이 막히다 | murmur 중얼거리다

"Oh, Father, dear Father! If you were only here!"
"오, 아빠, 사랑하는 아빠! 아빠만 여기 계셨어도!"

These were his last words. He closed his eyes, / opened
이것이 그의 마지막 말이었다. 그는 눈을 감았고,

his mouth, / stretched out his legs, / and hung there, / as if
입을 벌렸고, 두 다리를 뻗었다. 거기에 매달린 채,

he were dead.
마치 죽은 것처럼.

🎩 12 🎩

The Lovely Maiden / with Azure Hair / sends for the poor
아름다운 소녀는　　　　　　하늘색 머리를 가진　　　불쌍한 꼭두각시를 구해 주고,

Marionette, / puts him to bed, / and calls three Doctors to
그를 침대에 눕히고,　　　　세 명의 의사를 불러 말해 달라고 했다

tell her / if Pinocchio is dead or alive.
피노키오가 살았는지 죽었는지를.

If the poor Marionette had dangled / there / much longer,
불쌍한 꼭두각시가 매달렸다면　　　　거기에서　좀 더 오래,

/ all hope would have been lost. Luckily for him, / the
모든 희망은 사라졌을 것이다.　　　　하지만 다행스럽게도,

Lovely Maiden / with Azure Hair / once again / looked
아름다운 소녀는　　하늘색 머리를 가진　다시 한 번

out of her window. Filled with pity / at the sight of the
창 밖을 내다보았다.　연민으로 가득 차서　불쌍한 친구를 보고는

poor little fellow / being knocked / helplessly about / by
　　　　　　　　　묶여 있어　　부질없이 흔들리고 있는

the wind, / she clapped her hands / sharply together /
바람에,　　그녀는 손뼉을 쳤다　　빠르게

three times.
세 번.

At the signal, / a loud whirr of wings / in quick flight /
신호에 맞춰,　날개가 윙 하는 큰 소리가　빠른 비행으로

was heard / and a large Falcon came / and settled itself /
들렸다　　그리고 큰 매 한 마리가 와서　앉았다

on the window ledge.
창가에.

"What do you command, / my charming Fairy?" / asked
"무슨 일입니까,　　　나의 아름다운 요정님?"

the Falcon, / bending his beak / in deep reverence / (for
매가 물었다,　부리를 구부리며　깊은 존경의 표시로

it must be known that, / after all, / the Lovely Maiden /
(사실은,　　　　　　결국엔,　아름다운 소녀는

with Azure Hair / was none other than / a very kind Fairy
하늘색 머리를 가진   바로   마음 착한 요정이었다

/ who had lived, / for more than a thousand years, / in the
살아온,   천 년 넘게,

vicinity of the forest).
숲에서).

"Do you see that Marionette / hanging from the limb / of
"저 꼭두각시가 보이지   가지에 매달린

that giant oak tree?"
저기 큰 떡갈나무의?"

"I see him."
"네, 보입니다."

"Very well. Fly immediately / to him. With your strong
"좋아.   당장 날아가라   그에게.   네 강한 부리로,

beak, / break the knot / which holds him tied, / take him
       매듭을 끊어   그를 묶고 있는,   그를 내려놓고,

down, / and lay him softly / on the grass / at the foot of the
조심해서 눕혀 놓아라   잔디 위에   떡갈나무 아래."

oak."

The Falcon flew away / and after two minutes / returned, /
매는 멀리 날아갔다   그리고 2분 후에   돌아왔다,

saying, / "I have done / what you have commanded."
말하면서,   "했습니다   분부대로."

> ### Key Expression 🎵
>
> **no[none] other than~ : 다름 아닌 바로 ~**
> no[none] other than~은 '~이외의 아무도[아무 것도] 아닌'이란 의미로, 즉
> '다름 아닌 바로 ~'라는 뜻을 나타내는 숙어입니다.
>
> ex) The Lovely Maiden with Azure Hair was none other than a very kind Fairy
>   그 하늘색 머리의 아름다운 소녀는 다름 아닌 바로 마음 착한 요정이었다.

---

dangle 매달려 늘어지다 | knock 때리다 두드리다 | clap 손뼉을 치다 | whirr 윙 하는[윙윙거리는] 소리 | Falcon
매 | ledge 절벽에서 (선반처럼) 튀어나온 바위 | bend 구부리다 | reverence 숭배 | vicinity (~의) 부근 | beak (
새의) 부리

"How did you find him? Alive or dead?"
"아이는 어떻더냐?   살았는가 죽었는가?"

"At first glance, / I thought he was dead. But / I found / I
"언뜻 보기에,   죽었다고 생각했습니다.   하지만   알았습니다

was wrong, / for as soon as I loosened the knot / around
내가 틀렸다는 걸,   왜냐하면 매듭을 느슨하게 하자마자   그의 목에 있는,

his neck, / he gave a long sigh / and mumbled / with a
그의 목에 있는,   그는 깊은 숨을 쉬고   중얼거렸습니다

faint voice, / 'Now I feel better!'"
희미한 목소리로,   '이제야 살 것 같아!'라고"

The Fairy clapped her hands / twice. A magnificent
요정은 손뼉을 쳤다   두 번.   멋진 푸들이 나타났다,

Poodle appeared, / walking on his hind legs / just like a
        뒷다리로 서서 걸어오는,   마치 사람처럼.

man. He was dressed / in court livery. A tricorn / trimmed
그 개는 입고 있었다   저택의 제복을.   삼각모자가   금장식을 두른

with gold lace / was set / at a rakish angle / over a wig
금장식을   놓여져 있었다   비스듬한 각도로   하얗고 구불구불한

of white curls / that dropped down / to his waist. He
가발 위에   내려오는   허리까지.   그는

wore a jaunty coat / of chocolate-colored velvet, / with
의기양양하게 외투를 입고 있었다 초콜릿 색의 벨벳으로 만든,   다이아몬드

diamond buttons, / and with two huge pockets / which
단추가 달린,   두 개의 커다란 주머니가 있는

were always filled / with bones, / dropped there at dinner /
항상 가득 찬   뼈다귀로,   저녁으로 던져 주는

by his loving mistress. Breeches / of crimson velvet, / silk
사랑스런 여 주인이.   반바지와   진홍색 벨벳으로 만든,

stockings, / and low, / silver-buckled slippers / completed
실크 스타킹,   그리고 굽 낮은,   은이 박힌 슬리퍼가   그의 복장을 완성

his costume. His tail was encased / in a blue silk covering,
시켰다.   그의 꼬리는 싸여 있었다   파란 실크 덮개로,

/ which was to protect it / from the rain.
보호하기 위해   비로부터.

loosen 느슨하게 하다 | mumble 중얼거리다 | magnificent 참으로 아름다운 | trim (가장자리를) 장식하다 | livery
제복 | tricorn 세 개의 뿔이 있는 〈모자 등〉 | rakish (모자를) 비스듬히 쓴 | jaunty 경쾌한, 의기양양한 | breeches

"Come, Medoro," / said the Fairy / to him. "Get my best
"서둘러, 메도로," 요정이 말했다 그에게. "가장 멋진 마차를 준비

coach ready / and set out / toward the forest. On reaching
시키고 출발해라 숲을 향해. 떡갈나무에 도착하면,

the oak tree, / you will find / a poor, half-dead Marionette
찾게 될 거야 불쌍하게, 거의 죽어가는 꼭두각시를

/ stretched out / on the grass. Lift him up / tenderly, / place
뻗어 있는 잔디 위에. 그 애를 들어 올려서 부드럽게,

him / on the silken cushions of the coach, / and bring him
놓아라 마차의 실크 쿠션 위에, 그리고 여기로 데려와

here / to me."
나한테.'

The Poodle, / to show / that he understood, / wagged / his
푸들은, 알리기 위해 이해했다는 것을, 흔들었다

silk-covered tail / two or three times / and set off / at a
실크로 덮인 꼬리를 두 세 번 그리고 출발했다

quick pace.
부리나케.

In a few minutes, / a lovely little coach, / made of glass,
잠시 후, 사랑스럽고 작은 마차가, 유리로 만들어진,

/ with lining as soft / as whipped cream / and chocolate
부드러운 선을 그리며 휘핑 크림처럼 그리고 초콜릿 푸딩처럼,

pudding, / and stuffed / with canary feathers, / pulled out
속이 채워진 카나리아 깃털로, 마구간에서 나왔다.

of the stable. It was drawn / by one hundred pairs of white
마차가 끌려졌다 흰 쥐 백 쌍에 의해,

mice, / and the Poodle sat / on the coachman's seat / and
그리고 푸들은 앉아서 마부의 자리에

snapped his whip / gayly / in the air, / as if he were a real
채찍을 휘둘렀다 경쾌하게 공중에다, 마치 진짜 마부인 것처럼

coachman / in a hurry / to get to his destination.
서둘러 도착지를 향해 가며.

(무릎 바로 아래서 여미게 되어 있는) 반바지 | crimson 진홍색 | silver-buckled 은 죔쇠가 달린 | encased (
특히 보호하기 위해) 감싸다[둘러싸다] | wag 동물이 꼬리 등을 흔들다 | stuffed with ~로 속을 채운 | canary
카나리아 | table 마구간 | coachman 마부 | gayly 제멋대로, 경쾌하게

In a quarter of an hour / the coach was back. The Fairy,
15분이 지나자   마차가 돌아왔다.   요정은,

/ who was waiting / at the door of the house, / lifted the
기다리고 있던   문에서,

poor little Marionette / in her arms, / took him / to a
불쌍한 꼭두각시를 들어 올렸다   그녀의 팔에 안고,   데려갔다

dainty room / with mother-of-pearl walls, / put him to
앙증맞은 방으로   진주빛 자개로 벽을 장식한,   그를 침대에 눕히고

bed, / and sent immediately / for the most famous doctors
즉시 불렀다   가장 유명한 의사들을

/ of the neighborhood / to come to her.
그 근처의   그녀에게 오도록.

One after another / the doctors came, / a Crow, / and Owl,
차례차례   의사들이 들어왔다.   까마귀,   올빼미,

/ and a Talking Cricket.
그리고 말하는 귀뚜라미였다.

"I should like to know, / signori," / said the Fairy, /
"알려 주세요,   여러분,"   요정이 말했다,

turning to the three doctors / gathered about Pinocchio's
세 의사들을 보면서   피노키오의 침대에 모인,

bed, / "I should like to know / if this poor Marionette is
"알려 주세요   이 불쌍한 꼭두각시가 죽었는지

dead / or alive."
아니면 살았는지."

At this invitation, / the Crow stepped out / and felt /
이에 응대하여,   까마귀가 나가서   짚어봤다

Pinocchio's pulse, / his nose, / his little toe. Then / he
피노키오의 맥박과,   코와,   작은 발가락을.   그리고 나서

solemnly pronounced / the following words:
그는 엄숙히 말했다   다음과 같이:

"To my mind / this Marionette is dead and gone; / but if, /
"제 생각엔   이 꼭두각시는 죽었습니다;   하지만 만약,

by any evil chance, / he were not, / then / that would be a
혹시,   죽지 않았다면,   그때는   그게 확실한 증거입니다

sure sign / that he is still alive!"
                    그가 살아있다는!"

"I am sorry," / said the Owl, / "to have to contradict the
"미안하지만," 올빼미가 말했다, "까마귀 선생과 의견이 다릅니다,

Crow, / my famous friend / and colleague. To my mind
훌륭한 친구이자 동료인. 제 생각엔

/ this Marionette is alive; / but if, / by any evil chance, /
이 꼭두각시는 살아있어요; 하지만 만약, 혹시,

he were not, / then / that would be a sure sign / that he is
살지 않았다면, 그때는 그게 확실한 증거입니다 그가 죽었다는!"

wholly dead!"
그가 죽었다는!"

"And do you hold / any opinion?" / the Fairy asked / the
"선생님은 있나요 다른 의견이?" 요정이 물었다

Talking Cricket.
말하는 귀뚜라미에게.

"I say that a wise doctor, / when he does not know / what he
"현명한 의사란, 잘 알지 못할 때

is talking about, / should know enough / to keep his mouth
자신이 무엇을 말하고 있는지 알아야 합니다 입을 다물 줄.

shut. However, / that Marionette is not a stranger / to me. I
그러나, 저 꼭두각시는 낯설지 않아요 내게.

have known him / a long time!"
그를 알고 있습니다 오래 전에!"

Pinocchio, / who until then / had been very quiet, /
피노키오는, 그때까지 매우 조용했던,

shuddered so hard / that the bed shook.
몸을 부르르 떨었다 침대가 흔들릴 만큼.

dainty 앙증맞은 | mother-of-pearl (조개껍데기 속의, 진주 광택이 나는) 진주층, 광채 나는 자개 조각을 여러가지 형상으로 박아 붙여 만든 공예품 | one after another 차례차례 | by any evil chance 혹시라도 | contradict 반박하다 | colleague (같은 직장이나 직종에 종사하는) 동료 | shudder 전율하다

"That Marionette," / continued the Talking Cricket, / "is a
"저 꼭두각시는," 말하는 귀뚜라미가 계속했다.

rascal / of the worst kind."
"악동입니다 가장 지독한."

Pinocchio opened his eyes / and closed them again.
피노키오는 눈을 떴다가 다시 감았다.

"He is rude, / lazy, / a runaway."
"그는 무례하고, 게으르고, 가출한 떠돌이입니다."

Pinocchio hid his face / under the sheets.
피노키오는 얼굴을 숨겼다 이불 밑에.

"That Marionette is a disobedient son / who is breaking
"저 꼭두각시는 말을 안 듣는 아들입니다 아비의 마음을 찢어놓는!"

his father's heart!"

Long shuddering sobs were heard, / cries, / and deep sighs.
몸을 떨며 흐느끼는 소리가 들렸다. 울음 소리와, 깊은 한숨이.

Think / how surprised everyone was / when, on raising
생각해 보세요 얼마나 놀랐을지 이불을 들춰보고,

the sheets, / they discovered Pinocchio / half melted in
피노키오를 발견했을 때 눈물에 거의 녹을 것

tears!
같은!"

"When the dead weep, / they are beginning to recover," /
"눈물을 흘리는걸 보니, 회복하기 시작했습니다,"

said the Crow / solemnly.
까마귀가 말했다 엄숙하게.

"I am sorry / to contradict / my famous friend / and
"죄송하지만 의견이 다릅니다 나의 훌륭한 친구이자

colleague," / said the Owl, "but as far as I'm concerned, /
동료와," 올빼미가 말했다, "제가 보기에는,

I think / that when the dead weep, / it means / they do not
생각합니다 우는 건, 의미한다고

want to die."
죽고 싶지 않다는 걸."

as far as I'm concerned 내 생각에는

13

Pinocchio eats sugar, / but refuses to take medicine.
피노키오는 설탕은 먹고,　　　약은 먹지 않으려 한다.

When the undertakers come for him, / he drinks the
장의사가 데리러 오자,　　　　　　　　약을 마시고

medicine / and feels better. Afterwards / he tells a lie and,
나아진다.　　　그 후로는　　　거짓말을 하면,

/ in punishment, / his nose grows / longer and longer.
그 벌로,　　　코가 늘어난다　　　점점 더 길게.

As soon as the three doctors had left / the room, / the
세 명의 의사가 떠나자 마자　　　　　　방을,

Fairy went to Pinocchio's bed and, / touching him on the
요정은 피노키오 침대로 가서,　　　　이마를 만지면서,

forehead, / noticed that he was burning / with fever.
펄펄 끓고 있는 것을 알았다　　　열이.

She took a glass of water, / put a white powder into it, /
그녀는 물 한 잔을 가져와,　　　거기에 하얀 가루를 타서,

and, handing it / to the Marionette, / said lovingly to him:
건네 주면서　　　꼭두각시에게,　　　사랑스럽게 말했다:

"Drink this, / and in a few days / you'll be up and well."
"이걸 마셔,　　　며칠 지나면　　　나아질 거야."

Pinocchio looked at the glass, / made a wry face, / and
피노키오는 잔을 쳐다보고,　　　얼굴을 찡그리며,

asked / in a whining voice: / "Is it sweet or bitter?"
물었다　　우는 소리로:　　　"달아요, 써요?"

"It is bitter, / but it is good for you."
"쓸 거야,　　　하지만 몸에는 좋아."

"If it is bitter, / I don't want it."
"쓰다면,　　　안 먹을래요."

"Drink it!"
"마셔!"

---

undertaker 장의사 | whine 우는 소리를 하다

"I don't like anything bitter."
"쓴 건 싫어요."

"Drink it / and I'll give you / a lump of sugar / to take
"마셔   그러면 줄게   각설탕을

the bitter taste / from your mouth."
쓴 맛을 없애주는   네 입에서부터."

"Where's the sugar?"
"설탕은 어디 있어요?"

"Here it is," / said the Fairy, / taking a lump / from a
"여기 있지,"   요정이 말했다.   한 조각을 들면서

golden sugar bowl.
금으로 된 설탕 단지에서.

"I want the sugar first, / then I'll drink the bitter water."
"설탕을 먼저 주면,   쓴 물을 마실게요."

"Do you promise?"
"약속하는 거지?"

"Yes."
"네."

The Fairy gave him / the sugar / and Pinocchio, / after
그에게 주었다   설탕을   그러자 피노키오는,

chewing and swallowing it / in a twinkling, / said, /
씹고 삼킨 후   금새,   말했다,

smacking his lips:
입맛을 다시면서:

"If only sugar were medicine! I should take it every day."
"설탕이 약이라면 좋겠어요!   매일 먹을 텐데."

"Now keep your promise / and drink / these few drops of
"자 약속을 지켜야지   이제 마셔   이 물 몇 방울을.

water. They'll be good for you."
몸에 좋을 거야."

Pinocchio took the glass / in both hands / and stuck his
피노키오는 유리잔을 잡고   두 손으로   코를 집어넣었다

nose / into it. He lifted it / to his mouth / and once more /
그 안에.   잔을 들어   입으로 가져갔다   그리고 다시 한 번

lump 덩어리 | smack one's lips 입맛을 다시다 | pillow 베개 | bother 괴롭히다

stuck his nose into it.
코를 집어넣었다.

"It is too bitter, / much too bitter! I can't drink it."
"너무 써요,   너무 너무 써요!   못 마시겠어요."

"How do you know, / when you haven't even tasted it?"
"어떻게 알지,   맛도 아직 안 보고서?"

"I can imagine it. I smell it. I want / another lump of
"상상으로 알죠.   냄새를 맡아요. 원해요   각설탕을 하나 더,

sugar, / then I'll drink it."
          그럼 마실게요."

The Fairy, / with all the patience / of a good mother, / gave
요정은,   인내심을 가진   좋은 엄마의,   그에게

him / more sugar / and again / handed him the glass.
주었다 설탕을 더   그리고 다시   유리잔을 건넸다.

"I can't drink it / like that," / the Marionette said, /
"못 마시겠어요   그런 건,"   꼭두각시가 말했다,

making more wry faces.
얼굴을 더 찡그리며.

"Why?"
"왜?"

"Because that feather pillow / on my feet / bothers me."
"왜냐하면 깃털 베개가   발 밑에 있는   거슬려요."

The Fairy took away / the pillow.
요정이 치웠다   베개를.

"It's no use. I can't drink it / even now."
"소용없어요.   마실 수 없어요   지금도."

Key Expression 🎯

명령문, and … : ~해라, 그러면 …할 것이다

명령문에 and/or로 시작하는 문장을 덧붙이면 '그러면 …할 것이다'라는 의미
로 명령을 수행했을 때의 결과를 부연설명하는 표현이 됩니다. 반대로 '그렇지 않
으면 ~할 것이다'라고 표현하려면 and 대신 or를 사용하지요.

또한 이 구문은 if 조건문으로 바꾸어 쓸 수 있어요.

▶ 명령문, and ~ : ~해라, 그러면 …할 것이다 (= If you ~, you will ~.)
▶ 명령문, or ~ : ~해라, 그렇지 않으면 …할 것이다 (= If you don't ~, you will ~.)

ex) Drink it and I'll give you a lump of sugar to take the bitter taste from your
mouth.
이걸 마시렴, 그러면 내가 너에게 쓴 맛을 없애 줄 각 설탕을 줄게.

"What's the matter now?"
"뭐가 문제니?"

"I don't like / the way that door looks. It's half open."
"싫어요   저 문의 모습이.   반쯤 열려 있잖아요."

The Fairy closed the door.
요정은 문을 닫았다.

"I won't drink it," / cried Pinocchio, / bursting out crying.
"안 마실 거예요."   피노키오가 소리쳤다   눈물을 터뜨리며.

"I won't drink / this awful water. I won't. I won't! No, no,
"안 마실 거야   이 이상한 물은.   안 마셔요.   안 마신다고요! 싫어, 싫어,

no, no!"
싫어, 싫어!"

"My boy, you'll be sorry."
"애야, 나중에 후회할 거야."

"I don't care."
"상관없어요."

"You are very sick."
"넌 지금 많이 아파."

"I don't care."
"상관없어요."

"In a few hours / the fever will take you / far away / to
"몇 시간 안에   열이 널 데려갈 거야   멀리

another world."
저 세상으로."

"I don't care."
"상관없어요."

"Aren't you afraid of death?"
"죽음이 두렵지 않니?"

"Not a bit. I'd rather die / than drink / that awful
"조금도요.   차라리 죽는 게 나아요 마시는 것 보단   저 끔찍한 약을."

medicine."

At that moment, / the door of the room flew / open / and
그 순간,   방문이 열렸고   활짝

in came four Rabbits / as black as ink, / carrying a small
네 마리의 토끼가 들어왔다   잉크처럼 검은,   작고 검은 관을 가지고

black coffin / on their shoulders.
어깨에.

"What do you want / from me?" / asked Pinocchio.
"뭘 원하니   나한테?"   피노키오가 물었다.

"We have come for you," / said the largest Rabbit.
"널 데리러 왔다,"   제일 큰 토끼가 말했다.

"For me? But I'm not dead yet!"
"나를?   하지만 난 아직 안 죽었어!"

"No, not dead yet; / but you will be in a few moments
"그래, 아직은 아니지;   하지만 넌 몇 분 안에 죽을 거다

/ since you have refused to take the medicine / which
약을 먹지 않으려 하기 때문에

would have made you well."
널 치료해 줄."

"Oh, Fairy, my Fairy," / the Marionette cried out, / "give
"아, 요정님, 나의 요정님,"   꼭두각시가 외쳤다,

me that glass! Quick, please! I don't want to die! No, no,
"그 컵을 주세요!   빨리요, 제발!   난 죽기 싫어요!   안 돼, 안 돼,

not yet —— not yet!"
아직 아니야 — 아직 아니야!"

And holding the glass / with his two hands, / he
그러고는 잔을 잡고   두 손으로,

swallowed the medicine / at one gulp.
약을 삼켰다   단숨에.

Key Expression ✏

would rather : 차라리 ~하는 게 낫다
rather는 '약간, 상당히, 오히려' 등의 의미를 가진 부사지요. 하지만 rather와
함께 쓰인 would rather는 '차라리 ~하는 게 낫다'는 본인의 의지나 희망을
나타내는 조동사입니다. 이때 A than B를 덧붙여서 'B 하느니 차라리 A 하는
게 낫다'라는 의미로 쓰이도 합니다.
또한 would rather는 조동사이므로 뒤에는 동사원형이 따라오며 부정형은
would rather not입니다.

ex) I'd rather die than drink that awful medicine.
    그렇게 끔찍한 약을 먹느니 차라리 죽는 게 나아요

awful 몹시 싫은 | gulp 한입에 삼키는 양

95

"Well," / said the four Rabbits, / "this time / we have made
"이런," 네 마리 토끼가 말했다, "이번에는

the trip for nothing."
헛걸음을 했군."

And turning on their heels, / they marched solemnly /
발길을 돌리면서, 그들은 엄숙하게 행진했다

out of the room, / carrying their little black coffin / and
방 밖으로, 작고 검은 관을 들고

muttering and grumbling / between their teeth.
중얼거리고 툴툴대면서 입으로.

In a twinkling, / Pinocchio felt fine. With one leap / he was
눈 깜짝할 새에, 피노키오는 나아졌다. 한걸음에

out of bed / and into his clothes.
침대에서 나와 옷을 입었다.

The Fairy, / seeing him run and jump / around the room /
요정은, 피노키오가 뛰는 걸 보면서 방 안을

gay as a bird on wing, / said to him:
날갯짓하는 새처럼 즐겁게, 말했다:

"My medicine was good for you, / after all, / wasn't it?"
"내 약을 먹으니 나아졌지, 결국, 안 그러니?"

"Good indeed! It has given me / new life."
"정말이에요! 그 약이 제게 주었어요 새 생명을."

"Why, then, did I have to beg you / so hard / to make you
"그런데, 왜 그렇게 나를 애 먹였니 힘들게

drink it?"
그걸 마시게 하는데?"

"I'm a boy, / you see, / and all boys hate medicine / more
"전 어린애잖아요, 아시다시피, 그리고 모든 아이들은 약을 싫어해요

than they do sickness."
아픈 것보다도."

---

solemnly 장엄하게, 진지하게 | mutter 중얼거리다 불평하다 | what a shame 그것 참 너무[깨씸]하군, 그거 안
됐구나[유감이다]

"What a shame! Boys ought to know, / after all, / that
"어처구니 없구나!   아이들도 알아야지,   결국엔,

medicine, / taken in time, / can save them / from much
그 약이,   시간이 좀 걸려도,   구해 준다는 걸   많은 고통으로부터

pain / and even from death."
목숨까지도."

"Next time / I won't have to be begged / so hard. I'll
"다음 번엔   애 먹이지 않을게요   너무 심하게.

remember / those black Rabbits / with the black coffin /
기억할게요   그 까만 토끼들을   검은 관을 들고 온

on their shoulders / and I'll take the glass / and pouf!——
어깨에   그리고 유리잔을 들고   마실 거예요! —

down / it will go!"
당장!"

"Come here now / and tell me / how it came about / that
"이리로 와서   말해 보렴   어떻게 된 건지

you found yourself / in the hands of the Assassins."
네가 잡히게 됐는지   강도들 손에."

"It happened / that Fire Eater gave me / five gold pieces
"그러니까   불 먹는 사나이가 주었어요   금화 다섯 닢을

/ to give to my Father, / but on the way, / I met a Fox and
아빠에게 주라고,   그런데 가는 길에,   여우와 고양이를 만났어요,

a Cat, / who asked me, / 'Do you want the five pieces / to
내게 물었죠,   '다섯 닢을 원하느냐

become two thousand?' And I said, / 'Yes.' And they said,
2천 개로 만들기를?'   내가 말했죠,   '네.'   그들이 말했어요,

/ 'Come with us / to the Field of Wonders.' And I said, /
'우리랑 함께 가자   기적의 땅으로.'   그래서 제가 말했죠,

'Let's go.' Then they said, / 'Let us stop / at the Inn of the
'같이 가요.'   그러자 그들이 말했어요,   '들르자   빨간 가재 여관에

Red Lobster / for dinner / and after midnight / we'll set
                저녁을 먹으러   그리고 한밤 중에

out again.' We ate and went to sleep. When I awoke / they
다시 떠날 거야.' 우리는 밥을 먹고 잠이 들었어요.   내가 잠에서 깨어났을 때

were gone / and I started out / in the darkness / all alone.
그들은 사라졌고   난 떠났어요   어둠 속에서   혼자서.

On the road / I met two Assassins / dressed in black coal
길에서   두 강도를 만났어요   검은 석탄 자루를 입은,

sacks, / who said to me, / 'Your money or your life!' / and
            그들이 나에게 말했어요,   '돈 아니면 목숨을 내놔라!'

all alone 홀로; 혼자서, 남의 도움 없이

98   The Adventures of Pinocchio

I said, / 'I haven't any money'; / for, you see,/ I had put
그래서 내가 말했죠, '한 푼도 없어요'; 아시다시피, 나는 돈을 넣었어요

the money / under my tongue. One of them tried to put
혀 밑에. 둘 중 하나가 손을 집어넣으려고 했어요

his hand / in my mouth / and I bit it off / and spat it out;
내 입에 그래서 내가 물어 뜯어서 뱉었어요;

/ but it wasn't a hand, / it was a cat's paw. And they ran
하지만 그건 손이 아니었어요, 고양이의 발이었어요. 그들이 나를 계속 쫓아왔고

after me / and I ran and ran, / till at last / they caught me /
나는 계속 달렸어요, 마침내 잡혀서

and tied my neck / with a rope / and hanged me / to a tree,
내 목을 묶었고 로프로 매달았어요 나무에다,

/ saying, / 'Tomorrow / we'll come back / for you / and
말하면서, '내일 다시 오겠다 널 보러

you'll be dead / and your mouth will be open, / and then
넌 죽어있겠지 입은 벌어져 있을 테고, 그러면

/ we'll take the gold pieces / that you have hidden / under
우린 금화를 가져갈 것이다 네가 숨긴

your tongue.'"
혀 밑에.'"

"Where are the gold pieces now?" / the Fairy asked.
"지금 금화는 어디 있니?" 요정이 물었다.

"I lost them," / answered Pinocchio, / but he told a lie, /
"잃어버렸어요," 피노키오가 대답했다, 하지만 거짓말이었다,

for he had them / in his pocket.
왜냐하면 갖고 있었으니까 주머니에.

Key Expression 🎵

접속사 for

for가 접속사로 쓰이는 경우에는 '왜냐하면(그 이유는) ~니까'라는 의미를 나타
내며 앞의 말을 하게 된 근거를 부연설명 하는 역할을 합니다.
접속사 for는 ',와 함께 '~, for 주어 + 동사'의 형태로 쓰이는 경우가 많아요. 또한
회화체에서는 거의 쓰이지 않고 문학작품에 주로 등장합니다.

ex) He told a lie, for he had them in his pocket.
그는 거짓말을 했다, 왜냐하면 주머니 속에 그것을 감추고 있었으니까.
We'll look for them and find them, for everything that is lost there is always
found.
우린 그걸 찾아 나설 것이고 발견하게 될 거야. 왜냐하면 잃어버린 모든 것은 언
제나 발견되는 법이거든.

As he spoke, / his nose, / long though it was, / became at
그가 말하자,   코가,   원래도 길었는데,   적어도

least / two inches longer.
2인치가 더 길어졌다.

"And / where did you lose them?"
"그럼   어디에서 잃어버렸니?"

"In the wood / near by."
"숲에서요   근처."

At this second lie, / his nose grew / a few more inches.
두 번째 거짓말을 하자,   코가 길어졌다   몇 인치 더.

"If you lost them / in the near-by wood," / said the Fairy, /
"네가 잃어버렸다면   근처 숲에서,"   요정이 말했다,

"we'll look for them / and find them, / for everything that is
"우리가 샅샅이 찾아볼게   찾을 수 있어,   왜냐하면 잃어버린 모든 건

lost / there is always found."
    항상 발견되는 법이니까."

"Ah, now I remember," / replied the Marionette, / becoming
"아, 지금 생각났어요,"   꼭두각시가 대답했다,

more and more confused. "I did not lose the gold pieces, /
점점 더 당황하며.   "금화를 잃어버린 게 아니에요,

but I swallowed them / when I drank the medicine."
삼켰어요   약을 마실 때."

At this third lie, / his nose became / longer than ever, /
세 번째 거짓말을 하자,   그의 코는 변했다   엄청나게 길게,

so long / that he could not even turn around. If he turned
너무 길어서   고개도 못 돌릴 정도로.   오른쪽으로 고개를 돌리면,

to the right, / he knocked it / against the bed / or into the
    부딪쳤다   침대에   또는 창 유리에;

windowpanes; / if he turned to the left, / he struck the walls
    왼쪽으로 돌리면,   벽에 걸렸다

/ or the door; / if he raised it a bit, / he almost put the Fairy's
또는 문에;   그가 살짝 일어나려 하자,   요정의 눈을 찌를 뻔했다.

eyes out.

windowpane 창유리

The Fairy sat / looking at him / and laughing.
요정은 앉았다   그를 보고   웃으면서.

"Why do you laugh?" / the Marionette asked her, /
"왜 웃으세요?"   꼭두각시가 그녀에게 물었다.

worried now / at the sight of his growing nose.
걱정스럽게   길어진 코를 보며.

"I am laughing / at your lies."
"웃는 거야   네 거짓말 때문에."

"How do you know / I am lying?"
"어떻게 아셨어요   내가 거짓말한 걸?"

"Lies, / my boy, / are known / in a moment. There are
"거짓말은,   애야,   알 수 있어   금방.

two kinds of lies, / lies with short legs / and lies with long
두 종류의 거짓말이 있는데,   다리가 짧아지는 거짓말과   코가 길어지는 거짓말이지.

noses. Yours, / just now, / happen to have long noses."
네 거짓말로,   방금,   길어진 코를 갖게 된 거야."

Pinocchio, / not knowing / where to hide his shame,
피노키오는,   몰라서   부끄러움을 어디다 숨겨야 할지,

/ tried to escape / from the room, / but his nose had
도망치려 했다   방에서,   하지만 코가 너무 길어서

become so long / that he could not get it / out of the door.
나갈 수 없었다   문 밖으로.

Key Expression

where to ~ : 어디에서 ~할지

where to ~ 는 '어디에서 ~(해야) 할지'의 뜻입니다. 이와같이 의문사가 이끄는 명사절은 의문사 + to부정사의 형태로 축약하여 사용하는 경우가 많아요. 또한 의문사 + 주어 + should + 동사원형의 절로 바꾸어 쓸 수 있습니다.

ex) Pinocchio, not knowing where to hide his shame, tried to escape from the room.
피노키오는, 부끄러움을 어디에 숨겨야 할지 몰라서 방에서 도망치려 했다.

mini test 4

A. 다음 문장을 해석해 보세요.

(1) As he ran, / the Marionette felt / more and more certain / that he would have to give himself up / into the hands of his pursuers.
   →

(2) With a voice so weak / that it hardly / could be heard, / she whispered.
   →

(3) When we return / in the morning, / we hope you'll be polite / enough to let us find / you dead and gone / and with your mouth wide open.
   →

(4) Pinocchio, / not knowing / where to hide his shame, / tried to escape / from the room, / but his nose had become so long / that he could not get it / out of the door.
   →

B. 다음 주어진 문구가 알맞은 문장이 되도록 순서를 맞춰 보세요.

(1) 그를 매다는 것 밖에는 남은 할 일이 없어.
   (to hang / nothing / There is / but / left / him / to do)
   →

(2) 처음 흘깃 보았을 땐, 나는 그가 죽었다고 생각했어요.
   (first / glance, / thought / he / I / dead / At)
   →

(3) 이 불쌍한 꼭두각시가 죽었는지 살았는지 알고 싶어요.
   (should like to / dead / I / if / is / or / this poor Marionette / know / alive)
   →

Answer

A. (1) 달리면서, 꼭두각시는 그가 추격자들의 손에 잡히고야 말 것이라고 더욱 더 확신했다. (2) 너무 작아서 거의 들리지 않는 목소리로, 그녀가 속삭였다. (3) 아침에 우리가 돌아오면, 네가 입을 벌린 채 죽어 있는 것을 발견하도록 공손해 지길 바란다. (4) 피노키오는 부끄러움을 어디에 감춰야할 지 몰라서, 방에

(4) 이걸 마시면 내가 네게 각설탕을 하나 줄게.
   (it / sugar / and / give / a lump of / Drink / I'll / you)
   →

C. 다음 주어진 문장이 본문의 내용과 맞으면 T, 틀리면 F에 동그라미 하세요.

(1) Pinocchio was hung to the branch of a giant oak tree by the assassins.
   [T / F]

(2) Pinocchio was stolen the money by the assassins.
   [T / F]

(3) Pinocchio was revived thanks to the Lovely Maiden with Azure Hair.
   [T / F]

(4) Pinocchio's ears became longer and longer as he lied.
   [T / F]

D. 의미가 비슷한 것끼리 서로 연결해 보세요.

(1) jaunty   ▶   ◀ ① shine
(2) assassin   ▶   ◀ ② cheerful
(3) mutter   ▶   ◀ ③ mumble
(4) gleam   ▶   ◀ ④ killer

14

Pinocchio weeps / upon learning / that the Lovely Maiden
피노키오는 눈물을 흘린다   알게 되자   아름다운 소녀가

/ with Azure Hair / is dead. He meets a Pigeon, / who
하늘색 머리카락을 가진   죽었다는 것을.   그는 비둘기를 만난다,

carries him / to the seashore. He throws himself into the
그를 데려다 줄   바닷가로.   그는 바다에 뛰어든다

sea / to go to the aid / of his father.
구하기 위해   아빠를.

As soon as Pinocchio no longer felt / the shameful weight
더 이상 없다고 느끼자 마자   수치스러운 개 목걸이가

of the dog collar / around his neck, / he started to run /
목에서,   뛰기 시작했다

across the fields / and meadows, / and never stopped / till
들판을 가로질러   목초지와,   멈추지 않았다

he came to the main road / that was to take him / to the
큰 길에 도착할 때까지   그를 인도해 주었던

Fairy's house.
요정의 집까지.

When he reached it, / he looked into the valley / far below
도착했을 때,   그는 계곡을 들여다 보았다   저 멀리 아래를

him / and there / he saw the wood / where unluckily / he
거기에서   숲을 보았다   불행히도

had met the Fox and the Cat, / and the tall oak tree / where
여우와 고양이를 만났던 곳을   그리고 떡갈나무도

he had been hanged; / but though he searched / far and
매달렸던;   하지만 아무리 찾아도   여기 저기를,

near, / he could not see the house / where the Fairy with
그 집을 찾을 수 없었다   하늘색 머리카락의 요정이 살았던.

the Azure Hair lived.

pigeon 비둘기 | aid 원조, 지원, 도움 | shameful 수치스러운 | collar (개 등의 목에 거는) 목걸이 | meadows (특히 건초를 만들기 위한) 목초지

He became terribly frightened and, / running as fast as
그는 공포에 질려서,　　　　　　　　　힘껏 달렸고,

he could, / he finally came to the spot / where it had once
　　　　마침내 그곳에 도착했다　　　　한때 집이 있었던.

stood. The little house was no longer there. In its place /
그 작은 집은 더 이상 없었다.　　　　　　그 자리에 대신,

lay a small marble slab, / which bore this sad inscription:
작은 대리석 조각이 놓여져 있었다.　이러한 슬픈 문구가 새겨진:

HERE LIES
이곳에 잠들다

THE LOVELY FAIRY WITH AZURE HAIR
하늘색 머리의 아름다운 요정

WHO DIED OF GRIEF
슬픔으로 인해 죽음을 맞이한

WHEN ABANDONED BY
버림을 받아서

HER LITTLE BROTHER PINOCCHIO
동생 피노키오에게

The poor Marionette was heartbroken / at reading these
가여운 꼭두각시는 가슴이 찢어졌다　　　　　　이 글을 읽으면서.

words. He fell to the ground / and, covering the cold
　　　그는 땅바닥에 쓰러져서　　차가운 대리석에 입을 맞추고,

marble with kisses, / burst into bitter tears. He cried / all
　　　　　쓰디 쓴 눈물을 터뜨렸다.　　　그는 울었다

night, / and dawn found him still there, / though his tears
밤새도록,　그리고 새벽까지 계속 거기에 있었다,　눈물이 말랐어도

had dried / and only hard, dry sobs / shook his wooden
　　　그리고 눈물이 마른 채 흐느끼며　　나무로 된 몸을 흔들었다.

frame. But these were so loud / that they could be heard /
하지만 그 소리가 너무 커서　　　들렸다

by the faraway hills.
저 멀리 언덕까지.

As he sobbed / he said to himself:
그는 흐느끼며　　혼잣말을 했다:

marble 대리석 | slab 두껍고 반듯한 조각 | inscription 새겨진 글 | abandon (돌볼 책임이 있는 사람을) 버리다 |
heartbroken 비통해 하는 | faraway 멀리 떨어진

"Oh, my Fairy, my dear, dear Fairy, / why did you die?
"오, 나의 요정님, 나의 사랑하는, 사랑하는 요정님,　　　　왜 돌아가셨나요?

Why did I not die, / who am so bad, / instead of you, / who
왜 내가 죽지 않고,　　　이렇게 나쁜 아이인,　　당신 대신에,

are so good? And my father / —— where can he be? Please
아주 착하신?　　우리 아빠는　　　　　— 어디에 계시나요?

dear Fairy, / tell me / where he is / and I shall never, never
제발 요정님,　　말씀해 주세요　아빠가 어디에 게신지　그러면 그를 절대로, 절대로 떠나지 않을

leave him / again! You are not really dead, / are you? If you
게요　　　다시는!　요정님 정말 죽은 건 아니죠,　　　그렇죠?　　나를

love me, / you will come back, / alive / as before. Don't
사랑한다면,　돌아오세요,　　　　살아서　이전처럼.

you feel sorry / for me? I'm so lonely. If the two Assassins
안쓰럽지도 않나요　내가?　　나는 너무 외로워요.　두 강도가 온다면,

come, / they'll hang me / again / from the giant oak tree /
나를 매달 거예요　　다시　큰 떡갈나무에

and I will really die, / this time. What shall I do alone / in
그러면 나는 죽을 거예요,　　이번에는.　나 혼자 어떻게 하죠

the world? Now that you are dead / and my father is lost, /
이 세상에서?　당신은 죽었고　　　아빠는 잃어버렸는데,

where shall I eat? Where shall I sleep? Who will make my
어디에서 먹어야 하죠?　어디에서 자야 해요?　　누가 나에게 새 옷을 만들어

new clothes? Oh, I want to die! Yes, I want to die! Oh, oh,
줄까요?　오, 죽고 싶어요!　네, 죽고 싶어요!　　오, 오, 오!

oh!"

Poor Pinocchio! He even tried to tear his hair, / but as it
가엾은 피노키오!　　그는 머리를 쥐어 뜯으려 했지만,　　머리는 단지 그림

was only painted / on his wooden head, / he could not
이었기 때문에,　　나무 머리에 그려진,　　잡아당길 수조차 없었어요.

even pull it.

Just then / a large Pigeon flew / far above him. Seeing the
바로 그 때　커다란 비둘기 한 마리가 날아왔다　그의 머리 위에.　　꼭두각시를 보면서,

Marionette, / he cried to him:
비둘기가 외쳤다:

"Tell me, / little boy, / what are you doing / there?"
"말해 보렴,   애야,   뭘 하고 있지   거기에서?"

"Can't you see? I'm crying," / cried Pinocchio, / lifting his
"보면 몰라?   울고 있잖아,"   피노키오가 외쳤다,   머리를 들어

head / toward the voice / and rubbing his eyes / with his
목소리가 나는 쪽으로   눈을 문지르며   소매로.

sleeve.

"Tell me," / asked the Pigeon, / "do you by chance / know
"말해 보렴,"   비둘기가 물었다,   "너는 혹시

of a Marionette, / Pinocchio by name?"
꼭두각시를 알고 있니,   이름이 피노키오인?"

"Pinocchio! Did you say Pinocchio?" / replied the
"피노키오!   피노키오라 했니?"   꼭두각시가 대답했다,

Marionette, / jumping to his feet. "Why, I am Pinocchio!"
벌떡 일어서며.   "내가 피노키오야!"

At this answer, / the Pigeon flew / swiftly / down to the
피노키오의 대답에,   비둘기는 날아왔다   빠르게   땅 아래로.

earth. He was much larger / than a turkey.
그 새는 훨씬 컸다   칠면조보다.

"Then / you know Geppetto also?"
"그럼   제페토도 알겠구나?"

"Do I know him? He's my father, my poor, dear father!
"아느냐고?   그는 우리 아빠야, 나의 불쌍하고, 사랑하는 아빠!

Has he, perhaps, / spoken to you of me? Will you take me
아빠가, 혹시,   네게 나에 대해 말했니?   날 데려다 줄 수 있니

/ to him? Is he still alive? Answer me, / please! Is he still
아빠한테?   아직 살아 계시지?   대답해 줘,   제발!   살아 계신 거 맞지?"

alive?"

"I left him / three days ago / on the shore / of a large sea."
"그를 두고 왔어   3일 전에   해변에   넓은 바다의."

"What was he doing?"
"뭘 하고 계셨어?"

"He was building / a little boat / with which to cross the
"만들고 계셨어   작은 배를   바다를 건너는 데 필요한.

ocean. For the last four months, / that poor man has been
지난 넉 달 동안,   불쌍한 노인은 헤매고 다녔어,

wandering / around Europe, / looking for you. Not having
유럽을   널 찾으려고.   널 찾지 못하자,

found you yet, / he has made up his mind / to look for you /
결심하셨지   널 찾겠다고

in the New World, / far across the ocean."
'신세계'에서,   바다 건너 멀리."

"How far is it from here / to the shore?" / asked Pinocchio /
"여기에서 얼마나 멀지   해변까지?"   피노키오가 물었다

anxiously.
걱정스럽게.

"More than fifty miles."
"50마일이 넘어."

"Fifty miles? Oh, dear Pigeon, / how I wish / I had your
"50마일?   아, 비둘기야,   얼마나 좋을까   내가 네 날개를

wings!"
가졌다면!"

"If you want to come, / I'll take you with me."
"가고 싶으면,   내가 데려다 줄게."

"How?"
"어떻게?"

"Astride my back. Are you very heavy?"
"내 등에 올라타.   넌 많이 무겁니?"

"Heavy? Not at all. I'm only a feather."
"무거우냐고?   천만에.   난 깃털처럼 가벼워."

"Very well."
"좋았어."

Saying nothing more, / Pinocchio jumped / on the Pigeon's
아무 말도 없이,   피노키오는 뛰어올랐다   비둘기의 등에

---

wander 돌아다니다, 헤매다 | anxiously 열망하여 | astride 양쪽으로 두 다리를 벌리고 | gallop 전속력으로 (말을)
달리다 | steed (승마용) 말 | clutch (꽉) 움켜잡다

back / and, as he settled himself, / he cried out gayly:
그리고, 앉으면서,   즐겁게 소리쳤다:

"Gallop on, gallop on, my pretty steed! I'm in a great
"이랴, 이랴, 나의 작은 말아!   한시가 급하구나."

hurry."

The Pigeon flew away, / and in a few minutes / he had
비둘기는 멀리 날았고,   몇 분도 안 돼서

reached the clouds.
구름에 도착했다.

The Marionette looked to see / what was below them. His
꼭두각시는 보았다   발 아래를.

head swam / and he was so frightened / that he clutched
머리는 어지러웠고   너무 무서워서   꽉 움켜잡았다

wildly / at the Pigeon's neck / to keep himself from falling.
마구   비둘기의 목을   떨어지지 않으려고.

They flew / all day. Toward evening / the Pigeon said:
그들은 날았다   하루 종일. 저녁이 되자   비둘기가 말했다:

"I'm very thirsty!"
"목이 너무 말라!"

"And I'm very hungry!" / said Pinocchio.
"나도 너무 배고파!"   피노키오가 말했다.

Key Expression 🎵

I wish 가정법

I wish 가정법은 '~하면[했더라면] 좋을 텐데[좋았을 텐데]'라는 의미로 실현 불가능한 소망을 나타내는 가정법의 특수한 형태입니다.
특히 I wish 가정법에는 '이루지 못해서 유감'이라는 속뜻이 숨어 있으며 'I'm sorry that+부정문'을 직설법 문장으로 바꿀 수 있습니다.

▶ I wish+주어+과거동사/were ~ : ~하면 좋을 텐데
  (현재 또는 미래의 실현될 수 없는 소망)

▶ I wish+주어+had+과거분사 ~ : ~했더라면 좋았을 텐데
  (과거에 이루지 못한 일에 대한 소망)

ex) How I wish I had your wings!
    내게 당신의 날개가 있다면 얼마나 좋을까요!

"Let us stop / a few minutes / at that pigeon coop / down
"들렀다 가자　　　잠시　　　　　　비둘기 집에　　　　　　　저 아래의.

there. Then / we can go on / and be at the seashore / in the
그러고 나서　계속 갈 수 있어　해변에 도착할 거야

morning."
아침이면."

They went / into the empty coop / and there / they found
그들은 들어갔다　빈 집으로　　　　　　그리고 거기에서　발견했다

/ nothing but / a bowl of water / and a small basket / filled
오직　　　　　물 한 대야와　　　　작은 바구니를

with chick-peas.
병아리 콩으로 가득 찬.

The Marionette had always hated / chick-peas. According
꼭두각시는 항상 싫어했다　　　　　　병아리 콩을.　그에 따르면,

to him, / they had always made him sick; / but that night
병아리 콩은 항상 그를 아프게 했다;　　　하지만 그 날 밤

/ he ate them / with a relish. As he finished them, / he
그는 콩들을 먹었다　너무나 맛있게.　다 먹고 나자,

turned to the Pigeon / and said:
비둘기를 보며　　　　　말했다:

"I never should have thought / that chick-peas could be so
"미처 몰랐어　　　　　　　　　병아리 콩이 이렇게 맛있을 줄!"

good!"

Key Expression 🍗

with + 추상명사 = 부사

추상명사 앞에 전치사를 붙여 부사의 의미를 나타내는 경우가 있습니다. 이때 사
용되는 전치사로는 with가 가장 많으며 그 외에도 in, on, by 등도 사용됩니다.
단어에 따라 사용되는 전치사가 다르므로 알아두세요.
또한 of + 추상명사는 형용사의 의미가 된다는 점도 함께 기억하세요.

with ease = **easily** | with care = **carefully** | with fluency = **fluently**
with courage = **courageously** | with accuracy =**accurately**
in public = **publicly** | in private = **privately** | in triumph = **triumphantly**
by accident = **accidentally** | on purpose = **purposely**

ex) He ate them with a relish. 그는 그것들을 맛있게 먹었다.

"You must remember, / my boy," / answered the Pigeon, /
"알아두렴, 얘야," 비둘기가 말했다.

"that hunger is the best sauce!"
"배고픔이 최고의 반찬이란다!"

After resting a few minutes longer, / they set out again.
몇 분을 더 쉬고 나서, 그들은 다시 출발했다.

The next morning / they were at the seashore.
다음 날 아침 그들은 해변에 도착했다.

Pinocchio jumped off / the Pigeon's back, / and the Pigeon,
피노키오는 뛰어 내렸다 비둘기의 등에서, 그런데 비둘기는,

/ not wanting any thanks / for a kind deed, / flew away /
고맙다는 인사도 받지 않은 채 친절한 행동에 대한, 멀리 날아갔다

swiftly / and disappeared.
재빨리 그리고 사라졌다.

The shore was full of people, / shrieking and tearing their
바닷가는 사람들로 가득했다. 소리지르며 머리를 뜯고 있는

hair / as they looked / toward the sea.
바라보면서 바다를.

"What has happened?" / asked Pinocchio / of a little old
"무슨 일이 있어났나요?" 피노키오가 물었다

woman.
한 할머니에게.

"A poor old father lost his only son / some time ago / and
"불쌍한 아버지가 자식을 잃었어 얼마 전에 그리고

today / he built a tiny boat / for himself / in order to go / in
오늘 작은 배를 만들었대 혼자서 떠나기 위해

search of him / across the ocean. The water is very rough /
아들을 찾으려 바다를 건너. 파도가 심해서

and we're afraid / he will be drowned."
걱정이야 그가 빠져 죽을까 봐."

"Where is the little boat?"
"그 배는 어디에 있는데요?"

coop 닭장. (짐승) 우리 | chick-pea 병아리 콩 | relish 즐거움

"There. Straight down there," / answered the little old
"저기. 바로 저기란다." 할머니가 대답했다.

woman, / pointing to a tiny shadow, / no bigger than a
작은 점을 가리키며, 호두껍질보다 작은,

nutshell, / floating on the sea.
바다 위에 떠 있는.

Pinocchio looked / closely / for a few minutes / and then
피노키오는 보았다 자세히 몇 분 동안

gave a sharp cry:
그리고 나서 크게 소리쳤다:

"It's my father! It's my father!"
"아빠예요! 우리 아빠예요!"

Meanwhile, / the little boat, / tossed about / by the angry
잠시 후, 작은 배는, 흔들거리면서 성난 파도에 의해,

waters, / appeared and disappeared / in the waves. And
나타났다 사라졌다 파도 속에서.

Pinocchio, / standing on a high rock, / tired out with
피노키오는, 높은 바위에 올라서서, 찾으려고 애썼다,

searching, / waved to him with hand / and cap / and even
그에게 손을 흔들며 모자도

with his nose.
그리고 코마저.

It looked / as if Geppetto, / though far away from the
보였다 마치 제페토가, 해변에서 멀리 떨어져 있음에도,

shore, / recognized his son, / for he took off his cap / and
아들을 알아본 것처럼, 왜냐하면 그도 모자를 벗어

waved also. He seemed to be trying / to make everyone
흔들었기 때문이었다. 그는 애쓰는 것처럼 보였다 모두에게 말하려고

understand / that he would come back / if he were able,
돌아가겠다고 할 수 있다면.

/ but the sea was so heavy / that he could do nothing /
하지만 바다가 너무 거세어 아무것도 할 수 없었다

with his oars. Suddenly / a huge wave came / and the boat
그의 노를 가지고는. 갑자기 커다란 바다가 덮쳤고 배가 사라졌다.

disappeared.

They waited and waited / for it, / but it was gone.
기다리고 기다렸지만, 배가 나타나기를, 그러나 배는 사라지고 없었다.

"Poor man!" / said the fisher folk / on the shore, /
"불쌍한 양반!" 어부들이 말했다 해변에 있던,

whispering a prayer / as they turned to go home.
기도를 중얼거리며 집으로 돌아가면서.

Just then / a desperate cry was heard. Turning around, /
바로 그때 절망적인 외침이 들렸다. 돌아서서,

the fisher folk saw Pinocchio / dive into the sea / and heard
어부들은 피노키오를 보았다 바다에 뛰어드는 것을 그리고 들었다

him / cry out:
울부짖는 소리를:

"I'll save him! I'll save my father!"
"내가 구할 거야! 아빠를 구할 거야!"

The Marionette, / being made of wood, / floated easily
꼭두각시는, 나무로 만들어졌기 때문에, 물에 쉽게 떴고,

along / and swam like a fish / in the rough water. Now and
물고기처럼 수영했다 거친 물 속을. 때때로

again / he disappeared / only to reappear / once more. In a
그는 사라졌고 다시 나타났다 한 번 더.

twinkling, / he was far away / from land. At last / he was
눈 깜짝할 사이, 그는 멀어졌다 육지에서. 마침내

completely lost to view.
완전히 시야에서 사라졌다.

"Poor boy!" / cried the fisher folk / on the shore, / and
"불쌍한 꼬마군!" 어부들이 외쳤다 해변에 있던, 그리고 다시

again / they mumbled a few prayers, / as they returned
기도를 몇 마디 중얼거렸다 집으로 돌아가면서.

home.

meanwhile 그 동안에 | oars 노 | folk (일반적인) 사람들 | desperate 자포자기한

15

Pinocchio promises / the Fairy / to be good / and to study,
피노키오는 약속한다　　　요정에게　　　착한 사람이 되겠다고 그리고 공부하겠다고,

/ as he is growing tired / of being a Marionette, / and
　점점 지겨워져서　　　꼭두각시로 사는 게,　　　되고 싶어 한다

wishes / to become a real boy.
　진짜 어린이가.

If Pinocchio cried / much longer, / the little woman
피노키오가 울었다면　　더 오래,　　작은 여인은 생각했다

thought / he would melt away, / so she finally admitted /
그가 녹아서 없어질 거라고,　　그래서 마침내 인정했다

that she was the little Fairy / with Azure Hair.
자신이 요정이라는 사실을　　하늘색 머리의.

"You rascal of a Marionette! How did you know / it was
"말썽꾸러기 피노키오야!　　어떻게 알았니　　나라는 걸?

I?" / she asked, / laughing.
그녀가 물었다,　　웃으면서.

"My love for you / told me / who you were."
"당신을 향한 나의 사랑이　알려 줬어요　당신이 누구라는 걸."

"Do you remember? You left me / when I was a little girl
"기억하니?　　네가 나를 떠났을 때　나는 작은 소녀였어

/ and now / you find me / a grown woman. I am so old, / I
그런데 지금　나를 찾았구나　어른이 된.　　난 나이를 먹어서,

could almost be your mother!"
네 엄마 뻘이 되었어!"

"I am very glad of that, / for then / I can call you mother /
"전 좋아요,　　왜냐하면　당신을 엄마라고 부를 수 있어서

instead of sister. For a long time / I have wanted a mother,
누나가 아니라.　　오랫동안　　엄마가 생기길 바랐어요,

/ just like other boys. But how did you grow / so quickly?"
다른 아이들처럼.　　그런데 어떻게 자랄 수 있었죠　그렇게 빨리?"

melt away 차츰 사라지다[사라지게 하다] | disgustedly 넌더리를 내며 | it's about time ~을 해야 할 때이다[(곧)
~을 해야 할 것 같다]

"That's a secret!"
"비밀이란다!"

"Tell it / to me. I also want to grow a little. Look at me!
"가르쳐 주세요 내게.   나도 자라고 싶어요.   나를 보세요!

I have never grown / higher than a penny's worth of
전혀 자라지 않았어요   1페니 어치의 치즈만큼도."

cheese."

"But you can't grow," / answered the Fairy.
"하지만 넌 자랄 수 없단다,"   요정이 대답했다.

"Why not?"
"왜요?"

"Because Marionettes never grow. They are born
"꼭두각시는 절대 자랄 수 없기 때문이야.   꼭두각시로 태어나면,

Marionettes, / they live Marionettes, / and they die
꼭두각시로 살다가,   꼭두각시로 죽는 거야."

Marionettes."

"Oh, I'm tired of / always being a Marionette!" / cried
"아, 너무 지겨워요   항상 꼭두각시라는 게!"   피노키오가

Pinocchio / disgustedly. "It's about time / for me / to
소리쳤다   넌더리를 치며.   "때가 되었는데   내가

grow into a man / as everyone else does."
어른으로 자랄   다른 사람들과 똑같이."

Key Expression ❓

that is why 그것이 바로 ~한 이유이다

'that is why~'는 why 앞에 the reason 이라는 선행사가 생략된 관계부
사 구문이에요. '그것이 바로 ~한 이유이다' 혹은 앞문장의 결과를 나타내는 의미
로 '그래서 ~하는 것이다'로 해석할 수 있어요.
또한 이 구문은 '왜냐하면'이라는 뜻을 가진 접속사 because를 사용한 구문과
비교해서 알아둘 필요가 있어요.

▶ (원인), That's why ~(결과)
▶ (결과), That's because~(원인)

ex) This is the reason why I have come so far to look for you.
    이게 바로 내가 너를 찾으러 여기까지 온 이유야.
    (=그래서 내가 너를 찾으러 여기까지 왔어)

"And you will / if you deserve it —— "
"넌 그럴 수 있어   그럴 만한 자격이 되면 — "

"Really? What can I do / to deserve it?"
"정말이에요?   어떻게 하면 되나요   그럴 만한 자격이 되려면?"

"It's a very simple matter. Try to act / like a well-behaved
"아주 쉬워.   행동하려고 노력해 봐 착한 아이처럼."

child."

"Don't you think I do?"
"내가 착한 아이가 아니라고 생각하시죠?"

"Far from it! Good boys are obedient, / and you, / on the
"물론이지!   착한 아이는 말을 잘 듣지만,   너는,

contrary —— "
반대로 — "

"And I never obey."
"절대로 안 듣죠."

"Good boys love / study and work, / but you —— "
"착한 아이는 좋아해   공부도 일도,   하지만 너는 — "

"And I, / on the contrary, / am a lazy fellow / and a tramp
"나는,   반대로,   게으른 아이고   돌아다니기나 해요

/ all year round."
일 년 내내."

"Good boys always tell / the truth."
"착한 아이는 항상 말한다   진실을."

"And I always tell lies."
"난 늘 거짓말을 해요."

"Good boys go gladly / to school."
"착한 아이는 기쁘게 간다   학교에."

"And I get sick / if I go to school. From now on / I'll be
"난 아파요   학교에 가면.   지금부터는

different."
달라질 거예요."

"Do you promise?"
"약속하니?"

"I promise. I want to become a good boy / and be a
"약속해요.   나는 착한 아이가 되고 싶어요   위로가 되는 사람이

comfort / to my father. Where is my poor father / now?"
아빠한테.　불쌍한 우리 아빠는 어디 계시죠　지금?"

"I do not know."
"나도 모르겠구나."

"Will I ever be lucky / enough to find him / and embrace
"나에게 행운이 있을까요　아빠를 찾을 만큼　아빠를 안아볼 수 있

him / once more?"
을 만큼　다시 한 번?"

"I think so. Indeed, / I am sure of it."
"그렇게 하길 바라. 정말로,　틀림없이 그럴 거야."

At this answer, / Pinocchio's happiness was very great.
이 대답을 듣고,　피노키오는 매우 행복했다.

He grasped the Fairy's hands / and kissed them / so hard /
그는 요정의 손을 잡고　입맞췄다　너무 열심히

that it looked / as if he had lost his head. Then lifting his
그래서 보였다　미친 사람처럼.　그리고는 얼굴을 들어,

face, / he looked at her / lovingly / and asked: / "Tell me,
그녀를 보았다　사랑스럽게　그리고 물었다:　"말해 주세요,

little Mother, / it isn't true / that you are dead, / is it?"
엄마,　아니죠　돌아가신 게,　그렇죠?"

"It doesn't seem so," / answered the Fairy, / smiling.
"아마도 그럴 거야."　요정이 대답했다,　웃으면서.

"If you only knew / how I suffered / and how I wept /
"엄마가 알았다면　내가 얼마나 슬펐는지　얼마나 울었는데

when I read / 'Here lies ——'"
읽었을 때　'여기 잠들다 —'라는 글을"

"I know it, / and for that / I have forgiven you. The depth
"알고 있단다,　그렇기 때문에　널 용서했단다.

of your sorrow / made me see / that you have a kind
네 깊은 슬픔 때문에　알게 되었어　네가 착한 마음을 가졌다는 것을.

heart. There is always hope / for boys / with hearts / such
항상 희망은 있단다　아이들에게는　착한 마음을 가진

as yours, / though they may often be very mischievous.
너처럼,　아무리 말썽을 피웠더라도.

---

on the contrary 그와는 반대로 | tramp (특히 오랫동안) 터벅터벅[저벅저벅] 걷다 | embrace (껴)안다, 포옹하다

This is the reason / why I have come / so far / to look for
이게 바로 이유야   내가 돌아온   여기까지   너를 찾으러.

you. From now on, / I'll be your own little mother."
지금부터는,   내가 네 엄마가 되어 줄게."

"Oh! How lovely!" / cried Pinocchio, / jumping / with joy.
"오! 너무 기뻐요!"   피노키오가 소리쳤다.   펄쩍펄쩍 뛰면서 기뻐서.

"You will obey me / always / and do / as I wish?"
"내 말을 잘 들어야 한다   항상   그리고 해야 돼 내가 원하는걸?"

"Gladly, / very gladly, / more than gladly!"
"기꺼이,   매우 기꺼이   그 이상으로!"

"Beginning tomorrow," / said the Fairy, / "you'll go to
"내일부터 시작이야."   요정이 말했다,   "학교에 가는 거야

school / every day."
매일."

Pinocchio's face fell a little.
피노키오의 표정이 약간 가라앉았다.

"Then you will choose / the trade you like best."
"그리고 찾아보는 거야   네가 가장 잘할 수 있는 일을."

Pinocchio became more serious.
피노키오는 더 심각해졌다.

"What are you mumbling / to yourself?" / asked the Fairy.
"뭐라고 중얼거리고 있니   혼자서?"   요정이 물었다.

"I was just saying," / whined the Marionette / in a
"말한 것 뿐이에요,   피노키오는 울먹였다

whisper, / "that it seems too late / for me / to go to school
속삭이듯,   "너무 늦은 것 같다고   내가   학교에 가는 건

/ now."
지금."

"No, / indeed. Remember / it is never too late / to learn."
"아니야, 절대로.   기억하렴   너무 늦은 때란 없단다   배우는데 있어서."

"But I don't want / either trade or profession."
"하지만 하고 싶지 않아요   일도 직업도."

weary 지치게[피곤하게] 하다 | woe betide somebody ~는 화를 당할지니라(경고의 뜻으로 하는 말) | touch
마음을 움직이다, 감동시키다 | tiresome 성가신, 짜증스러운

"Why?"
"왜?"

"Because work wearies me!"
"일을 하면 피곤하니까요!"

"My dear boy," / said the Fairy, / "people who speak / as
"애야," 요정이 말했다. "말하는 사람들은

you do / usually / end their days / either in a prison / or
너처럼 대부분 생을 마감하지 감옥 안에서

in a hospital. A man, / remember, / whether rich or poor,
혹은 병원에서. 사람은, 기억해 두렴, 부자든 가난뱅이든,

/ should do something / in this world. No one can find
일을 해야 한단다 이 세상에서는. 아무도 행복해질 수 없어

happiness / without work. Woe betide the lazy fellow!
일을 하지 않으면. 게으른 사람은 화를 당할 거야!

Laziness is a serious illness / and one must cure it /
게으름은 심각한 병이야 그러니까 꼭 고쳐야 해

immediately; / yes, even from early childhood. If not, / it
즉시; 맞아, 아주 어렸을 때부터. 그러지 않으면,

will kill you / in the end."
게으름 때문에 죽을 거야 결국엔."

These words touched Pinocchio's heart. He lifted his
요정의 말에 피노키오의 마음이 움직였다. 그는 고개를 들어

eyes / to his Fairy / and said seriously: / "I'll work; I'll
요정에게 심각하게 말했다: "일을 할게요;

study; / I'll do all / you tell me. After all, / the life of a
공부도 할게요; 다 할게요 엄마가 하라는 대로. 어쨌든,

Marionette has grown very tiresome / to me / and I want
꼭두각시로 사는 건 너무 지겨워요 내게 그래서 난 어린이가

to become a boy, / no matter how hard it is. You promise
되고 싶어요. 그것이 아무리 힘든 일이라도. 약속하신 거예요,

that, / do you not?"
맞죠?"

"Yes, I promise, / and now / it is up to you."
"그래, 약속하마, 이제 네게 달렸어."

16

Pinocchio, / instead of becoming a boy, / runs away to the
피노키오는,　　　아이가 되지 못하고,　　　　　몰래 '장난감 나라'에 간다

Land of Toys / with his friend, Lamp-Wick.
친구인, '램프 심지'와 함께.

Coming at last out of the surprise / into which the Fairy's
놀라움에서 막 정신을 차리고　　　　　요정의 말이 그에게 안겨 준,

words had thrown him, / Pinocchio asked for permission /
피노키오는 허락을 청했다

to give out the invitations.
초대장을 돌려도 되는지.

"Indeed, / you may invite your friends / to tomorrow's
"그럼,　　　친구들을 초대해도 좋다　　　　내일의 파티에.

party. Only remember / to return home / before dark. Do
다만 기억하렴　　　집에 돌아오도록　　　어둡기 전에.

you understand?"
알겠니?"

"I'll be back / in one hour / without fail," / answered the
"돌아올게요　　한 시간 내로　　틀림없이."　　꼭두각시가 대답했다.

Marionette.

"Take care, Pinocchio! Boys give promises / very easily, /
"조심하렴, 피노키오!　　아이들은 약속을 하지　　너무 쉽게,

but they as easily forget them."
하지만 그만큼 쉽게 잊는단다."

"But I am not like those others. When I give my word / I
"하지만 전 그들과 달라요.　　　　　내가 한 말은

keep it."
꼭 지켜요."

---

lampwick [-wik] 램프 심지 | permission 허락, 허가 | give out (전단지나 초대장을) 돌리다 | without fail
틀림없이, 반드시 | disobey 불복종하다[거역하다/반항하다]

"We shall see. In case you do disobey, / you will be the
"두고 보자꾸나. 약속을 지키지 않으면, 네가 바로 고통을 겪게 된다.

one to suffer, / not anyone else."
다른 사람이 아닌."

"Why?"
"왜요?"

"Because / boys / who do not listen to their elders / always
"왜냐하면 아이들은 어른들의 충고를 듣지 않는

come to grief."
항상 곤경에 빠지니까."

"I certainly have," / said Pinocchio, "but from now on, / I
"알았어요." 피노키오는 말했다. "하지만 지금부터는,

obey."
잘 들을게요."

"We shall see / if you are telling the truth."
"알게 되겠지 네가 진실을 말하고 있는지."

Without adding another word, / the Marionette bade the
더 이상 대구하지 않은 채, 꼭두각시는 착한 요정에게 작별인사를 하고,

good Fairy good-by, / and singing and dancing, / he left
노래하고 춤추며,

the house.
집을 떠났다.

In a little more than an hour, / all his friends were invited.
한 시간이 조금 지나자, 모든 친구들이 초대되었다.

Some accepted / quickly and gladly. Others had to be
어떤 친구들은 초대에 응해 주었다 바로 기뻐하며, 다른 친구들은 졸라야 했다,

coaxed, / but when they heard / that the toast was to be
하지만 그들은 말을 듣고 토스트에 버터를 발랐다는

buttered / on both sides, / they all ended by accepting the
양면에, 결국 모두들 초대에 응했다

invitation / with the words, / "We'll come to please you."
이런 말을 하면서, "널 기쁘게 하려고 가는 거야."

Now / it must be known that, / among all his friends, /
이제 여러분은 알아야 해요, 친구들 중에,

Pinocchio had one / whom he loved / most of all. The
피노키오에게 한 명이 있다는 것을 그가 사랑하는 가장.

boy's real name was Romeo, / but everyone called him
그 아이의 이름은 로미오였는데, 친구들은 그를 불렀다

/ Lamp-Wick, / for he was long / and thin / and had a
'램프 심지'라고, 왜냐하면 그는 키가 컸고 마르고

woebegone look about him.
항상 비탄에 잠긴 얼굴을 했기 때문이었다.

Lamp-Wick was the laziest boy / in the school / and the
램프 심지는 가장 게으른 아이였다   학교에서

biggest mischief-maker, / but Pinocchio loved him / dearly.
그리고 가장 말썽꾸러기였다,   하지만 피노키오는 그를 사랑했다   너무나도.

That day, / he went straight / to his friend's house / to
그 날,   그는 곧장 달려갔다   친구의 집으로

invite him to the party, / but Lamp-Wick was not at home.
파티에 초대하기 위해,   하지만 램프 심지는 집에 없었다.

He went a second time, / and again a third, / but still /
다시 한 번 갔을 때도,   세 번째 갔을 때도,   여전히

without success.
헛수고였다.

Where could he be? Pinocchio searched / here and there
도대체 어디에 있는 걸까?   피노키오는 찾아 다녔다   여기 저기

/ and everywhere, / and finally / discovered him / hiding
모든 곳을,   그리고 마침내   그를 찾았다

near a farmer's wagon.
농부의 마차 근처에 숨어 있는.

"What are you doing there?" / asked Pinocchio, / running
"거기서 뭐 하니?"   피노키오가 물었다,

up to him.
그에게 달려가면서.

"I am waiting for midnight / to strike to go ——"
"자정이 될 때까지 기다리고 있어   그때 가려고 — "

"Where?"
"어디를?"

"Far, far away!"
"아주, 아주 멀리!"

"And I have gone / to your house / three times / to look for
"찾아갔었어   너네 집에   세 번이나

you!"
널 찾으려고!"

"What did you want from me?"
"무슨 일인데?"

"Haven't you heard / the news? Don't you know / what
"아직 못 들었니   소식을?   넌 모르는구나

good luck is mine?"
내게 어떤 행운이 왔는지?"

"What is it?"
"그게 뭔데?"

"Tomorrow / I end my days / as a Marionette / and become
"내일이면   생을 마감하고   꼭두각시로서의   그리고 진짜 아이가

a boy, / like you / and all my other friends."
된다고,   너처럼   다른 친구들처럼."

"May it bring you luck!"
"정말 잘됐구나!"

"Shall I see you / at my party / tomorrow?"
"와 줄 수 있니   파티에   내일?"

"But I'm telling you / that I go / tonight."
"하지만 말했잖니   난 떠난다고   오늘 밤."

"At what time?"
"몇 시에?"

"At midnight."
"자정에."

"And where are you going?"
"그럼 어디를 가는데?"

"To a real country —— / the best in the world —— / a
"진짜 세계로 —   세계 최고의 —

wonderful place!"
멋진 곳으로!"

"What is it called?"
"나라 이름이 뭐야?"

"It is called the Land of Toys. Why don't you come, / too?"
""장난감 나라'야.   같이 가지 않을래,   너도?"

"I? Oh, no!"
"나? 오, 안 돼!"

morn (문예체) 아침 | nod (고개를) 끄덕이다

"You are making a big mistake, / Pinocchio. Believe me,
"넌 지금 실수하는 거야.   피노키오.   나를 믿어,

/ if you don't come, / you'll be sorry. Where can you find
가지 않으면,   후회할 거야.   어디에서 그런 곳을 찾을 수 있겠어

a place / that will agree better / with you and me? No
딱 맞는   너와 나한테?

schools, / no teachers, / no books! In that blessed place
학교도 없지,   선생님도 없지,   책도 없어!   그렇게 축복 받은 곳에는

/ there is no such thing / as study. Here, / it is only on
전혀 없어   공부 같은 건. 여기에서는, 오직 토요일뿐이지

Saturdays / that we have no school. In the Land of Toys,
학교를 쉬는 날인.   하지만 장난감 나라에서는,

/ every day, / except Sunday, / is a Saturday. Vacation
매일이,   일요일은 빼고,   토요일이야.   방학이 시작돼

begins / on the first of January / and ends / on the last
1월 1일부터   그리고 끝나   12월 마지막 날에.

day of December. That is the place for me! All countries
그곳은 나를 위한 곳이야!

should be like it! How happy we should all be!"
모든 나라가 그와 같다면!   우린 얼마나 행복할까!"

"But how does one spend / the day / in the Land of Toys?"
"그런데 무엇을 하며 지내   하루를   장난감 나라에서는?"

"Days are spent in play and enjoyment / from morn till
"놀면서 신나게 보내면 돼   아침부터 밤까지.

night. At night / one goes to bed, / and next morning, / the
밤에는   잠자리에 들고,   다음 날 아침이면,

good times begin / all over again. What do you think of
재미있는 시간이 시작되지   계속해서.   어떻게 생각해?"

it?"

"H'm ── !" / said Pinocchio, nodding his wooden head,
"음 ─ !"   피노키오는 말했다,   나무 머리를 끄덕이며,

/ as if to say, / "It's the kind of life / which would agree
마치 말하는 것처럼, "그렇게 사는 건   나한테 꼭 맞는군

with me / perfectly."
완벽하게."

"Do you want to go / with me, / then? Yes or no? You
"같이 갈래   나랑,   그럼?   갈래 안 갈래?

must make up your mind."
네가 결정해."

"No, no, and again no! I have promised my kind Fairy
"아니, 아니, 절대 안 돼!   난 친절한 요정과 약속했어

/ to become a good boy, / and I want to keep my word.
착한 아이가 되겠다고,   그리고 난 약속을 지키고 싶어.

Just see: / The sun is setting / and I must leave you / and
저길 봐: 태양이 지고 있어   난 떠나야 해   달려야 해.

run. Good-by / and good luck to you!"
안녕   그리고 행운을 빌어!"

"Where are you going / in such a hurry?"
"어디를 가는데   그리 서둘러?"

"Home. My good Fairy wants me / to return home /
"집에.   착한 요정이 내게 원해   집에 돌아오기를

before night."
밤이 되기 전에."

"Wait two minutes more."
"2분만 더 기다려."

"It's too late!"
"너무 늦었어!"

"Only two minutes."
"딱 2분만."

---

in a hurry 서둘러, 급히 | scold 야단치다, 꾸짖다 | wagon 마차 | boundary 경계(선) | marvelous 신기한,

훌륭한 | strike (시간을 알리기 위해 시계가) 치다[알리다]

"And if the Fairy scolds me?"
"요정이 날 야단치면?"

"Let her scold. After she gets tired, / she will stop," /
"야단치게 놔 둬.   그러다 지치면,   그만두겠지."

said Lamp-Wick.
램프 심지가 말했다.

"Are you going alone / or with others?"
"넌 혼자 가니   아니면 여럿이 함께 가니?"

"Alone? There will be more than a hundred of us!"
"혼자냐고?   우린 백 명도 넘어!"

"Will you walk?"
"걸어서 가니?"

"At midnight / the wagon passes here / that is to take us /
"자정에   마차가 여길 지나가   우리를 데려다 줄

within the boundaries / of that marvelous country."
국경 안으로   마법의 나라의."

"How I wish / midnight would strike!"
"얼마나 좋을까   자정이 지금이라면!"

"Why?"
"왜?"

"To see you all / set out together."
"너희 모두를 볼 수 있으니까   함께 떠나는 걸."

"Stay here / a while longer / and you will see us!"
"여기에서 기다려   조금만 더   그러면 우리를 볼 수 있어!"

"No, no. I want to return home."
"안 돼, 안 돼. 난 집에 돌아가고 싶어."

"Wait two more minutes."
"2분만 더 기다려 줘."

"I have waited too long / as it is. The Fairy will be
"너무 오래 기다렸어   지금도.   요정이 걱정할 거야."

worried."

"Poor Fairy! Is she afraid / the bats will eat you up?"
"불쌍한 요정이네! 걱정하는 거니 박쥐가 널 먹어 치울까봐?"

"Listen, Lamp-Wick," / said the Marionette, / "are you
"음, 램프 심지야," 꼭두각시가 말했다. "정말로 확실하니

really sure / that there are no schools / in the Land of
학교가 없다는 것이 장난감 나라에는?"

Toys?" "Not even the shadow of one."
"그럼, 학교라고는 그림자도 없어."

"Not even one teacher?"
"선생님도 없고?"

"Not one."
"한 명도."

"And one does not have to study?"
"공부를 안 해도 되고?"

"Never, never, never!"
"절대로, 결코, 정말로!"

"What a great land!" / said Pinocchio, / feeling his mouth
"정말로 멋진 나라구나!" 피노키오가 말했다. 입에 침이 고이는 걸 느끼며.

water. "What a beautiful land! I have never been there, /
"정말로 아름다운 곳이야! 한 번도 간 적도 없지만,

but I can well imagine it."
아주 상상이 잘 가는구나."

Key Expression ♥

remember me to~ : ~에게 나의 안부 전해 줘

remember A to B는 '기억하다'라는 의미라기 보다 'B에게 A의 안부를 전하다'라는 의미로 쓰입니다. 보통 remember me to~의 형식으로 '~에게 안부 전해줘'라고 많이 쓰여요. 같은 의미로 쓰이는 다른 표현들도 함께 알아두세요.

remember me to~
= say hello to~
= give my regards to~
= give my best wishes to~

ex) Good-by, then, and remember me to the grammar schools.
그럼 안녕, 그리고 문법 학교에 안부 전해 줘.

"Why don't you come, too?"
"너도 같이 가지 않을래?"

"It is useless / for you / to tempt me! I told you / I promised
"소용없어   네가   날 유혹해도!   말했잖아   요청과 약속했다고

my good Fairy / to behave myself, / and I am going to keep
          얌전히 굴기로,   난 약속을 지킬 거야."

my word."

"Good-by, then, / and remember me / to the grammar
"안녕, 그럼,   안부 전해줘   문법 학교에,

schools, / to the high schools, / and even to the colleges / if
          고등학교에,   대학에도

you meet them on the way."
혹시 길에서 지나가게 되면."

"Good-by, Lamp-Wick. Have a pleasant trip, / enjoy
"안녕, 램프 심지야.   즐거운 여행하고,   재미있게 지내,

yourself, / and remember your friends / once in a while."
          그리고 네 친구들을 기억해 줘   이따금."

With these words, / the Marionette started / on his way
이 말을 하고는,   꼭두각시는 출발했다   집으로 가는 길을.

home. Turning once more / to his friend, / he asked him:
          한 번 더 뒤돌아서   친구를 향해,   물었다:

"But are you sure that, / in that country, / each week is
"그런데 확실하니,   그 나라에서는,   일주일이 구성된다는 게

composed of / six Saturdays and one Sunday?"
          여섯 개의 토요일과 하나의 일요일로?"

"Very sure!"
"확실하지!"

"And that vacation begins / on the first of January / and
"그럼 방학이 시작된다는 것도   1월 1일에   그리고 끝나

ends / on the thirty-first of December?"
는 것도   12월 31일에?"

tempt 유혹하다 | behave (oneself)! 얌전히 굴어라!

"Very, very sure!"
"아주, 아주 확실하지!"

"What a great country!"/ repeated Pinocchio, / puzzled as
"정말 멋진 나라구나!"   피노키오가 대답했다,   어찌할 바를 몰라

to what to do.
당황하며.

Then, / in sudden determination, / he said hurriedly:
"그러다가,   갑자기 마음을 다잡고,   서둘러 말했다:

"Good-by / for the last time, / and good luck."
"안녕   마지막으로,   행운을 빌어."

"Good-by."
"안녕."

"How soon will you go?"
"언제쯤 떠날 거니?"

"Within two hours."
"두 시간 이내로."

"What a pity! If it were only one hour, / I might wait for
"안타깝군!   딱 한 시간이면,   기다릴 텐데.

you."

"And the Fairy?"
"그럼 요정은?"

"By this time I'm late, / and one hour more or less / makes
"이미 늦었어,   한 시간 정도로

very little difference."
달라질 것도 없지."

"Poor Pinocchio! And if the Fairy scolds you?"
"불쌍한 피노키오!   그러다 요정이 널 야단치면?"

"Oh, I'll let her scold. After she gets tired, / she will stop."
"어, 야단치게 내버려 둘 거야.   그러다 지치면,   그만하겠지."

In the meantime, / the night became darker and darker. All
잠시 후,   밤은 점점 더 어두워졌다.

at once / in the distance / a small light flickered. A queer
갑자기   멀리서   작은 불빛이 깜박였다.

sound could be heard, / soft as a little bell, / and faint and
괴상한 소리가 들리더니,   작은 방울 소리처럼 부드럽게,   그리고 희미하고 약하게

muffled / like the buzz of a far-away mosquito.
저 멀리 모기 소리처럼.

"There it is!" / cried Lamp-Wick, / jumping to his feet.
"왔다!"   램프 심지가 외쳤다,   벌떡 일어서며.

"What?" / whispered Pinocchio.
"뭐가?"   피노키오가 속삭였다.

"The wagon / which is coming / to get me. For the last
"마차가   오고 있어   나를 태우러.   마지막으로,

time, / are you coming or not?"
갈 거야 안 갈 거야?"

"But is it really true / that in that country / boys never
"그런데 정말 사실이니   그 나라에서는

have to study?"
아이들이 공부할 필요가 없는 게?"

"Never, never, never!"
"절대로, 절대로, 절대로!"

"What a wonderful, beautiful, marvelous country! Oh
"정말 멋지고, 아름답고, 놀라운 나라구나!

—— h —— h!!"
오 — 오 — 오!"

Key Expression 🎵

how/what으로 시작하는 감탄문

영어의 감탄문은 how와 what을 사용하여 만들어요. 이때 how는 형용사나 부
사가 있는 문장에, what은 명사가 있는 문장에 사용하는데 각각의 어순이 다르므로
잘 기억하세요.

▶ How + 형용사 / 부사 + (주어 + 동사)!
▶ What + (a / an) + 형용사 + 명사 + (주어 + 동사)!

ex) What a wonderful, beautiful, marvelous country!
　　정말 멋지고, 아름답고, 놀라운 나라구나!
　　How happy we should all be!
　　얼마나 행복할까!

determination (공식적인) 결정 | (in the) meantime 그 동안[사이]에(= meanwhile) | flicker 깜박거리다 | queer
기묘한, 괴상한 | faint 희미한[약한] | muffle (소리를) 죽이다[약하게 하다] | buzz 윙윙거림

131

mini test 5

A. 다음 문장을 해석해 보세요.

(1) He saw the wood / where unluckily / he had met the Fox and the Cat, / and the tall oak tree / where he had been hanged.
→

(2) It looked / as if Geppetto, / though far away from the shore, / recognized his son, / for he took off his cap / and waved also.
→

(3) The Marionette, / being made of wood, / floated easily along / and swam like a fish / in the rough water.
→

(4) Pinocchio promises / the Fairy / to be good / and to study, / as he is growing tired / of being a Marionette, / and wishes to become / a real boy.
→

B. 다음 주어진 문장이 되도록 빈칸에 써 넣으세요.

(1) 그는 너무 놀랐고, <u>최대한 빨리 달려서</u>, 마침내 그 장소에 도착했다.

He became terribly frightened and,
                      , he finally came to the spot.

(2) 그는 너무 놀라서 <u>떨어지지 않으려고</u> 비둘기의 목을 꽉 잡았다.

He was so frightened that he clutched wildly at the Pigeon's neck   .

(3) <u>이게 바로</u> 내가 너를 찾아서 여기 까지 <u>온 이유야.</u>

                                              I have come so far to look for you.

Answer

A. (1) 그는 불운하게도 여우와 고양이를 만났던 그 나무와 그가 매달렸던 그 키 큰 떡갈나무를 보았다. (2) 바닷가에서 멀었음에도 불구하고 제페토는 그의 아들을 알아본 듯 보였다. 왜냐하면 그도 모자를 벗고 손을 흔들었기 때문이다. (3) 그 꼭두각시는 나무로 만들어졌기 때문에, 거친 바다에서도 쉽게 떠다니며 물고

(4) 내가 지금 학교에 가기는 너무 늦은 것 같아요.

It seems _____ now.

C. 다음 주어진 문구가 알맞은 문장이 되도록 순서를 맞춰 보세요.

(1) 여기에서 바닷가까지는 얼마나 멀어?
(far / the shore? / How / it / is / from / to / here)
→

(2) 내가 네 날개를 가진다면 얼마나 좋을까!
(I / How / had / wish / your wings! / I)
→

(3) 아무리 힘들더라도 나는 아이가 되고 싶어요.
(matter / it / how / no / hard / is)
→

(4) 그건 네게 달렸어.
(to / is / It / you / up)
→

D. 다음 단어에 대한 맞는 설명과 연결해 보세요.

(1) clutch ▶   ◀ ① very sad
(2) tramp ▶   ◀ ② hold something tightly
(3) flickers ▶   ◀ ③ walk slowly for a long time
(4) woebegone ▶   ◀ ④ shine unsteadily

기처럼 헤엄쳤다. (4) 피노키오는 꼭두각시가 되는 것에 싫증이 나서 진짜 아이가 되고 싶었기 때문에 착한 사람이 되고 공부도 하겠다고 요정에게 약속했다. | B. (1) running as fast as he could (2) to keep himself from falling (3) This is the reason why (4) too late for me to go to school | C. (1) How far is it from here to the shore? (2) How I wish I had your wings! (3) I want to become a boy, no matter how hard it is. (4) It is up to you. | D. (1) ② (2) ③ (3) ④ (4) ①

133

Pinocchio's ears become / like those of a Donkey. In a
피노키오의 귀가 변한다   당나귀 귀처럼.

little while / he changes / into a real Donkey / and begins
잠시 후   피노키오는 변한다   진짜 당나귀로   그리고 당나귀 울음

to bray.
소리를 내기 시작하다.

Everyone, / at one time or another, / has found some
모두들,   차례로,   놀라운 일들은 발견해 왔지요

surprise / awaiting him. Of the kind / which Pinocchio
          그를 기다리고 있는.   그런 놀라움은   피노키오가 경험했던

had / on that eventful morning / of his life, / there are
      그 파란만장했던 아침에   그의 인생에서,   아마 없을 겁니다.

but few.

What was it? I will tell you, / my dear little readers. On
그게 뭐였을까요?   말해 줄게요,   어린이 독자 여러분에게는.

awakening, / Pinocchio put his hand up / to his head /
일어나자 마자,   피노키오는 손을 올려 놓았을 때   머리 위에

and there / he found —— Guess!
거기서   그가 발견한 것은 — 알아 맞춰 보세요!

Key Expression 🍋

접속사 while과 명사 while

접속사 while에는 '~하는 동안'이란 뜻의 시간의 접속사, '~하는 반면에'란 의미의 양보 접속사, 그리고 상반되는 두 문장을 연결하는 역접의 의미로 사용됩니다. 명사인 while은 '잠깐, 잠시 동안'의 의미로 쓰이며 주로 for a while(잠시 동안), after a while(잠시 후에), once in a while(가끔, 때때로)와 같이 표현합니다.

ex) In a little while he changes into a real Donkey and begins to bray.
   잠시 후 그는 진짜 당나귀로 변하여 울기 시작한다.
   While talking in the darkness, Pinocchio thought he saw a faint light in the distance.
   어둠 속에서 이야기하는 동안, 피노키오는 멀리서 희미한 불빛을 본 것 같았다.

He found that, / during the night, / his ears had grown /
그는 발견했다.   밤 사이에,   귀가 자랐다는 것을

at least ten full inches!
적어도 10인치나!

You must know / that the Marionette, / even from his
여러분들은 알고 있겠지만 꼭두각시는,   태어날 때조차,

birth, / had very small ears, / so small indeed / that to
귀가 아주 작았어요,   정말 너무도 작아서

the naked eye / they could hardly be seen. Fancy / how
맨 눈으로는   거의 보이지도 않을 정도였죠.   상상해 보세요

he felt / when he noticed / that overnight / those two
그가 어떻게 느꼈을지   알아차렸을 때   밤새   그 두 개의 앙증맞은

dainty organs / had become as long / as shoe brushes!
귀가   길어졌다는 것을   구두 솔만큼이나!'

He went / in search of a mirror, / but / not finding any, /
피노키오는 갔다 거울을 찾으러,   하지만 어디에서도 찾을 수 없어서,

he just filled a basin / with water / and looked at himself.
대야를 가득 채우고   물로   그리고 자신의 모습을 비춰보았다.

There / he saw / what he never could have wished to
거기에서   그는 보았다   절대로 보고 싶지 않았던 모습을.

see. His manly figure was adorned and enriched / by a
     인간의 모습인 그의 얼굴에 붙어 있었다

beautiful pair of donkey's ears.
아름다운 당나귀 귀 한 쌍이.

I leave you to think of / the terrible grief, / the shame, /
여러분의 상상에 맡길게요   끔찍한 슬픔과,   창피함,

the despair / of the poor Marionette.
절망에 대해서는   불쌍한 꼭두각시의.

He began to cry, / to scream, / to knock his head /
그는 울기 시작했고,   소리 지르고,   머리를 부딪쳤다

against the wall, / but the more he shrieked, / the longer
벽에다,   하지만 점점 더 소리칠수록,

and the more hairy / grew his ears.
더 길고 많은 털들이   귀에서 자라났다.

---

bray (당나귀가 시끄럽게) 울다 | dainty 앙증맞은, 얌전한 | shoe brush 구둣솔 | basin 양푼(같이 생긴 그릇); 대야
| manly 남자다운 | adorn 꾸미다, 장식하다 | enrich 질을 높이다, 풍요롭게 하다; (식품에 어떤 영양소를) 강화하다

At those piercing shrieks, / a Dormouse came / into the
날카로운 울음 소리를 듣고, 다람쥐가 왔다 방으로,

room, / a fat little Dormouse, / who lived upstairs. Seeing
통통하고 작은 다람쥐인데, 위층에 살았다.

Pinocchio so grief-stricken, / she asked him / anxiously:
절망에 빠진 피노키오를 보고, 다람쥐가 물었다 걱정스럽게:

"What is the matter, / dear little neighbor?"
"무슨 일이니, 옆집 친구?"

"I am sick, / my little Dormouse, / very, very sick —— / and
"몸이 아파, 친구 다람쥐야, 너무, 너무 아파 —

from an illness / which frightens me! Do you understand /
병 때문에 나를 겁에 질리게 한! 너는 아니

how to feel the pulse?"
맥 짚는 방법을?"

"A little."
"조금."

"Feel mine then / and tell me / if I have a fever."
"그럼 나 좀 봐 줘 그리고 말해 줘 열이 있는지."

The Dormouse took Pinocchio's wrist / between her paws
다람쥐는 피노키오의 손목을 잡았다 앞 발 사이로

/ and, after a few minutes, / looked up at him / sorrowfully
그리고, 몇 분 후, 그를 보더니 슬프게

/ and said: / "My friend, I am sorry, / but I must give you
말했다: "친구야, 미안하지만,

some very sad news."
나쁜 소식을 전해야겠어."

no longer
no longer는 '더 이상 ~아닌' 혹은 '이미 ~가 아니다'라는 의미로 쓰이는 숙어입
니다. 또한 not ~ any longer로 풀어 쓰기도 합니다.

ex) Within two or three hours, you will no longer be a Marionette, nor a boy.
두세 시간 후면, 너는 더 이상 꼭두각시도, 소년도 아니게 될 거야.
I can no longer stand up.
나는 더 이상 견딜 수 없어요.

"What is it?"
"뭔데?"

"You have a very bad fever."
"넌 나쁜 열병에 걸렸어."

"But what fever is it?"
"무슨 열병?"

"The donkey fever."
"당나귀 열병."

"I don't know anything about / that fever," / answered the
"난 들어본 적이 없어   그 열병을,"   꼭두각시가 말했다,

Marionette, / beginning to understand even too well / what
그러나 너무나 잘 이해하기 시작하며

was happening to him.
자신에게 무슨 일이 일어나고 있는지.

"Then I will tell you / all about it," / said the Dormouse.
"그럼 내가 말해 줄게   모든 걸,"   다람쥐가 말했다.

"Know then that, / within two or three hours, / you will no
"알아둬,   두세 시간 후면,

longer be a Marionette, / nor a boy."
너는 더 이상 꼭두각시가 아닐 거야,   어린 아이도 아니고.

"What shall I be?"
"그럼 뭐가 되는데?"

"Within two or three hours / you will become a real
"두세 시간이면   너는 진짜 당나귀가 될 거야,

donkey, / just like the ones / that pull the fruit carts / to
바로 그들처럼   과일 수레를 끌고 가는

market."
시장에."

"Oh, what have I done? What have I done?" / cried
"아, 어쩌다 그런 거지?   어떻게 된 거야?"   피노키오가 외쳤다,

Pinocchio, / grasping his two long ears / in his hands /
그의 긴 두 귀를 잡고서   손으로

and pulling and tugging at them / angrily, / just as if they
잡아당기면서   화를 내며,   마치 남의 귀라도 되는 양.

belonged to another.

piercing 날카로운 | dormouse 동면쥐 류 | grief-stricken 비탄에 빠진 | pulse 맥박, 맥 | wrist 손목, 팔목 |
cart 수레, 우마차 | tug 잡아당기다

"My dear boy," / answered the Dormouse / to cheer him
"이 친구야." 다람쥐가 말했다 조금이라도 위로하려고,

up a bit, / "why worry / now? What is done / cannot be
"왜 걱정을 하니 지금? 일어난 일은 돌이킬 수 없어,

undone, / you know. Fate has decreed / that all lazy boys /
너도 알다시피. 다 운명이란다 모든 게으른 아이들은

who come to hate books / and schools / and teachers / and
책을 싫어하며 학교와 선생님도

spend all their days / with toys and games / must sooner
온종일 시간을 보내는 장난감과 게임으로 반드시 조만간

or later / turn into donkeys."
당나귀로 변한다는 것을."

"But is it really so?" / asked the Marionette, / sobbing
"그게 정말이야?" 꼭두각시가 말했다,

bitterly.
크게 흐느끼며.

"I am sorry / to say it is. And tears now are useless. You
"미안하지만 이렇게 말해서. 눈물은 이제 소용없어.

should have thought of all this / before."
이렇게 될 줄 알았어야지 미리."

"But the fault is not mine. Believe me, / little Dormouse, /
"하지만 내 잘못이 아니야. 믿어줘, 다람쥐야,

the fault is all Lamp-Wick's."
모두 램프 심지의 잘못이라고."

"And who is this Lamp-Wick?"
"그럼 램프 심지는 누군데?"

"A classmate of mine. I wanted to return home. I wanted
"같은 반 친구야. 난 집에 돌아가고 싶었어. 난 말 잘 듣는

to be obedient. I wanted to study / and to succeed in
아이가 되고 싶었어. 난 공부해서 성공하고 싶었어 학교에서,

school, / but Lamp-Wick said to me, / 'Why do you want
그런데 램프 심지가 말했어,

to waste your time studying? Why do you want to go to
'왜 시간을 공부에 허비하려고 하니? 왜 학교에 가고 싶어 하니?

school? Come with me / to the Land of Toys. There / we'll
나랑 같이 가자   장난감 나라로.   거기에서는

never study / again. There / we can enjoy ourselves / and
절대로 공부하지 않아 다시는.   거기에서는 즐겁게 놀 수 있고

be happy / from morn till night.'"
행복할 수 있어   아침부터 밤까지'라고."

fate 운명 | decree (법령, 판결 등에 따라) 명하다 | bitterly 비통하게, 몹시 | obedient 말을 잘 듣는, 순종적인,
복종하는

139

"And why did you follow / the advice / of that false friend?"
"왜 따랐니   충고를   그렇게 나쁜 친구의?"

"Why? Because, / my dear little Dormouse, / I am a
"왜냐고?   왜냐하면,   다람쥐야,

heedless Marionette / —— heedless and heartless. Oh! If I
나는 조심성 없는 꼭두각시잖아   — 조심성 없고 양심도 없는.   아!

had only had a bit of heart, / I should never have abandoned
내가 양심이 조금이라도 있었다면,   저버리진 않았을 텐데

/ that good Fairy, / who loved me so well / and who has
그 착한 요정을,   나를 엄청 사랑해 주고

been so kind / to me! And by this time, / I should no longer
아주 친절했던   내게!   그리고 지금쯤이면,   난 더 이상 꼭두각시도 아니었을

be a Marionette. I should have become a real boy, / like
텐데.   진짜 아이가 되어 있을 텐데,

all these friends of mine! Oh, if I meet Lamp-Wick / I am
내 친구들처럼!   아, 램프 심지를 만나면

going to tell him / what I think of him / —— and more, too!"
말해야겠다   내가 어떤 기분인지   — 혼내 줘야겠어!"

After this long speech, / Pinocchio walked / to the door
긴 넋두리가 끝난 후,   피노키오는 걸어갔다   방문으로.

of the room. But / when he reached it, / remembering his
하지만, 문에 이르자,   당나귀 귀가 생각났고,

donkey ears, / he felt ashamed / to show them / to the public
부끄러워서   보이는 게   사람들 앞에

/ and turned back. He took a large cotton bag / from a shelf,
돌아왔다.   그는 커다란 면 주머니를 꺼내   선반에서,

/ put it on his head, / and pulled it far down / to his very
머리에 썼다,   푹 잡아당겨서   코까지.

nose.

Thus adorned, / he went out. He looked for Lamp-Wick /
그렇게 변장한 후,   밖으로 나갔다.   램프 심지를 찾아 다녔다

everywhere, / along the streets, / in the squares, / inside the
이곳저곳으로,   거리며,   광장이며,   극장 안에도,

theatres, / everywhere; / but he was not to be found. He
모든 곳을; 하지만 찾을 수 없었다.

asked everyone / whom he met / about him, / but no one
그는 모두에게 물어봤다 만났던 그에 대해, 하지만 그를 본

had seen him. In desperation, / he returned home / and
사람은 아무도 없었다. 실망하면서, 그는 집으로 돌아가서

knocked at the door.
문을 두드렸다.

"Who is it?" / asked Lamp-Wick from within.
"누구세요?" 램프 심지가 안에서 물었다.

"It is I!" / answered the Marionette.
"나야!" 꼭두각시가 대답했다.

"Wait a minute."
"잠깐만 기다려."

After a full half hour / the door opened. Another surprise
30분이나 지난 후 문이 열렸다. 또 다른 놀라운 광경이 피노

awaited Pinocchio! There in the room / stood his friend,
키오를 기다리고 있었다! 방 안에는 그의 친구가 서있었다,

/ with a large cotton bag on his head, / pulled far down to
커다란 면 주머니를 머리에 쓴 채, 아래로 잡아당겨서

his very nose.
코까지.

At the sight of that bag, / Pinocchio felt slightly happier /
그 주머니를 보자, 피노키오는 약간 행복해져서

and thought to himself:
생각했다:

"My friend must be suffering / from the same sickness /
"내 친구도 아픈 게 틀림없구나 똑같은 병으로

that I am! I wonder / if he, too, has donkey fever?"
나와 같이! 궁금하군 그도, 역시, 당나귀 열병일까?"

But pretending he had seen nothing, / he asked / with a
하지만 아무것도 보지 못한 척하며, 물었다 웃음을 띠며:

smile:

---

heedless 세심한 주의를 기울이지 않는 | heartless 양심 없는, 무정한, 비정한 | ashamed 부끄러운 | shelf 선반 |
adorn 꾸미다 | slightly 약간, 조금 | suffer from 병을 앓다

"How are you, / my dear Lamp-Wick?"
"잘 있었니,   램프 심지야?"

"Very well. Like a mouse / in a Parmesan cheese."
"잘 지내. 마치 쥐처럼   파마산 치즈 속에 들어 있는."

"Is that really true?"
"정말 사실이니?"

"Why should I lie / to you?"
"왜 거짓말을 하겠니   네게?"

"I beg your pardon, / my friend, / but why then are you
"미안한데,   친구야,   그런데 왜 쓰고 있는 거니

wearing / that cotton bag / over your ears?"
그 면 주머니를   귀에다?

"The doctor has ordered it / because one of my knees hurts.
"의사가 그렇게 지시했어   왜냐하면 한쪽 무릎을 다쳤거든.

And you, dear Marionette, / why are you wearing / that
그런데 너는, 꼭두각시야,   왜 쓰고 있니

cotton bag down / to your nose?"
그 면 주머니를   코까지 내려서?

"The doctor has ordered it / because I have bruised my
"의사가 그렇게 처방했어   왜냐하면 다리가 멍들었거든."

foot."

"Oh, my poor Pinocchio!"
"아, 불쌍한 피노키오!"

"Oh, my poor Lamp-Wick!"
"아, 불쌍한 램프 심지!"

An embarrassingly long silence followed these words, /
이렇게 말하고는 당황스럽게 긴 침묵이 흘렀고,

during which time / the two friends looked at each other /
그 동안   두 친구는 서로를 보았다

in a mocking way.
놀리는 눈초리로.

Finally / the Marionette, / in a voice / sweet as honey / and
마침내   꼭두각시가,   목소리로   꿀처럼 달콤하고

Parmesan 파르메산 치즈(아주 단단한 이탈리아 치즈. 보통 이탈리아 음식 위에 갈아서 얹어 먹음) | bruise 타박상을
입다 | embarrassingly 난처하게 | mocking 비웃는

soft as a flute, / said to his companion:
플루트처럼 부드러운,   친구에게 말했다:

"Tell me, Lamp-Wick, dear friend, / have you ever suffered
"말해 봐, 램프 심지, 내 친구야,   혹시 앓은 적 있니

/ from an earache?"
   귓병을?"

"Never! And you?"
"전혀!   너는?"

"Never! Still, / since this morning / my ear has been
"전혀!   그런데,   오늘 아침부터   귀가 아프더라."

torturing me."

"So has mine."
"나도 그랬는데."

"Yours, too? And which ear is it?"
"너도?   어느 쪽 귀가 아픈데?"

"Both of them. And yours?"
"양쪽 다.   너는?"

"Both of them, too. I wonder / if it could be the same
"나도, 양쪽 다.   궁금하군   똑같은 병인지."

sickness."

"I'm afraid / it is."
"아무래도   그런 것 같아."

"Will you do me a favor, Lamp-Wick?"
"부탁 하나만 들어줄래, 램프 심지야?"

"Gladly! With my whole heart."
"기꺼이!   내 마음을 다해서."

"Will you let me see / your ears?"
"보게 해 줄래   네 귀를?"

"Why not? But before I show you mine, / I want to see
"왜 안 되겠니?   하지만 내 것을 보여 주기 전에,   네 귀를 보고 싶어,

yours, / dear Pinocchio."
     피노키오."

---

flute 플루트 | companion 동반자 | earache 귓병 | torture 고문하다

143

"No. You must show yours first."
"안 돼. 네가 먼저 보여 줘."

"No, my dear! Yours first, / then mine."
"아냐, 친구야! 네가 먼저, 그럼 나도 보여 줄게."

"Well, then," / said the Marionette, / "let us make a
"좋아, 그렇다면," 곡두각시가 말했다, "협상을 하자."

contract."

"Let's hear the contract!"
"그럼 협상을 들어보자고!"

"Let us take off our caps / together. All right?"
"우리가 모자를 벗는 거야 동시에. 어때?"

"All right."
"좋아."

"Ready then!"
"자 준비!"

Pinocchio began to count, / "One! Two! Three!"
피노키오가 숫자를 세기 시작했다, "하나! 둘! 셋!"

At the word "Three!" / the two boys pulled off their caps /
"셋!"하는 소리에 두 아이는 모자를 벗어

and threw them high in air.
공중으로 높이 던졌다.

And then / a scene took place / which is hard to believe,
그러자 광경이 벌어졌다 믿기 힘든,

/ but it is all too true. The Marionette and his friend,
하지만 모두 사실인. 곡두각시와 그 친구, 램프 심지는,

Lamp-Wick, / when they saw each other / both stricken
서로를 보았을 때

by the same misfortune, / instead of feeling sorrowful and
둘 다 똑같은 불행을 겪고 있는, 슬프고 부끄러운 감정 대신,

ashamed, / began to poke fun / at each other, / and after
놀리기 시작했다 서로를, 그리고 터무니없는

much nonsense, / they ended by bursting out / into hearty
일들 끝에, 결국 터뜨리고 말았다

contract 계약[약정](서) | stricken ~으로 시달리는 | hearty 진심 어린, (감정의 정도가) 강한 | ache (계속
무지근히) 아프다 | totter 비틀거리다 | stumble 비틀[휘청]거리다 | helplessly 어찌해 볼 수도 없이

laughter.
큰 웃음을.

They laughed and laughed, / and laughed again —— /
그들은 웃고 웃었다,   그리고 또 웃었다 —

laughed till they ached —— / laughed till they cried.
아플 때까지 웃었다 —   눈물이 날 때까지 웃었다.

But all of a sudden / Lamp-Wick stopped laughing. He
하지만 갑자기   램프 심지는 웃음을 멈추었다.

tottered / and almost fell. Pale as a ghost, / he turned to
비틀거리면서 거의 쓰러질 뻔했다.   유령처럼 창백해져서,   피노키오를 돌아보았다

Pinocchio / and said:
                    그리고 말했다:

"Help, help, Pinocchio!"
"도와줘, 도와줘, 피노키오!"

"What is the matter?"
"왜 그러니?"

"Oh, help me! I can no longer stand up."
"아, 도와줘!   더 이상 서 있을 수 없어."

"I can't either," / cried Pinocchio; / and his laughter turned
"나도 마찬가지야,"   피노키오가 소리쳤다   그의 웃음은 눈물이 되었다

to tears / as he stumbled about / helplessly.
              휘청거리면서   어찌해 볼 수 없이.

Key Expression

should have p.p~ : ~했어야 했는데

should have p.p~는 '~했어야 했는데'라는 의미로 과거에 하지 않은 일에 대한 유감, 후회, 비난을 담고 있는 표현입니다. should 대신에 ought to를 사용해도 됩니다.
하지만 가정법 과거 문장의 주절에 쓰인 should have p.p는 '~할 것이다'라는 의미인 조동사 shall의 과거형으로 '~했을 텐데'의 뜻이며 이때는 should 대신 would로 바꾸어 쓸 수 있습니다.

ex) You should have thought of all this before.
    넌 이 모든 것에 대해 미리 생각했어야 했어.
    If I had only had a bit of heart, I should never have abandoned that good Fairy.
    내가 조금만 더 생각이 있었더라면, 그렇게 착한 요정을 저버리진 않았을 텐데.

145

They had hardly finished speaking, / when both of them
좀처럼 그들은 말도 다 끝내지 못했다.　　　　　　　둘 다 네 발로 땅을 짚더니

fell on all fours / and began running and jumping / around
　　　　　　　　달리고 점프하기 시작했다　　　　　　　방 안을 빙빙.

the room. As they ran, / their arms turned into legs, / their
　　　　　달리는 도중에,　　　두 팔은 다리로 변했고,

faces lengthened / into snouts / and their backs became
얼굴은 길쭉해져서　　　주둥이가 되었고　　등은 뒤덮였다

covered / with long gray hairs.
　　　　　긴 잿빛 털로.

This was humiliation enough, / but the most horrible
이것도 충분히 수치스러웠지만,　　　　　가장 끔찍한 순간은

moment was the one / in which the two poor creatures felt
불쌍한 두 아이들이 알았을 때였다　꼬리가 나오고 있음을.

their tails appear. Overcome with shame and grief, / they
　　　　　　　　수치와 슬픔을 이기려고,

tried to cry / and bemoan their fate.
그들은 울기 시작했고　자신들의 신세를 한탄했다.

But what is done / can't be undone! Instead of moans and
하지만 이미 일어난 일은　　되돌릴 수 없는 법!　　탄식과 통곡 대신,

cries, / they burst forth into / loud donkey brays, / which
터뜨렸다　　　　　　　커다란 당나귀 울음 소리를,

sounded very much like, / "Haw! Haw! Haw!"
마치 당나귀와 똑같은 소리처럼,　　"히힝!　히힝!　히힝!"

At that moment, / a loud knocking was heard / at the door /
그 순간,　　　　　큰 노크 소리가 들렸다　　　　　문에서

and a voice called to them:
그리고 목소리가 그들에게 말했다:

"Open! I am the Little Man, / the driver of the wagon /
"문 열어! 난 마부다,　　　　　　마차를 끌고 온 사람이지,

which brought you here. Open, I say, or beware!"
너희들을 여기에 데려온.　　　　문 열지 않으면 혼내줄테다!"

---

snout 돌출부, 주둥이 | humiliation 창피, 굴욕 | bemoan 한탄하다 | beware 조심[주의]하다

18

Pinocchio, / having become a Donkey, / is bought by the
피노키오는, 당나귀가 된, 서커스 단장에게 팔린다,

owner of a Circus, / who wants to teach him to do tricks.
그에게 재주를 가르치고 싶어 하는.

The Donkey becomes lame / and is sold to a man / who
그 당나귀는 다리를 절게 되고 한 남자에게 팔린다

wants to use his skin for a drumhead.
가죽으로 북을 만들려는.

Very sad and downcast were / the two poor little fellows
너무나 슬프고 의기소침 했다 불쌍한 두 친구는

/ as they stood and looked / at each other. Outside the
서서 바라보았다 서로를. 방 밖에서,

room, / the Little Man grew more and more impatient, /
작은 남자는 점점 더 조바심이 나서,

and finally / gave the door such a violent kick / that it flew
결국 문을 과격하게 차서 활짝 열었다.

open. With his usual sweet smile / on his lips, / he looked
그러고는 평소처럼 미소를 띄고 입가에,

at Pinocchio and Lamp-Wick / and said to them:
피노키오와 림프 심지를 보고 그들에게 말했다:

"Fine work, boys! You have brayed well, / so well / that I
"잘했다, 얘들아! 아주 잘 울었다, 너무 잘 울어서

recognized your voices / immediately, / and here I am."
내가 소리를 듣고 알아냈지 즉시, 그래서 여기에 왔단다."

On hearing this, / the two Donkeys bowed their heads / in
그 말을 듣고, 두 당나귀는 머리를 숙이고

shame, / dropped their ears, / and put their tails / between
부끄러움에, 귀를 떨어뜨렸고, 꼬리를 넣었다

their legs.
다리 사이로.

drumhead 북 가죽 | violent 격렬한.

At first, / the Little Man petted / and caressed them / and
먼저,   작은 남자는 어루만지고   그들을 토닥여 주었다

smoothed down their hairy coats. Then / he took out a
그런 다음에 털을 부드럽게 쓸었다.   그리고 나서   말빗을 꺼내어

currycomb / and worked over them / till they shone like
             잘 빗겨 주었다   거울처럼 빛날 때까지.

glass. Satisfied with the looks / of the two little animals,
모습에 만족하면서   두 동물의,

/ he bridled them / and took them / to a market place /
굴레를 씌우고   데려갔다   시장에

far away / from the Land of Toys, / in the hope of selling
멀리 떨어진   장난감 나라로부터,   팔리기를 바라면서

them / at a good price.
        좋은 가격에.

In fact, / he did not have to wait very long / for an offer.
사실,   그는 그리 오래 기다릴 필요도 없었다   제안을 받는데.

Lamp-Wick was bought by a farmer / whose donkey had
램프 심지는 농부가 샀다   당나귀가 죽었다는

died / the day before. Pinocchio went to the owner of a
바로 전날.   피노키오는 서커스 단장에게 팔렸다,

circus, / who wanted to teach him / to do tricks / for his
가르치고 싶어 하는   재주를

audiences.
청중을 위해.

And now / do you understand / what the Little Man's
자 이제   여러분은 아시겠지요   작은 남자의 직업이 무엇인지?

profession was? This horrid little being, / whose face
                이 불쾌하고 작은 사람은,   빛나는 얼굴을 가지고

shone / with kindness, / went about the world / looking
있지만   친절함으로,   세계를 돌아다녔다   아이들을 찾으러.

for boys. Lazy boys, / boys who hated books, / boys who
        게으른 아이들,   책을 싫어하는 아이들,

---

pet (동물·아이를 다정하게) 어루만지다[쓰다듬다] | caress 애무하다, 어루만지다 | currycomb 말빗 | bridle (말에게)
굴레를 씌우다 | horrid 진저리나는, 지독한| hardships 고충 | stable 마구간 | manger (소·말의) 여물통[구유] |
straw 짚 | mouthful (음식) 한 입, 한 모금

wanted to run away from home, / boys who were tired
가출하려는 아이들,   학교가 싫증난 아이들 —

of school —— / all these were his joy / and his fortune.
                  이 모든 아이들은 그의 기쁨이었고   그의 돈이었다.

He took them with him / to the Land of Toys / and let
그는 그들을 데려가서   장난감 나라로   즐겁게 내버려

them enjoy themselves / to their heart's content. When,
두었다   마음껏.

after months of all play and no work, / they became little
몇 달 동안 놀기만 하고 일하지 않으면,   아이들은 작은 당나귀가 되었고,

donkeys, / he sold them / on the market place. In a few
          그는 당나귀를 팔았다   시장에서.   몇 년 만에,

years, / he had become a millionaire.
         그는 백만장자가 되었다.

What happened to Lamp-Wick? My dear children, I do
램프 심지는 어떻게 되었을까요?   어린이 여러분, 잘 모르겠어요.

not know. Pinocchio, / I can tell you, / met with great
              피노키오에 대해서는, 말해 줄 수 있지요,   너무 큰 시련을 만났다고

hardships / even from the first day.
             첫 날부터.

After putting him in a stable, / his new master filled his
피노키오를 마구간에 집어넣고,   새 주인은 여물통을 채웠다

manger / with straw, / but Pinocchio, / after tasting a
짚으로,   하지만 피노키오는,   한 입 맛보고는,

mouthful, / spat it out.
             뱉어버렸다.

Key Expression ❢

be tired of~ : ~에 싫증난

tired는 '피로한, 지친'(육체적 피로)의 의미와 '싫증난, 지긋지긋한'(정신적 피로)
의 두 가지 뜻을 지닌 형용사입니다. '피로한'의 뜻일 경우에는 from, with, to
부정사와 함께 쓰이며, '싫증난'의 뜻일 때에는 tired of로 사용합니다.

ex) ~ boys who were tired of school ~
    ~ 학교에 싫증난 아이들 ~
    I'm tired of always being a Marionette!
    난 항상 꼭두각시로 있는 것에 싫증이 나요!
    If we feel tired we can rest by the wayside.
    피곤함을 느끼면 길가에서 쉴 수 있어요.

Then / the man filled the manger / with hay. But
그러자   주인은 여물통을 채웠다   건초로.

Pinocchio did not like that any better.
그러나 피노키오는 건초도 마다했다.

"Ah, you don't like hay either?" / he cried angrily. "Wait,
"아하, 건초도 싫단 말이지?"   그는 화가 나서 외쳤다.

my pretty Donkey, I'll teach you / not to be so particular."
"기다려라, 요 당나귀 녀석, 가르쳐 주마   네가 특별하지 않다는 것을." 더 이상의

Without more ado, / he took a whip / and gave the Donkey
소동도 없이,   채찍을 들어   당나귀에게 세게 휘둘렀다

a hearty blow / across the legs.
              그의 다리에.

Pinocchio screamed with pain / and as he screamed / he
피노키오는 고통으로 소리쳤는데   소리를 질렀지만

brayed:
당나귀 소리가 났다:

"Haw! Haw! Haw! I can't digest straw!"
"히힝!   히힝!   히힝!   나는 짚을 소화 못 시킨다고요!"

"Then eat the hay!" / answered his master, / who
"그럼 건초를 먹어!"   주인이 말했다.

understood the Donkey / perfectly.
그는 당나귀의 말을 알아들었다   완벽하게.

"Haw! Haw! Haw! Hay gives me a headache!"
"히힝!   히힝!   히힝!   건초는 머리가 아프단 말이에요!"

"Do you pretend, / by any chance, / that I should feed you
"상상하는 거냐,   혹시라도,   내가 오리나 닭고기를 줄 거라 알고?"

duck or chicken?" / asked the man again, / and, angrier
              주인이 다시 물었다,   그리고, 더 화를 내며,

than ever, / he gave poor Pinocchio / another lashing.
          불쌍한 피노키오에게 휘둘렀다   또 다시 채찍을.

At that second beating, / Pinocchio became very quiet /
그렇게 두 번째로 맞자,   피노키오는 조용해졌고

and said no more.
더 이상 말하지 않았다.

---

hay 건초 | ado 야단법석(fuss), 소동; 노고, 고생, 고심(difficulty) | hearty 강력한, 애정어린 | digest (음식을)
소화하다 | pretend ~라고 가장[상상]하다

After that, / the door of the stable was closed / and he was
그 후로,　　　　마구간의 문이 닫히고　　　　　혼자 남겨졌다.

left alone. It was many hours / since he had eaten anything
몇 시간이 흘렀다　　　　아무것도 못 먹은 채

/ and he started to yawn / from hunger. As he yawned, / he
그는 하품하기 시작했다　　배가 고파서.　　하품을 하면서,

opened a mouth / as big as an oven.
입을 벌렸다　　　아궁이처럼 크게.

Finally, / not finding anything else / in the manger, / he
마침내,　　다른 게 없다는 걸 알고　　여물통에는,

tasted the hay. After tasting it, / he chewed it well, / closed
건초를 맛보았다.　　건초를 맛보고,　　잘 씹어서,

his eyes, / and swallowed it.
눈을 감고,　　삼켰다.

"This hay is not bad," / he said to himself. "But how much
"건초도 나쁘지 않군,"　　혼자 말했다.　　　"하지만 얼마나 행복했을까

happier I should be / if I had studied! Just now, instead
공부를 했더라면!　　지금쯤,

of hay, / I should be eating some good bread and butter.
건초 대신,　맛있게 버터 바른 빵을 먹고 있을 테지.

Patience!"
참자!"

Next morning, / when he awoke, / Pinocchio looked in the
다음 날 아침,　　잠에서 깨어나자,　　피노키오는 여물통을 들여다 보았다

manger / for more hay, / but it was all gone. He had eaten it
건초가 더 있는지,　　하지만 없었다.　　그가 모두 먹어 치운 것

all / during the night.
이었다　밤 사이에.

He tried the straw, / but, as he chewed away at it, / he
그는 짚을 맛보았는데,　　씹으면서,

noticed / to his great disappointment / that it tasted /
알아차렸다　실망스럽게도　　　그 맛이

neither like rice / nor like macaroni.
쌀도 아니고　　마카로니도 아니라는 것을.

"Patience!" / he repeated / as he chewed. "If only / my
"참자!" 반복해서 말했다 씹으면서. "좋을 텐데

misfortune might serve as a lesson / to disobedient boys /
이 불행이 교훈이 된다면 말 안 듣는 아이들에게

who refuse to study! Patience! Have patience!"
공부하기 싫어하는! 참자! 어쩌겠어!"

"Patience indeed!" / shouted his master / just then, / as he
"참아야지 당연히!" 주인이 소리 질렀다 바로 그때,

came into the stable. "Do you think, / perhaps, / my little
마구간으로 들어오면서. "생각하는 거냐, 혹시, 당나귀 녀석아,

Donkey, / that I have brought you here / only to give you
내가 널 여기 데려온 이유가 음식이랑 물이나 주려는

food and drink? Oh, no! You are to help me / earn some
것이라고? 오, 아니지! 너는 나를 도와서 금화를 벌어야 해,

fine gold pieces, / do you hear? Come along, now. I am
알아들어? 가자, 당장.

going to teach you / to jump and bow, / to dance a waltz
가르쳐 주마 점프하고 절하는 법을, 왈츠와 폴카를 추는 법을,

and a polka, / and even to stand on your head."
물구나무 서는 법까지."

Poor Pinocchio, / whether he liked it or not, / had to learn
불쌍한 피노키오는, 좋건 싫건 간에, 배워야 했다

/ all these wonderful things; / but it took him three long
이 모든 놀라운 일들을; 그렇게 하는데 석 달이 걸렸고

months / and cost him many, many lashings / before he
많고, 많은 채찍질이 가해졌다

was pronounced perfect.
완벽하게 하기까지.

The day came / at last / when Pinocchio's master was
그 날이 왔다 마침내 피노키오의 주인이 알릴 수 있는

able to announce / an extraordinary performance. The
기이한 공연을.

announcements, / posted all around the town, / and written
포스터에는, 동네 곳곳에 붙여진,

in large letters, / read thus:
큰 글씨로 쓰여 있었다. 다음과 같이:

GREAT SPECTACLE / TONIGHT
대 공연이   오늘 밤에 열립니다

LEAPS AND EXERCISES / BY THE GREAT ARTISTS
묘기와 공연이 펼쳐집니다   위대한 곡예사들과

AND THE FAMOUS HORSES of the COMPANY
유명한 말들의

First Public Appearance / of the FAMOUS DONKEY /
처음으로 선보입니다   그 유명한 당나귀가

called PINOCCHIO
피노키오라 불리우는

THE STAR OF THE DANCE
춤의 샛별이라고 알려진

The Theater will be as Light as Day
극장을 대낮처럼 환하게 빛내줄 것입니다

That night, / as you can well imagine, / the theater was filled
그날 밤,   여러분이 상상할 수 있듯이,   극장은 사람들로 넘쳐났다

to overflowing / one hour before / the show was scheduled to
          한 시간 전부터   공연이 시작되기.

start.

Not an orchestra chair could be had, / not a balcony seat, /
1등석도 구할 수 없었다,   발코니 석도,

nor a gallery seat; / not even for their weight in gold.
일반 방청석도;   금을 줘도 구할 수 없었다.

The place swarmed / with boys and girls / of all ages
그곳은 붐볐다   소년 소녀들로   모든 연령과 키를 막론하고,

and sizes, / wriggling and dancing about / in a fever of
          꿈틀거리고 춤을 추며   안달이 나서

impatience / to see the famous Donkey dance.
          유명한 당나귀 춤을 보려고.

---

if only ~이면 좋을 텐데 | stand on one's head 물구나무 서다 | announcement 발표, 소식 | overflow
넘치다 | an orchestra seat 1등석 | a balcony seat (극장 2층의) 발코니석 | a gallery seat (대형 홀의 위층
뒷면이나 옆면) 좌석 | swarm 떼[무리]를 지어 다니다

When the first part of the performance was over, / the
공연의 첫 파트가 끝나자,

Owner and Manager of the circus, / in a black coat, / white
서커스 단장은,   검은 외투를 입은,

knee breeches, / and patent leather boots, / presented
하얀 반바지와,   에나멜 가죽 부츠를 신고,

himself to the public / and in a loud, pompous voice /
관객 앞에 나가서   크고, 거만한 목소리로

made the following announcement:
다음 연설을 했다:

"Most honored friends, / Gentlemen and Ladies!
"존경하는 친구들,   신사 숙녀 여러분!"

"Your humble servant, / the Manager of this theater, /
"미천한 제가,   이 극장의 단장인,

presents himself before you / tonight / in order to introduce
여러분 앞에 섰습니다   오늘 밤   소개시켜 드리기 위해

to you / the greatest, / the most famous Donkey / in the
가장 위대하고,   가장 유명한 당나귀를

world, / a Donkey that has had the great honor / in his
이 세상에서, 대단한 영광을 가진 당나귀를

short life / of performing / before the kings and queens and
짧은 생애 동안   공연을 한   왕과 여왕과 황제 폐하들 앞에서

emperors / of all the great courts of Europe. We thank you
유럽 모든 왕궁의.   감사드립니다

/ for your attention!"
여러분의 관심에!"

This speech was greeted / by much laughter and applause.
이 연설은 받았다   많은 웃음 소리와 갈채를.

And the applause grew to a roar / when Pinocchio, / the
그리고 박수 소리는 함성이 되었다   피노키오가,

famous Donkey, / appeared / in the circus ring. He was
유명한 당나귀인,   나타났을 때   서커스장에.

handsomely arrayed. A new bridle / of shining leather
그는 멋지게 치장되었다.   새 굴레가   빛나는 가죽으로 된

breech 반바지 | patent 에나멜 가죽으로 만든 | pompous 젠체하는[거만한] | court 대궐, 궁궐 | applause 박수
| array (보기 좋게) 배열하다

/ with buckles / of polished brass / was on his back; /
징이 박힌   광택이 나는 황동의   등에 씌워졌다;

two white camellias were tied / to his ears; / ribbons
두 송이의 하얀 동백꽃은 꽂혀 있었다   양쪽 귀에;

and tassels / of red silk / adorned his mane, / which
리본과 술로   빨간 실크로 된   갈기를 장식했다,

was divided into many curls. A great sash of gold and
여러 갈래로 나눠 꼰,   금색과 은색의 멋진 띠가

silver / was fastened / around his waist / and his tail was
은색이   매어졌다   허리 둘레에   그리고 꼬리는 장식되었다

decorated / with ribbons / of many brilliant colors. He
           리본으로   다양하고 화려한 색의.

was a handsome Donkey / indeed!
그는 멋진 당나귀였다   정말로!

Key Expression ♥

mean의 다양한 의미

'의미하다'라는 의미의 동사로 흔히 쓰이는 mean은 동사, 형용사, 명사로서 다양한 의미를 지니고 있어요. 그 의미와 함께 이 책에서 쓰인 mean의 다양한 예를 살펴볼까요.

▶ 동사의 mean : 의미하다, ~라는 의미이다 / 의도하다, 작정하다(주로 to부정사와 함께) / ~의 의미가 있다, 가치가 있다

▶ 형용사의 mean : 인색한 / 비열한 / 심술궂은, 못된 / 보통의, 평균의 / 누추한, 보잘 것 없는

▶ 명사의 means : 중용, 중도 / 평균 / (항상 복수로) 수단, 방법

ex) All the means used by centuries of civilization in subduing wild beasts failed in this case.
수 세기 동안 문명사회에서 사용된 모든 수단은 이런 경우의 야생동물을 길들이는 데에는 실패했다.
He is so mean and cruel!
그는 너무 못된데다 잔인해!
Even mischievous boys understand what it means.
말썽꾸러기의 아이라도 그것이 의미하는 바를 이해한다.
What do you mean?
무슨 뜻이야?

polished (잘 닦아서) 광이 나는 | brass 황동 | camellia 동백나무 | tassel (쿠션·옷 등에 장식으로 다는) 술 | mane (말이나 사자 목덜미의) 갈기 | sash (특히 제복의 일부로 몸에 두르는) 띠

155

The Manager, / when introducing him to the public, /
단장은, 그를 소개하면서

added these words:
이렇게 덧붙였다:

"Most honored audience! I shall not take your time /
"존경하는 관객 여러분! 시간을 빼앗지 않겠습니다

tonight / to tell you / of the great difficulties / which I
오늘 밤 말하는데 많은 시련들에 대해

have encountered / while trying to tame this animal, /
제가 겪었던 이 동물을 길들이려고,

since I found him / in the wilds of Africa. Observe, / I
처음 발견한 후 아프리카 야생에서. 봐 주십시오,

beg of you, / the savage look of his eye. All the means
간청하건대, 저 사나운 눈빛을. 사용되었던 모든 수단들은

used / by centuries of civilization / in subduing wild
수세기 동안의 문명사회에 의한 야생동물을 길들이는데

beasts / failed / in this case. I had finally to resort / to
실패했습니다 이 경우엔. 결국 의지하게 되었죠

the gentle language / of the whip / in order to bring
다정한 언어에 채찍이라는 그를 만들기 위해

him / to my will. With all my kindness, / however, /
제 의지대로. 아무리 다정하게 대해줘도, 하지만,

I never succeeded / in gaining my Donkey's love. He
실패했습니다 당나귀의 사랑을 얻는데.

is still today / as savage / as the day / I found him. He
그는 오늘도 여전히 사납습니다 그 날처럼 그를 발견했던.

still fears / and hates me. But I have found in him / one
여전히 두려워하고 저를 싫어합니다. 하지만 그에게서 찾았습니다

great redeeming feature. Do you see / this little bump /
훌륭한 보완점을. 보입니까 이 작은 혹이

on his forehead? It is this bump / which gives him / his
이마에 있는? 바로 이 혹입니다 그에게 준

great talent of dancing / and using his feet / as nimbly /
위대한 춤의 재능을 그리고 발을 사용하는 것을 민첩하게

encounter 우연히 만나다 | wilds 미개척지 | savage 야만적인, 몹시 사나운 | subdue 부드럽게 하다 | resort
의지하다, 도움을 청하다 | redeem 결점 따위를 보완하다 | bump (부딪치거나 맞아서 생긴) 혹, 타박상

as a human being. Admire him, / O signori, / and enjoy
사람처럼.   칭찬해 주십시오,   여러분,   그리고 즐겨 주세요.

yourselves. I let you, now, be the judges / of my success
여러분의 판단에 맡기겠습니다   제가 성공했는지는

/ as a teacher of animals. Before I leave you, / I wish to
동물들의 조련사로서.   떠나기 전에,   알려 드리고

state / that there will be another performance / tomorrow
싶습니다 또 다른 공연이 있다는 걸   내일 밤에도.

night. If the weather threatens rain, / the great spectacle
만약 비가 오면,   대 공연은 시작할 것입니다

will take place / at eleven o'clock in the morning."
아침 11시에."

The Manager bowed / and then turned to Pinocchio
단장은 인사를 하고   피노키오를 돌아보며

/ and said: "Ready, Pinocchio! Before starting your
말했다: "준비해, 피노키오!   공연을 시작하기 전에,

performance, / salute your audience!"
관객들께 인사해야지!"

Pinocchio obediently bent / his two knees / to the ground
피노키오는 얌전히 굽혔다   두 무릎을   땅에

/ and remained kneeling / until the Manager, / with the
그리고 무릎을 꿇고 있었다   그때 단장이,

crack of the whip, / cried sharply: / "Walk!"
채찍을 휘두르며,   크게 소리쳤다: "걸어가!"

The Donkey lifted himself / on his four feet / and walked
당나귀는 일어났다   네 발로

around the ring. A few minutes passed / and again /the
그리고 서커스장을 걸었다. 몇 분이 흐르고   다시

voice of the Manager called:
단장이 소리쳤다:

"Quickstep!" / and Pinocchio obediently / changed his
"빨리!"   피노키오는 복종하며   걸음을 바꿨다.

step.

take place 개최되다[일어나다] | salute 경의를 표하다 | kneel 무릎을 꿇다

"Gallop!" / and Pinocchio galloped.
"달려!" 그러자 피노키오는 달렸다.

"Full speed!" / and Pinocchio ran / as fast as he could. As
"전속력으로!" 피노키오는 달렸다 아주 힘껏.

he ran / the master raised his arm / and a pistol shot rang /
달리는 동안 주인이 팔을 들어올렸다 그리고 총소리가 울렸다

in the air.
공중에서.

At the shot, / the little Donkey fell / to the ground / as if he
총소리에, 당나귀는 쓰러졌다 땅 위로

were really dead.
마치 진짜 죽은 것처럼.

A shower of applause / greeted the Donkey / as he arose to
수많은 갈채가 당나귀에게 쏟아졌다 발로 일어났을 때.

his feet. Cries and shouts / and handclappings / were heard
외침과 환호와 박수 소리가 들렸다

/ on all sides.
사방에서.

At all that noise, / Pinocchio lifted his head / and raised
환호 소리를 듣고, 피노키오는 고개를 들어 위를 보았다.

his eyes. There, / in front of him, / in a box / sat a beautiful
그곳에 그의 앞에, 객석에 아름다운 여인이 앉아

woman. Around her neck / she wore a long gold chain, /
있었다. 목에는 긴 금 목걸이를 둘렀다,

from which hung a large medallion. On the medallion / was
큰 메달이 달린. 메달에는

painted / the picture of a Marionette.
그려져 있었다 꼭두각시의 모습이.

"That picture is of me! That beautiful lady is my Fairy!"
"저건 나잖아! 저 아름다운 여인은 나의 요정이다!"

/ said Pinocchio to himself, / recognizing her. He felt so
피노키오는 중얼거렸다, 그녀를 알아보며. 너무 기뻐서

happy / that he tried his best / to cry out:
최선을 다했다 외치는 데:

handclap 박수 | spectator 구경꾼 | lick 핥다 | fainting 기절, 졸도, 실신; 의기소침

"Oh, my Fairy! My own Fairy!"
"오, 나의 요정님! 나만의 요정님!"

But instead of words, / a loud braying was heard / in the
하지만 말 대신, 커다란 당나귀 울음이 들렸다

theater, / so loud and so long / that all the spectators / ——
극장 안에, 너무 크고 길게 울어서 모든 관객들이

men, women, and children, / but especially the children
— 남자건, 여자건, 아이들이건, 특히 아이들은 —

—— / burst out laughing.
웃음을 터뜨렸다.

Then, / in order to teach the Donkey / that it was not
그러자, 당나귀를 가르치려고 좋은 태도가 아니라는 것을

good manners / to bray / before the public, / the Manager
당나귀 울음을 우는 것은 관객들 앞에서,

hit him on the nose / with the handle of the whip.
단장은 그의 코를 때렸다 채찍 손잡이로.

The poor little Donkey / stuck out a long tongue / and
불쌍한 당나귀는 긴 혀를 내밀어

licked his nose / for a long time / in an effort to take
코를 핥았다 오랫동안 고통을 없애고자.

away the pain.

And what was his grief / when on looking up / toward
그리고 슬픈 일은 올려다 보았을 때 객석을 향해,

the boxes, / he saw / that the Fairy had disappeared!
그는 알았던 것이다 요정이 사라져버린 걸!

He felt himself fainting, / his eyes filled with tears, / and
그는 기절할 것 같았다, 두 눈은 눈물이 고였고,

he wept bitterly. No one knew it, / however, / least of all
서럽게 울었다. 아무도 몰랐다, 하지만,

the Manager, / who, cracking his whip, / cried out:
단장마저도, 채찍을 휘두르며, 외쳤다:

"Bravo, Pinocchio! Now show us / how gracefully / you
'힘내라, 피노키오! 이제 보여 줘 얼마나 멋지게

can jump / through the rings."
점프할 수 있는지 굴렁쇠를 통과하면서."

Pinocchio tried / two or three times, / but / each time he
피노키오는 시도했다   두세 번,   하지만 다가갈 때마다

came / near the ring, / he found it more to his taste / to go
굴렁쇠로,   그는 하고 싶어졌다   그 아래로

under it. The fourth time, / at a look from his master / he
지나가기를.   네 번째 시도에서,   그는 주인의 표정을 보고,

leaped through it, / but as he did so / his hind legs caught /
뛰어올라 통과했다,   하지만 그러다가   뒷다리가 걸렸다

in the ring / and he fell to the floor / in a heap.
굴렁쇠에   그리고 땅에 떨어졌다   털썩.

When he got up, / he was lame / and could hardly limp / as
일어섰을 때,   다리를 절었고,   간신히 절룩거리며 갔다

far as the stable.
마구간까지.

"Pinocchio! We want Pinocchio! We want the little
"피노키오!   우리는 피노키오를 원한다!   당나귀 나와라!"

Donkey!" / cried the boys / from the orchestra, / saddened
아이들이 소리쳤다   관중석에서,

by the accident.
사고에 실망한.

No one saw Pinocchio / again / that evening.
아무도 피노키오를 볼 수 없었다   다시는   그 날 저녁.

The next morning / the veterinary / —— that is, the animal
다음 날 아침   수의사는   — 즉, 동물 의사는 —

doctor —— / declared / that he would be lame / for the rest
말했다   그는 절름발이가 되었다고

of his life.
남은 평생 동안.

"What do I want / with a lame donkey?" / said the
"어디다 쓰겠어   절름발이 당나귀를?"

Manager / to the stableboy. "Take him to the market / and
단장이 말했다   소년 마부에게.   "시장으로 가져가

sell him."
팔아라."

in a heap 한 덩어리[무더기]가 되어 | limp 다리를 절다[절뚝거리다] | sadden 슬프게 하다 | veterinary 수의사 |
stableboy 소년 마부 | change hands 주인이 바뀌다 | overlook 올려보다 | cliff 절벽

When they reached the square, / a buyer was soon found.
광장에 도착하자,   사려는 사람이 금방 나타났다.

"How much do you ask / for that little lame Donkey?"/ he
"얼마니   이 절름발이 당나귀는?"

asked.
그는 물었다.

"Four dollars."
"4달러요."

"I'll give you four cents. Don't think / I'm buying him / for
"4센트를 주지.   착각하지 마라   내가 이걸 사는 거라고   일을

work. I want only his skin. It looks very tough / and I can
시키려고. 난 단지 가죽이 필요해서란다.   아주 튼튼해 보이는군   사용할 수 있겠어

use it / to make myself a drumhead. I belong to a musical
북 가죽을 만드는데.   난 악대에 있는데

band / in my village / and I need a drum."
우리 마을의   북이 필요하거든."

I leave it to you, / my dear children, / to picture to
여러분에게 맡길게요,   어린이 여러분,   여러분의 상상에

yourself / the great pleasure / with which Pinocchio
얼마나 기뻐했는지   피노키오가 그 말을 듣고

heard / that he was to become a drumhead!
북 가죽이 된다는!

As soon as the buyer had paid the four cents, / the Donkey
4센트를 지불하자 마자,

changed hands. His new owner took him / to a high cliff /
당나귀는 주인이 바뀌었다. 새 주인은 그를 데려갔다   높은 절벽으로

overlooking the sea, / put a stone / around his neck, / tied
바다가 보이는,   돌을 매달고,   목에

a rope / to one of his hind feet, / gave him a push, / and
밧줄을 묶고 한쪽 뒷다리에,   그를 떠밀어,

threw him / into the water.
던졌다   물 속으로.

Pinocchio sank / immediately. And his new master sat / on
피노키오는 가라앉았다   곧.   그리고 새 주인은 앉아 있었다

the cliff / waiting for him to drown, / so as to skin him /
절벽 위에   그가 물에 빠져 죽기를 기다리면서   가죽을 벗기기 위해

and make himself a drumhead.
북을 만들려고.

161

🎩 mini test 6

A. 다음 문장을 해석해 보세요.

(1) Know then that, / within two or three hours, / you will no longer be a Marionette, / nor a boy.
→

(2) If I had only had a bit of heart, / I should never have abandoned / that good Fairy, / who loved me so well / and who has been so kind / to me!
→

(3) This was humiliation enough, / but the most horrible moment was the one / in which the two poor creatures felt their tails appear.
→

(4) How much happier I should be / if I had studied!
→

B. 다음 주어진 문구가 알맞은 문장이 되도록 순서를 맞춰보세요.

(1) 그곳에서 그는 <u>결코 볼 수 있을 거라 상상하지 못했던 것을</u> 보았다.
[could have wished / never / what / to see / he]
→ There he saw _____.

(2) 그가 비명을 지르면 지를수록, 그의 귀는 더욱 길고 털이 풍성하게 자랐다.
[shrieked, / grew / and / he / the longer / The more / his ears. / the more hairy]
→

(3) 일어난 일은 되돌릴 수 없는 거야.
[be / is / What / undone. / cannot / done]
→

A. (1) 그럼 알아둬, 두 세 시간 안에 너는 더 이상 꼭두각시도 아이도 아니게 되어버릴 거야. (2) 내가 좀 더 생각이 있었다면, 나를 그토록 사랑하고 친절하게 대해준 착한 요정을 저버리는 짓은 하지 않았을 텐데! (3) 이것으로도 충분히 수치스러운 일이었지만, 가장 끔찍한 순간은 불쌍한 두 아이들이 자신들의 꼬

162　The Adventures of Pinocchio

(4) 너는 이 모든 것을 미리 생각했어야만 했어.
   [before / should / You / all this / thought of / have]
   →

C. 다음 주어진 문장이 본문의 내용과 맞으면 T, 틀리면 F에 동그라미 하세요.

(1) Both of the boys became donkeys.
   [T / F]

(2) Pinocchio succeeded in finishing his first performance at the circus.
   [T / F]

(3) At the circus, Pinocchio saw the Fairy at the box.
   [T / F]

(4) New owner of Pinocchio intended to let him drown to death.
   [T / F]

D. 의미가 서로 비슷한 것끼리 연결해 보세요.

(1) enrich   ►   ◄ ① torment
(2) torture   ►   ◄ ② be careful
(3) beware   ►   ◄ ③ restore
(4) redeem   ►   ◄ ④ develop

19

Pinocchio is thrown into the sea, / eaten by fishes, / and
피노키오는 바다에 던져진다,　　　　　　　물고기에 뜯어 먹힌 뒤,

becomes a Marionette / once more. As he swims to land, /
꼭두각시가 된다　　　　　다시 한 번.　　　육지를 향해 헤엄치다가,

he is swallowed / by the Terrible Shark.
삼켜진다　　　　　무시무시한 상어에 의해.

Down into the sea, / deeper and deeper, / sank Pinocchio,
깊은 바다 속으로,　　　　점점 더 깊이,　　　　피노키오는 가라앉았다,

/ and finally, / after fifty minutes of waiting, / the man / on
그리고 마침내,　50분을 기다린 후,　　　　　　절벽 위의 남자는

the cliff / said to himself:
혼잣말로 했다:

"By this time / my poor little lame Donkey / must be
"지금쯤이면　　불쌍한 절름발이 당나귀가　　　　물에 빠져 죽었을 거야.

drowned. Up with him / and then I can get to work / on
그를 올려서　　　일을 시작해야지

my beautiful drum."
내 멋진 북을 만드는."

He pulled the rope / which he had tied / to Pinocchio's leg
그는 밧줄을 잡아당겼다　　그가 묶었던　　　피노키오의 다리에

/ ── pulled and pulled and pulled / and, at last, / he saw
── 당기고 당기고 당겼다,　　　　　그리고 마침내,　나타난 걸

appear / on the surface of the water / ── **Can you guess**
보았다　물 위로　　　　　　　── 그게 무엇이었을까요?

what? Instead of a dead donkey, / he saw / a very much
죽은 당나귀가 아니라,　　　　　보았다

alive Marionette, / wriggling and squirming / like an eel.
바로 살아있는 꼭두각시를,　꿈틀거리며 움직이는　　　장어처럼.

Seeing that wooden Marionette, / the poor man thought
나무로 된 꼭두각시를 보자,　　　　　　불쌍한 그는 생각했다

/ he was dreaming / and sat there / with his mouth wide
꿈꾸는 거라고　　　그리고 앉았다　　입을 크게 벌린 채

open / and his eyes popping / out of his head.
눈이 튀어나온 채   얼굴 밖으로.

Gathering his wits together, / he said:
정신을 차리자,   말했다:

"And the Donkey I threw / into the sea?"
"내가 던진 당나귀는   바다에?"

"I am that Donkey," / answered the Marionette / laughing.
"내가 그 당나귀예요,"   꼭두각시가 말했다   웃으며.

"You?"
"네가?"

"I."
"저예요!"

squirm 꿈지락대다

"Ah, you little cheat! Are you poking fun at me?"
"아, 요 장난꾸러기!   나를 놀리는 거지?'

"Poking fun at you? Not at all, / dear Master. I am talking
"놀리다니요?   전혀요,   주인님.   진담입니다."

seriously."

"But, then, / how is it that you, / who a few minutes ago /
"그런데,   어떻게 네가,   몇 분 전까지

were a donkey, / are now standing / before me / a wooden
당나귀였던,   지금 서 있지   내 앞에

Marionette?"
나무 꼭두각시로?"

"It may be the effect of salt water. The sea is fond / of
"소금물 때문이에요.   바다는 좋아하죠

playing these tricks."
재주 부리는걸."

"Be careful, / Marionette, / be careful! Don't laugh at me!
"말 조심해,   꼭두각시야,   조심하라고!   날 놀리지 마라!

Woe be to you, / if I lose my patience!"
널 혼내 줄 거야,   날 화나게 하면!"

"Well, then, / my Master, / do you want to know / my
"자, 그럼,   주인님,   알고 싶으세요

whole story? Untie my leg / and I can tell it / to you
제 얘기를?   다리를 풀어 주면   말할게요   당신께."

better."

The old fellow, / curious to know / the true story of the
남자는,   진짜 얘기가 궁금해서   꼭두각시의 일생에 대한,

Marionette's life, / immediately / untied the rope / which
얼른   밧줄을 풀었다

held his foot. Pinocchio, / feeling free / as a bird of the air,
다리를 묶었던.   피노키오는,   자유로워져서   하늘의 새처럼,

/ began his tale:
이야기를 시작했다:

---

be fond of ~을 좋아하다 | lose one's patience 더 이상 참지 못하다

"Know, then, that, / once upon a time, / I was a wooden
"자, 그럼, 예전에, 나는 나무 꼭두각시였어요,

Marionette, / just as I am today. One day / I was about to
바로 지금처럼. 어느 날 아이가 되려고 했어요,

become a boy, / a real boy, / but on account of my laziness
진짜 아이가, 하지만 게으름 때문에

/ and my hatred of books, / and because I listened to
책을 싫어하고, 나쁜 친구의 말을 들었기 때문에,

bad companions, / I ran away from home. One beautiful
집에서 도망쳤어요. 어느 멋진 아침에,

morning, / I awoke to find / myself changed into a donkey
잠에서 깨어 발견했어요 내가 당나귀로 바뀐 것을

/ —— long ears, / gray coat, / even a tail! What a shameful
— 긴 귀에, 잿빛 털에, 꼬리까지! 얼마나 창피했는지!

day for me! I hope / you will never experience one like it,
바라건데 주인님은 그런 경험을 겪지 않길,

/ dear Master. I was taken to the fair / and sold to a Circus
주인님. 난 시장으로 끌려가 서커스 단장에게 팔렸어요,

Owner, / who tried to make me / dance and jump / through
나를 만들려는 춤추고 뛰면서 굴렁쇠를 통과

the rings. One night, / during a performance, / I had a bad
하도록. 어느 날 밤, 공연 중에, 심하게 넘어져서

fall / and became lame. Not knowing what to do/ with a
절름발이가 되었어요. 뭘 해야 할지 몰랐기 때문에

lame donkey, / the Circus Owner sent me / to the market
절름발이 당나귀로, 서커스 주인은 나를 보냈어요 시장으로

place / and you bought me."
그리고 당신이 날 샀죠."

"Indeed I did! And I paid four cents / for you. Now / who
"그랬지! 4센트를 주고 널 샀지. 이제

will return my money / to me?"
내 돈을 누가 돌려주지 나한테?"

"But / why did you buy me? You bought me / to do me harm
"그런데, 절 왜 사셨죠? 주인님은 날 샀죠 날 해치려고

/ —— to kill me —— / to make a drumhead out of me!"
— 날 죽이려고 — 나를 북 가죽으로 만들기 위해!"

"Indeed I did! And now / where shall I find another skin?"
"그랬지!   그럼 이제   어디에서 다른 가죽을 구하지?"

"Never mind, / dear Master. There are so many donkeys /
"걱정 마세요,   주인님.   당나귀는 얼마든지 많아요

in this world."
이 세상에는."

"Tell me, / impudent little rogue, / does your story end /
"말해 봐라,   요 버릇없는 녀석,   네 얘기는 끝난 거냐

here?"
여기서?"

"One more word," / answered the Marionette, / "and I am
"한 마디만 더 하면,"   꼭두각시가 말했다,   "끝날 거예요.

through. After buying me, / you brought me here / to kill
나를 산 후,   주인님은 여기에 데려왔지요   날 죽이려고.

me. But feeling sorry for me, / you tied a stone to my neck
하지만 불쌍한 생각이 들어,   내 목에 돌을 묶어서

/ and threw me / to the bottom of the sea. That was very
던졌어요   바다 밑으로.   그건 친절한 행동이었어요

good and kind / of you to want me / to suffer as little as
          주인님이 내게 원한 것은   가능한 한 적게 고통 받도록

possible / and I shall remember you / always. And now /
가능하면   그러니 주인님을 기억할게요   항상.   이제

my Fairy will take care of me, / even if you —— "
나의 요정이 날 보살펴 줄 거예요,   만일 주인님이 — "

"Your Fairy? Who is she?"
"네 요정?   누구지?"

"She is my mother, / and, like all other mothers / who love
"나의 엄마예요.   다른 엄마들처럼

their children, / she never loses sight of me, / even though
아이들을 사랑하는,   항상 날 보고 있어요,   내가 그럴 만한 자격이

I do not deserve it. And today / this good Fairy of mine,
없더라도.   오늘   요정은,

/ as soon as she saw me / in danger of drowning, / sent a
나를 보자마자   빠져 죽을 위험에 처한 것을,

rogue 악당[불한당] (같은 녀석) | lose sight of ~을 잊어버리다, ~이 더 이상 안 보이게 되다 | spot 곳, 장소 |
horrified 겁에 질린, 충격받은 | mullet 숭어과의 어류 | whitefish 흰빛의 물고기; 송어의 일종; 흰 돌고래

thousand fishes / to the spot where I lay. They thought /
천 마리의 물고기를 보냈어요 내가 누워 있는 곳으로. 물고기들은 생각했죠

I was really a dead donkey / and began to eat me. What
내가 정말로 죽은 당나귀라고 그래서 먹기 시작했어요.

great bites they took! One ate my ears, / another my nose,
어찌나 게걸스럽게 먹던지! 어떤 놈은 귀를 먹고, 어떤 놈은 코를,

/ a third my neck / and my mane. Some went at my legs /
다른 놈은 목을, 또 갈기를. 어떤 놈은 다리로 가고

and some at my back, / and among the others, / there was
어떤 놈은 등으로, 그 중에는, 작은 고기도

one tiny fish / so gentle and polite / that he did me the
있었죠 너무 친절하고 착하게도 나에게 큰 호의를 베풀었죠

great favor / of eating even my tail."
내 꼬리를 먹어 치워서."

"From now on," / said the man, horrified, / "I swear / I
"지금부터," 남자가 말했다, 몸서리치며, "맹세하지

shall never again taste fish. How I should enjoy / opening
다시는 물고기를 먹지 않겠다고. 좋을 게 없잖아 숭어나 송어의

a mullet or a whitefish / just to find there / the tail of a
배를 갈랐다가 거기서 발견하면 죽은 당나귀의 꼬리를!"

dead donkey!"

"I think / as you do," / answered the Marionette, / laughing.
"생각해요 그럴 거라고." 꼭두각시가 답했다, 웃으면서.

"Still, / you must know / that when the fish finished eating
"하지만, 알아두세요 물고기들이 내 당나귀 외투를 다 먹어 치웠을 때,

my donkey coat, / which covered me / from head to foot, /
나를 덮고 있던, 머리부터 발까지,

they naturally came to the bones / —— or rather, in my case,
자연스레 뼈만 남았죠 — 아니, 내 경우엔, 나무였지만,

to the wood, / for as you know, / I am made of very hard
아시다시피, 난 단단한 나무로 만들어졌죠.

wood. After the first few bites, / those greedy fish found out
몇 번 먹어보더니, 탐욕스러운 물고기들도 알았어요

/ that the wood was not good / for their teeth, / and, afraid of
나무는 안 좋다는 걸 이빨에, 그리고, 소화가 안 되

indigestion, / they turned and ran / here and there / without
는 게 걱정되는지, 돌아갔어요 여기 저기로

saying good-by / or even as much as thank you / to me.
안녕이란 인사도 없이 고맙다는 인사조차도 내게.

Here, dear Master, / you have my story. You know now /
여기까지예요, 주인님, 제 얘기였어요. 이제 알겠죠

why you found a Marionette / and not a dead donkey / when
어떻게 꼭두각시가 나왔는지 죽은 당나귀가 아니라

you pulled me / out of the water."
나를 끌어올렸을 때 물 밖으로."

"I laugh at your story!" / cried the man / angrily. "I know
"말도 안 되는 이야기군!" 남자가 소리쳤다 화가 나서. "난

/ that I spent four cents / to get you / and I want my money
4센트를 썼고 널 사려고 내 돈을 돌려 받아야겠다.

back. Do you know / what I can do; / I am going to take you
알겠냐 내가 뭘 할지; 널 데려갈 테다

/ to the market / once more / and sell you / as dry firewood."
시장으로 다시 한 번 그리고 팔아야지 마른 장작으로."

greedy 탐욕스러운 | porpoise 알락 돌고래, 쇠물돼지

"Very well, / sell me. I am satisfied," / said Pinocchio.
"아주 좋아요, 절 파세요. 전 상관없어요." 피노키오가 말했다.

But as he spoke, / he gave a quick leap / and dived into
하지만 말을 마치고는, 몸을 훌쩍 날려 바다 속으로 뛰어들었다.

the sea. Swimming away / as fast as he could, / he cried
멀리 헤엄치면서 가능한 한 빨리, 외쳤다,

out, / laughing:
웃으면서:

"Good-by, / Master. If you ever need a skin / for your
"안녕, 주인님. 가죽이 필요할 때마다 북을 만들려고,

drum, / remember me."
절 기억해 주세요."

He swam on and on. After a while, / he turned around
그는 계속 헤엄쳤다. 잠시 후, 또 뒤돌아보았다

again / and called louder / than before:
그리고 더 크게 소리쳤다 그 전보다:

"Good-by, / Master. If you ever need / a piece of good
"안녕, 주인님. 필요할 때마다 마른 장작이,

dry firewood, / remember me."
절 기억해 주세요."

In a few seconds / he had gone / so far / he could hardly
곧바로 그는 사라졌다 너무 멀리 거의 보이지 않을 정도로.

be seen. All that could be seen of him / was a very small
보이는 건 아주 작은 점뿐이었다

black dot / moving swiftly / on the blue surface / of the
빠르게 움직이는 파란 표면 위에서 물의,

water, / a little black dot / which now and then / lifted a
작은 까만 점은 이따금 다리나 팔을

leg or an arm / in the air. One would have thought / that
들어올렸다 공중으로. 아마 누군가는 생각할지 모른다

Pinocchio had turned into a porpoise / playing in the
피노키오가 돌고래가 되었다고 태양 아래 뛰노는.

sun.

After swimming / for a long time, / Pinocchio saw / a large
헤엄치고 나서 　　　　　　　한참을, 　　　　　피노키오는 보았다 　　큰 바위를

rock / in the middle of the sea, / a rock as white as marble.
바다 한가운데 있는, 　　　　　　　대리석처럼 하얀 바위를.

High on the rock / stood a little Goat / bleating and calling
바위 위에는 　　　　　작은 염소가 서 있었다 　　매에 소리를 내며 울면서

/ and beckoning to the Marionette / to come to her.
꼭두각시에게 손짓했다 　　　　　　　그녀에게 오라고.

There was something very strange / about that little Goat.
이상한 점이 있었다 　　　　　　　　작은 염소에게는.

Her coat was not white or black or brown / as that of
그녀의 털은 흰색도 검은색도 갈색도 아니라 　　다른 염소들처럼,

any other goat, / but azure, / a deep brilliant color / that
　　　　　　　하늘색이었다, 　아주 눈부신 색깔인

reminded one / of the hair of the lovely maiden.
상기시키는 　아름다운 소녀의 머리를.

Pinocchio's heart beat fast, / and then faster and faster.
피노키오의 심장은 빠르게 뛰었다, 　　그리고 점점 더 빨라졌다.

He redoubled his efforts / and swam / as hard as he could
그는 두 배로 힘을 내서 　　　헤엄쳤다 　최대한 열심히

/ toward the white rock. He was almost halfway over, /
흰 바위를 향해. 　　　　거의 반쯤 왔을 때,

when suddenly / a horrible sea monster / stuck its head /
갑자기 　　　무서운 바다 괴물이 　　　머리를 내밀었다

out of the water, / an enormous head / with a huge mouth,
물 밖으로, 　　　거대한 머리가 　　큰 입을 가진,

/ wide open, / showing three rows of gleaming teeth, / the
쫙 벌린 채, 　번쩍이는 이빨 세 줄을 드러내며,

mere sight / of which would have filled you with fear.
단지 보기만 해도 　공포로 가득 찰 정도였다.

Do you know / what it was?
여러분은 알겠지요 　그게 무엇인지?

bleat (양·염소가) 매에 하고 울다 | beckon to (오라고) 손짓하다, (손짓으로) 부르다 | remind 상기시키다 |
redouble one's efforts 노력을 배가하다, 한층 더 노력하다 | attila 아틸라 (5세기 전반에 동양에서 유럽에 침입한
흉노족(Huns)의 왕) | path 길, 방향

That sea monster was / no other than the enormous
바다 괴물은   다름 아닌 거대한 상어였다.

Shark, / which has often been mentioned / in this story
자주 언급되어 온   이 이야기에서

/ and which, / on account of its cruelty, / had been
그것은,   그 잔인함 때문에,   별명이 있었다

nicknamed / "The Attila of the Sea" / by both fish and
"바다의 아틸라"라는   물고기와 어부들이 부르는.

fishermen.

Poor Pinocchio! The sight of that monster / frightened
불쌍한 피노키오!   괴물을 보자   공포에 질려서

him / almost to death! He tried to swim / away from
거의 죽을 뻔했다!   그는 헤엄치려 했다   멀리,

him, / to change his path, / to escape, / but that immense
방향을 바꿔서,   도망치려고,   하지만 거대한 입이

mouth / kept coming / nearer and nearer.
계속 따라왔다   가까이 더 가까이.

"Hasten, Pinocchio, / I beg you!" / bleated the little Goat /
"서둘러,   피노키오,   제발!"   작은 염소가 매에 하고 울었다.

on the high rock.
높은 바위에서.

And Pinocchio swam / desperately / with his arms, / his
피노키오는 헤엄쳤다   필사적으로   두 팔로,

body, / his legs, / his feet.
온몸으로,   다리로,   발로.

"Quick, Pinocchio, / the monster is coming nearer!"
"빨리, 피노키오,   괴물이 더 가까이 온다!"

Pinocchio swam / faster and faster, / and harder and
피노키오는 헤엄쳤다   점점 더 빨리,   점점 더 세차게.

harder.

"Faster, Pinocchio! The monster will get you! There he
"더 빨리, 피노키오!   괴물이 널 잡으려 해!   그가 온다!

is! There he is! Quick, quick, / or you are lost!"
그가 온다!   빨리, 빨리,   안 그러면 죽어!"

Pinocchio went through the water / like a shot / —— swifter
피노키오는 물살을 가르며 갔다 　　　　　　　　총알처럼

and swifter. He came close / to the rock. The Goat leaned
— 점점 더 빨리. 　그는 가까이 왔다 　바위에. 　　염소는 몸을 기울여

over / and gave him one of her hoofs / to help him up / out
그에게 한쪽 말굽을 내밀었다 　　　　올라오는 걸 도와주려고

of the water.
물 밖으로.

Alas! It was too late. The monster overtook him / and
맙소사! 너무 늦었다 　　　괴물은 그를 추월했고

the Marionette found / himself in between the rows of
꼭두각시는 보았다 　　　　자신이 빛나는 하얀 이빨의 줄 사이에 끼어 있는 것을.

gleaming white teeth. Only for a moment, / however, / for
　　　　　　　　　그 순간. 　　　　　　하지만,

the Shark took a deep breath / and, as he breathed, / he
상어가 숨을 깊게 쉬었고 　　　숨을 들이키면서,

drank in the Marionette / as easily as he would have sucked
꼭두각시를 마셨다 　　　날달걀을 빨아들이듯 쉽게.

an egg. Then / he swallowed him so fast / that Pinocchio, /
그러자 너무 빨리 삼켜져서 　　　피노키오는,

falling down into the body of the fish, / lay stunned / for a
상어의 몸 속으로 떨어져, 　　　　정신을 잃고 누워 있었다

half hour.
30분씩이나.

When he recovered his senses / the Marionette could not
정신을 차렸을 때 　　　　　꼭두각시는 알지 못했다

remember / where he was. Around him / all was darkness,
어디에 있는 것인지. 　사방이 　　온통 깜깜했다,

/ a darkness / so deep and so black / that for a moment
어둠이 　　너무 깊고 검어서 　　잠시 동안

/ he thought / he had put his head / into an inkwell. He
그는 생각했다 　머리를 박고 있다고 　잉크병에.

listened / for a few moments / and heard nothing. Once in
귀를 기울여 봐도 　몇 분 동안 　아무것도 들리지 않았다. 잠시 후

a while / a cold wind blew / on his face. At first / he could
찬바람이 불었다   얼굴에.   처음에는

not understand / where that wind was coming from, / but
이해하지 못했다   어디에서 그 바람이 불어오는지,

after a while / he understood / that it came from the lungs
하지만 잠시 후   그는 알았다   그 바람은 괴물의 허파에서부터 온다는 것을.

of the monster. I forgot to tell you / that the Shark was
말하는 걸 잊었는데   상어는 앓고 있었어요

suffering / from asthma, / so that whenever he breathed
천식을,   그래서 숨을 쉴 때마다

/ a storm seemed to blow.
폭풍이 부는 것 같았지요.

Pinocchio at first / tried to be brave, / but as soon as he
피노키오는 처음에는   용기를 내려 했다,   하지만 확신이 들자마자

became convinced / that he was really and truly / in the
그가 정말로 진짜로

Shark's stomach, / he burst into sobs and tears. "Help!
상어의 뱃속에 있다는,   눈물이 터져 버렸다.   "도와주세요!

Help!" / he cried. "Oh, poor me! Won't someone come / to
도와주세요!" 그가 외쳤다.   "오, 불쌍한 내 신세! 누구 없어요

save me?"
날 구해 줄 사람이?"

"Who is there / to help you, / unhappy boy?" / said a rough
"누가 있겠니.   널 도와줄,   불쌍한 아이야?"   거친 목소리가 말했다,

voice, / like a guitar / out of tune.
기타 소리처럼   음정이 안 맞는.

"Who is talking?" / asked Pinocchio, / frozen with terror.
"누구세요?"   피노키오가 물었다,   공포로 얼어버린 채.

"It is I, / a poor Tunny / swallowed by the Shark / at the
"나야,   불쌍한 다랑어지   상어가 삼킨

same time as you. And what kind of a fish are you?"
너랑 동시에.   그런데 넌 무슨 물고기니?"

"I have nothing to do with fishes. I am a Marionette."
"난 물고기가 아냐.   꼭두각시야."

---

lung 폐 | asthma 천식 | convinced (전적으로) 확신하는 | terror (극심한) 공포 | tunny 다랑어(tuna); 그 살

"If you are not a fish, / why did you let / this monster
"물고기도 아닌데, 왜 가만히 있었니 이 괴물이 널 삼키도록?"

swallow you?"

"I didn't let him. He chased me / and swallowed me /
"가만히 있었던 게 아니야. 날 쫓아와서 삼켰어

without even a 'by your leave'! And now / what are we to
'실례지만'이란 말도 없이! 이제 여기에서 뭘 하지

do here / in the dark?"
이 캄캄한 곳에서?"

"Wait / until the Shark has digested / us both, / I suppose."
"기다려야지 상어가 소화시킬 때까지 우리 둘 다, 내 생각엔."

"But I don't want to be digested," / shouted Pinocchio, /
"하지만 난 소화되기 싫어." 피노키오가 소리쳤다,

starting to sob.
울기 시작하며.

"Neither do I," / said the Tunny, / "but I am wise / enough
"나도 마찬가지야." 다랑어가 말했다. "하지만 난 현명하지

to think that / if one is born a fish, / it is more dignified to
생각할 만큼 물고기로 태어났다면, 죽는 게 영광스럽다는 걸

die / under the water / than in the frying pan."
물 속에서 프라이팬 속에서 보다는."

"What nonsense!" / cried Pinocchio.
"말도 안 돼!" 피노키오가 소리쳤다.

"Mine is an opinion," / replied the Tunny, / "and opinions
"내 의견이 그렇다는 거야." 다랑어가 말했다.

should be respected."
"의견은 모두 존중되어야 한다고."

"But I want to get / out of this place. I want to escape."
"하지만 나가고 싶어 여기를. 도망치고 싶어."

"Go, / if you can!"
"가 봐, 할 수 있으면!"

"Is this Shark / that has swallowed us / very long?" /
"이 상어는 우리를 삼킨 얼마나 길어?"

by your leave 실례지만 | dignified 품위 있는 | nonsense 터무니없는 생각, 허튼소리

asked the Marionette.
꼭두각시가 물었다.

"His body, / not counting the tail, / is almost a mile long."
"몸통만, 꼬리를 빼더라도, 거의 1마일 정도 돼."

While talking / in the darkness, / Pinocchio thought / he
말하는 동안 어둠 속에서, 피노키오는 생각했다

saw a faint light / in the distance.
희미한 불빛을 보았다고 멀리서.

"What can that be?" / he said to the Tunny.
"저건 뭘까?" 다랑어에게 말했다.

"Some other poor fish, / waiting / as patiently as we / to be
"다른 불쌍한 물고기겠지, 기다리는 우리처럼 참을성 있게

digested / by the Shark."
소화되기를 상어에 의해."

"I want to see him. He may be an old fish / and may know
"그를 만나고 싶어. 어른 물고기라면 아마 알 거야

/ some way of escape."
도망치는 방법을."

"I wish you all good luck, / dear Marionette."
"행운을 빌어, 꼭두각시야."

"Good-by, Tunny."
"안녕, 다랑어."

"Good-by, Marionette, / and good luck."
"안녕, 꼭두각시야, 행운을 빌어."

"When shall I see you / again?"
"언제 널 볼 수 있을까 다시?"

"Who knows? It is better not / to think about it."
"누가 알겠니? 안 하는 게 좋을 거야 그런 생각은."

20

In the Shark's body / Pinocchio finds / whom? Read this
상어의 몸 속에서　　　피노키오는 찾는다　　　누구를?　이번 장을 읽어보면,

chapter, / my children, / and you will know.
어린이 여러분,　　　알게 될 것입니다.

Pinocchio, / as soon as he had said good-by / to his good
피노키오는,　　안녕하고 인사하자마자

friend, the Tunny, / tottered away / in the darkness / and
좋은 친구, 다랑어에게,　비틀거리며 떠났다　어둠 속에서

began to walk / as well as he could / toward the faint light /
걷기 시작했다　　최선을 다해　　희미한 불빛 쪽으로

which glowed in the distance.
멀리서 빛나는.

As he walked / his feet splashed / in a pool of greasy / and
걸을 때마다　발에 튀었다　기름투성이의 웅덩이에서

slippery water, / which had such a heavy smell / of fish
미끌미끌한 물이,　심한 냄새가 나는

fried in oil / that Pinocchio thought / it was Lent.
기름에 튀긴 생선의　피노키오는 생각했다　사순절 같다고.

The farther on he went, / the brighter and clearer grew /
더 멀리 감에 따라,　　더 밝고 선명해졌다

the tiny light. On and on / he walked / till finally / he found
작은 불빛은.　계속해서　걸어서　마침내　그는 발견했다

/ —— I give you a thousand guesses, / my dear children!
— 잘 생각하고 맞춰보세요,　　어린이 여러분!

He found / a little table set for dinner / and lighted by a
그는 보았다　작은 저녁 식탁이 차려진 것을　그리고 양초가 타고 있었다

candle / stuck in a glass bottle; / and near the table / sat a
유리병 안에 고정된;　식탁 근처에는

little old man, / white as the snow, / eating live fish. They
작은 노인이 앉아 있었다,　눈처럼 하얀,　살아있는 물고기를 먹으며. 물고기들

wriggled so that, / now and again, / one of them slipped /
은 어찌나 파닥거리는지,　이따금,　그 중 한 마리가 미끄러져 나왔다

out of the old man's mouth / and escaped / into the darkness
노인의 입 밖으로   그리고 도망쳤다   어둠 속으로

/ under the table.
　식탁 아래.

At this sight, / the poor Marionette was filled / with such
이 광경을 보자,   불쌍한 꼭두각시는 가득 차서   너무나 크고 갑작스

great and sudden happiness / that he almost dropped / in a
런 행복으로   쓰러질 지경이었다   현기증이

faint. He wanted to laugh, / he wanted to cry, / he wanted
나서.   그는 웃고 싶었고,   울고 싶었으며,   말하고 싶었다

to say / a thousand and one things, / but all he could do /
말하고   무수한 말들을,   하지만 할 수 있는 일이라곤

was to stand still, / stuttering and stammering brokenly. At
가만히 서 있는 것이었다,   말을 더듬고 우물우물하면서.

last, / with a great effort, / he was able to let out a scream
마침내,   간신히,   기쁨의 탄성을 지를 수 있었다

of joy / and, opening wide his arms / he threw them /
그리고, 두 팔을 크게 벌려   끌어안았다

around the old man's neck.
노인의 목을.

"Oh, Father, dear Father! Have I found you / at last? Now I
"오, 아빠, 사랑하는 아빠!   찾은 건가요   결국?   이제 나는

shall never, never / leave you / again!"
절대로, 절대로 않을 거예요   떠나지   다시는!'

"Are my eyes really telling me the truth?" / answered the
"내 눈에 보이는 게 진짜냐?"   노인이 대답했다,

old man, / rubbing his eyes. "Are you really / my own dear
눈을 비비며.   "네가 정말   내 아들 피노키오냐?"

Pinocchio?"

Key Expression

so that ~ : ~하도록

so that + 주어 + 동사는 '~가 …하도록/하기 위하여'라는 의미를 가지고 있어요. that절에는 주로 조동사를 동반하며, 이때 so that은 in order that 으로 바꾸어 쓸 수 있어요.
so와 that이 붙어있는 점에 유의하여 'so ~ that' 구문과 헷갈리지 않도록 하세요.

ex) You sold your old coat to buy me my A-B-C book so that I could go to school.
내가 학교에 갈 수 있도록 당신은 낡은 코트를 팔아 제 영어책을 사주었지요.

"Yes, yes, yes! It is I! Look at me! And you have forgiven
"네, 네, 네!   저예요!   나를 보세요!   절 용서해 주신 거죠,

me, / haven't you? Oh, my dear Father, / how good you
그렇죠?   오, 사랑하는 아빠,   정말 좋은 분이세요!

are! And to think / that I / —— Oh, / but if you only knew /
아신다면   내가   — 오,   만일 알았다면,

how many misfortunes have fallen / on my head / and how
얼마나 많은 불행이 떨어졌는지   내 앞에   얼마나 많은

many troubles I have had! Just think / that on the day / you
나쁜 일들이 일어났는지!   생각나네요   그 날

sold your old coat / to buy me my A-B-C book / so that I
아빠가 외투를 팔았던   내게 영어책을 사 주려고

could go to school, / I ran away to the Marionette Theater
내가 학교에 갈 수 있도록,   나는 꼭두각시 극장으로 도망갔는데

/ and the proprietor caught me / and wanted to burn me /
단장에게 잡혔고   나를 태우려 했어요

to cook his roast lamb! He was the one / who gave me the
양 구이 요리를 하려고!   그가 바로   내게 금화 다섯 닢을 줬어요

five gold pieces / for you, / but I met the Fox and the Cat,
아빠를 위해,   하지만 난 여우와 고양이를 만났고,

/ who took me / to the Inn of the Red Lobster. There they
그들은 나를 데려갔어요 빨간 가재 여관으로.   거기에서 그들은

ate / like wolves / and I left the Inn alone / and I met the
먹었죠 늑대들처럼   그리고 날 여관에 홀려 두고 떠났어요   난 강도를 만났어요

Assassins / in the wood. I ran / and they ran after me, /
숲에서.   난 도망갔고, 그들은 날 쫓아왔어요,

always after me, / till they hanged me / to the branch / of
계속 날 쫓아와서,   나를 매달았어요   가지에

a giant oak tree. Then / the Fairy of the Azure Hair / sent
큰 떡갈나무의.   그때   하늘색 머리 요정이   마차를

the coach / to rescue me / and the doctors, / after looking
보내줬어요   날 구하려고   그리고 의사들이,   나를 본 후에,

at me, / said, / 'If he is not dead, / then he is surely alive,'
말했죠,   '죽지 않았다면,   확실히 살아있는 겁니다,'

a thousand and one 무수한 | stutter 말을 더듬다, 더듬거리다 | stammer 말을 더듬다 | brokenly 말하는 것이
유창하지 못하게, 뚝뚝 끊어지게 | proprietor (사업체·호텔 등의) 소유주[자]

/ and then I told a lie / and my nose began to grow. It
그리고 거짓말을 했더니   내 코가 길어지기 시작했죠.

grew and it grew, / till I couldn't get it through / the door
자라고 자라서,   통과할 수 없었어요   문을

/ of the room. And then / I went / with the Fox and the
방의.   그리고 나서   갔어요   여우와 고양이와 함께

Cat / to the Field of Wonders / to bury the gold pieces.
기적의 땅으로   금화를 묻으려고.

The Parrot laughed at me / and, instead of two thousand
앵무새가 절 비웃었어요   그리고, 이천 개의 금화 대신,

gold pieces, / I found none. When the Judge heard / I had
난 아무것도 발견하지 못했죠. 판사가 듣고 나서

been robbed, / he sent me to jail / to make the thieves
내가 도둑맞았다는 걸, 날 감옥에 보냈어요   도둑을 기쁘게 해 주려고;

happy; / and when I came away / I saw / a fine bunch of
감옥에서 도망쳤을 때   보았죠   탐스런 포도송이를

grapes / hanging on a vine. The trap caught me / and the
포도넝쿨에 달린.   덫에 걸려서   농부가 나에게

Farmer put a collar on me / and made me a watchdog. He
개 목걸이를 채우고   날 감시견으로 만들었어요.

found out / I was innocent / when I caught the Weasels /
그는 알아냈죠   내가 결백하다는 걸   내가 족제비를 잡았을 때

and he let me go. The Serpent with the tail / that smoked
날 풀어줬어요.   꼬리를 가진 뱀이   연기가 나는

/ started to laugh / and a vein / in his chest / broke / and
웃기 시작했고   핏줄이   가슴에서   터졌어요

so I went back / to the Fairy's house. She was dead, /
그렇게 해서 난 돌아갔죠 요정의 집으로.   요정은 죽었어요,

and the Pigeon, / seeing me crying, / said to me, / 'I have
그런데 비둘기가,   내가 우는 걸 보고,   말했죠,

seen your father / building a boat / to look for you / in
'내가 네 아빠를 봤어   배를 만드는   널 찾으려고

America,' / and I said to him, / 'Oh, if I only had wings!'
미국에서,'라고,   그래서 내가 말했죠,   '오, 내게 날개가 있다면!'

vine 포도나무, 덩굴 식물 | watchdog 감시견, 감시인 | weasel 족제비 | serpent (특히 큰) 뱀 | whitecap 흰
물결, 흰 파도(breaker) | overturn 뒤집다

/ and he said to me, / 'Do you want / to go to your father?'
그러자 그가 말했어요,   '원하니   네 아빠한테 가기를?'

/ and I said, / 'Perhaps, but how?' / and he said, / 'Get on
그래서 내가 말했죠, '아마도, 하지만 어떻게?'   그가 말했어요,   '내 등에 타.

my back. I'll take you / there.' We flew / all night long, /
내가 데려다 줄게   그곳으로.' 우리는 날아갔어요 밤새도록,

and next morning / the fishermen were looking / toward
그리고 다음 날 아침   어부들이 보고 있었어요

the sea, / crying, / 'There is a poor little man / drowning,'
바다를,   소리치면서,   '불쌍한 노인이 있다   물에 빠진,'

/ and I knew / it was you, / because my heart told me so /
난 알았죠   그게 아빠라는 걸,   내 마음이 그렇게 말했으니까

and I waved to you / from the shore —— "
그리고 손을 흔들었어요   해변에서 — "

"I knew you also," / put in Geppetto, / "and I wanted to
"나도 널 알아보았다,"   제페토가 말했다,   "난 너한테 가고 싶었지만;

go to you; / but how could I? The sea was rough / and the
어떻게 할 수 있었겠니?   바다는 거칠었고

whitecaps overturned the boat. Then / a Terrible Shark
흰 파도들이 배를 뒤집었다.   그때   끔찍한 상어가 나타나

came up / out of the sea / and, / as soon as he saw me /
바다에서   그리고,   날 보자마자

in the water, / swam quickly / toward me, / put out his
물 속에서,   재빨리 헤엄쳐 왔단다   내게,   혀를 내밀고는,

tongue, / and swallowed me / as easily / as if I had been a
나를 삼켰지   쉽게   내가 초콜릿 페퍼민트인 듯.'

chocolate peppermint."

"And / how long have you been shut away / in here?"
"그럼   얼마나 오래 갇혀 계셨어요   여기에?"

"From that day / to this, / two long weary years / ——
"그 날부터   지금까지,   길고 지루했던 2년 동안

two years, / my Pinocchio, / which have been like two
— 2년이란,   피노키오야,   그건 마치 2백년 같았다."

centuries."

"And / how have you lived? Where did you find / the
"그럼   어떻게 살아계셨죠?   어디에서 찾았나요

candle? And the matches / with which to light it / ——
양초는?   성냥은   불을 밝힐

where did you get them?"
어디에서 났어요?"

"You must know that, / in the storm / which swamped
"곧 알겠지만,   폭풍 속에서   내 배를 뒤집어버린,

my boat, / a large ship also suffered / the same fate. The
큰 배 한 척도 겪었다   똑같은 운명을.

sailors were all saved, / but the ship went right / to the
선원들은 모두 구출되었지만,   그 배는 곧장 내려갔다

bottom of the sea, / and the same Terrible Shark / that
바다 밑으로,   그리고는 바로 그 무서운 상어가

swallowed me, / swallowed most of it."
나를 삼킨,   그걸 삼켰지."

"What! Swallowed a ship?" / asked Pinocchio / in
"뭐라고요!   배를 삼켰다고요?"   피노키오가 물었다

astonishment.
깜짝 놀라며.

"At one gulp. The only thing he spat out / was the main-
"한 입에 통째로.   그가 뱉은 유일한 것은   큰 돛대뿐이었지,

mast, / for it stuck in his teeth. To my own good luck,
왜냐하면 이빨에 끼었거든.   운 좋게도,

/ that ship was loaded / with meat, / preserved foods, /
그 배에는 실려 있었어   고기,   통조림,

crackers, / bread, / bottles of wine, / raisins, / cheese, /
비스킷,   빵,   포도주,   건포도,   치즈,

coffee, / sugar, / wax candles, / and boxes of matches.
커피,   설탕,   양초,   성냥들이.

With all these blessings, / I have been able to live happily
이 모든 축복 덕에,   난 행복하게 살 수 있었지

on / for two whole years, / but now / I am at the very last
2년 동안이나,   하지만 지금   이게 마지막 부스러기야.

crumbs. Today / there is nothing left / in the cupboard, /
오늘   남은 게 없어   찬장에는,

and this candle / you see here / is the last one / I have."
그리고 이 양초는   여기 보이는   마지막 양초야   내가 가진."

"And then?"
"그리고 나면?"

"And then, / my dear, / we'll find ourselves / in darkness."
"그리고 나면,   아들아,   우린 남게 되겠지   어둠 속에."

"Then, my dear Father," / said Pinocchio, / "there is no
"그럼, 아빠,"   피노키오가 말했다,   "시간이 없어요

time / to lose. We must try / to escape."
지체할.   시도해야 해요   탈출을."

"Escape! How?"
"탈출이라고! 어떻게?"

"We can run / out of the Shark's mouth / and dive into the
"뛰어 나가서   상어의 입 밖으로   바다에 뛰어들어요."

sea."

"You speak well, / but I cannot swim, / my dear
"말은 그럴 듯한데,   하지만 난 수영을 못한다,   피노키오야."

Pinocchio."

Key Expression

가목적어 it 구문

'think it possible to ~'는 '~하는 것을 가능하다고 생각하다'라는 의미로 쓰인 5형식 구문이에요. 여기에서 it은 가목적어, to 부정사가 진목적어이며 it은 따로 해석하지 않습니다. 또한 to 부정사의 주체가 주어가 다를 경우 'for + 목적격' 형태의 의미상 주어를 to 부정사 앞에 첨가하여 '...가 ~하는 것을'처럼 해석합니다.

이처럼 가목적어 it을 사용한 5형식 구문에 자주 쓰이는 동사로는 think, make, find 등이 있어요.

ex) Do you think it possible for a Marionette, a yard high, to have the strength to carry me on his shoulders and swim?"
너는 키가 1야드인 꼭두각시가 나를 어깨에 메고 수영할만한 힘을 가지는 것이 가능하다고 생각하니?

swamp (큰 파도 등이) 뒤덮다[집어삼키다] | astonishment 깜짝 놀람 | main-mast 큰 돛대 | crumb (특히 빵·케이크의) 부스러기

"Why should that matter? You can climb / on my shoulders
"뭐가 문제에요?   올라오세요   내 어깨에

/ and I, / who am a fine swimmer, / will carry you safely /
그러면 내가, 수영을 잘하거든요,   안전하게 모셔다 드릴게요.

to the shore."
바닷가로."

"Dreams, / my boy!" / answered Geppetto, / shaking his
"꿈 같은 말이야, 아들아!"   제페토가 답했다,   고개를 저으며

head / and smiling sadly. "Do you think / it possible / for
           슬프게 웃으면서   "생각하니   가능하다고

a Marionette,/ a yard high, / to have the strength / to carry
꼭두각시가,   키가 1야드밖에 안 되는, 힘을 가졌다는 게

me on his shoulders / and swim?"
나를 어깨에 싣고   헤엄칠?

"Try it / and see! And in any case, / if it is written / that we
"일단 해 보세요 그럼 알게 되요! 어떤 경우라도,   만약 쓰여 있다면

must die, / we shall at least / die together."
우리가 죽는다고, 우린 적어도   함께 죽는 거예요."

Not adding another word, / Pinocchio took the candle / in
더 이상의 말 없이,   피노키오는 양초를 들고

his hand / and going ahead / to light the way, / he said / to
손에   앞으로 갔다   길을 비추며,   말했다

his father:
아빠에게:

"Follow me / and have no fear."
"절 따라오세요   겁내지 말고."

They walked / a long distance / through the stomach /
그들은 걸었다   긴 거리를   뱃속을 통과하여

and the whole body / of the Shark. When they reached the
그리고 전체 몸통을   상어의.   목에 도착했을 때,

throat / of the monster, / they stopped / for a while / to wait
상어의,   멈추었다   잠시 동안

for the right moment / in which to make their escape.
적절한 때를 기다리기 위해   탈출할 수 있는.

I want you to know / **that the Shark,** / **being very old** /
여러분이 알아야 할 게 있어요   상어는,   너무 늙었고

and suffering from asthma and heart trouble, / was
천식과 심장병을 앓고 있어서,

obliged to **sleep** / **with his mouth open.** Because of this,
자야만 했다는 사실이에요.   입을 벌린 채로.   그런 이유로,

/ Pinocchio was able to catch a glimpse of / the sky filled
피노키오는 언뜻 볼 수 있었다   별들로 가득 찬 하늘을,

with stars, / as he looked up / through the open jaws / of
올려다 보았을 때   벌린 턱 사이를

his new home.
그의 새 집의.

"The time has come / for us to escape," / he whispered,
"때가 왔어요   우리가 탈출할,"   그는 속삭였다,

/ turning to his father. "The Shark is fast asleep. The sea
아빠를 보면서.   "상어는 곤히 자고 있어요.   바다는 고요하고

is calm / and the night is as bright / as day. Follow me
밤은 밝아요   낮처럼.   가까이 따라 오세요,

closely, / dear Father, / and we shall soon be saved."
사랑하는 아빠,   우린 곧 자유예요."

Key Expression 🎯

to make matters worse : 설상가상으로

to make matters worse는 숙어처럼 쓰이는 독립부정사 구문으로 나쁜 일
이 더욱 나쁘게 된다는 상황, 즉 '설상가상으로, 엎친 데 덮친 격'이라는 의미로 사
용됩니다.
이와 반대의 의미로 쓰이는 구문이 to make the matter better, 즉 '금
상첨화'가 있습니다.

ex) To make matters worse, the candle went out and father and son were left in
the dark.
설상가상으로, 초가 꺼지고 아버지와 아들은 어둠 속에 남겨졌다.

No sooner said than done. They climbed up / the throat
말하자마자 행동에 옮겼다.　　　　그들은 기어 올라갔다　　괴물의 목을

of the monster / till they came / to that immense open
　　　　　　도착할 때까지　　거대한 벌려진 입에.

mouth. There they had to walk / on tiptoes, / for if they
　　거기서는 걸어야 했다　　발끝으로,　　왜냐하면 만약 간지럽

tickled / the Shark's long tongue / he might awaken / ——
게 한다면　　상어의 긴 혀를　　　　깨어날 테니까

and where would they be / then? The tongue was so wide
— 그들은 어디에 있게 될까　　그렇게 되면? 혀는 아주 넓고

/ and so long / that it looked like a country road. The two
매우 길어서　　시골길처럼 보였다.

fugitives were just about to dive / into the sea / when the
두 도망자는 막 뛰어들려 했다　　　　바다로

Shark sneezed / very suddenly and, / as he sneezed, / he
그때 상어가 재채기를 했고　갑자기　　　　재채기를 하자,

gave Pinocchio and Geppetto / such a jolt / that they found
피노키오와 제페토에게 가했다　　　큰 충격을

themselves thrown / on their backs / and dashed once
그래서 그들은 다시 던져졌고　뒤쪽으로　　다시 한 번 내동댕이 당했다

more / and very unceremoniously / into the stomach / of
　　아주 인정사정 없이　　　　뱃속으로

the monster.
괴물의.

To make matters worse, / the candle went out / and father
설상가상으로,　　　　양초도 꺼져 버렸다

and son were left / in the dark.
아빠와 아들은 남겨졌다　　어둠 속에.

"And now?" / asked Pinocchio / with a serious face.
"이제 어쩌죠?"　　피노키오가 물었다　　심각한 표정으로.

"Now / we are lost."
"이제　우린 가망이 없어."

"Why lost? Give me your hand, / dear Father, / and be
"왜 가망이 없어요? 손을 주세요,　　아빠,　　미끄러지지 않게

careful not to slip!"
조심하세요!"

"Where will you take me?"
"어디로 날 데려 갈거니?"

"We must try again. Come with me / and don't be afraid."
"다시 시도해 봐야죠.   나와 함께 가요   겁내지 마세요."

With these words / Pinocchio took his father / by the hand
이렇게 말하고는   피노키오는 잡았다   아빠의 손을

/ and, always walking on tiptoes, / they climbed up / the
그리고, 계속 발끝으로 걸으면서,   기어올랐다

monster's throat / for a second time. They then crossed / the
괴물의 목을   다시.   그리고는 건넜다

whole tongue / and jumped / over three rows of teeth. But /
혓바닥 전체를   그리고 뛰어넘었다   세 줄의 이빨을.   하지만

before they took the last great leap, / the Marionette said to
마지막 도약을 하기 전,   꼭두각시는 아빠에게 말했다:

his father: / "Climb on my back / and hold on tightly / to my
"내 등에 올라와서   꽉 잡으세요

neck. I'll take care of everything else."
내 목을. 다른 건 내가 다 알아서 할게요."

As soon as Geppetto was comfortably seated / on his
제페토가 편안하게 앉자마자

shoulders, / Pinocchio, / very sure of what he was doing,
그의 어깨에,   피노키오는,   할 수 있다는 확신을 갖고,

/ dived into the water / and started to swim. The sea was
물속으로 뛰어들었고   헤엄치기 시작했다.   바다는 기름과 같았고,

like oil, / the moon shone / in all splendor, / and the Shark
달은 빛났으며   너무나 화려하게,   그리고 상어는 계속 잠을

continued to sleep / so soundly / that not even a cannon shot
잤다   너무나 깊게 자서   대포 총으로도 그를 깨우지 못했을 것이다.

would have awakened him.

---

tiptoes 발끝으로 살금살금 걷다 | tickle 간지럼을 태우다[간지럽히다] | country road 시골길 | fugitive 도망자,
탈주자 | sneeze 재채기하다 | jolt (갑자기 거칠게) 덜컥 하고 움직임 | dash 내동댕이치다 | unceremoniously
인정사정 없이 | be seated 앉다, 착석하다 | in splendor 화려하게 | soundly (잠이 든 모양이) 깊이, 곤히
| cannon 대포

A. 다음 문장을 해석해 보세요.

(1) Seeing that wooden Marionette, / the poor man thought / he
was dreaming / and sat there / with his mouth wide open /
and his eyes popping / out of his head.
→

(2) That was very good and kind / of you to want me / to suffer as
little as possible / and I shall remember you / always.
→

(3) All that could be seen of him / was a very small black dot /
moving swiftly / on the blue surface / of the water.
→

(4) Her coat was not white or black or brown / as that of any
other goat, / but azure, / a deep brilliant color / that reminded
one / of the hair of the lovely maiden.
→

B. 다음 주어진 문장이 되도록 빈칸에 써 넣으세요.

(1) 나는 잠에서 깨어 <u>자신이 당나귀로 변한 것을 발견했어요.</u>

I awoke _____.

(2) 나는 <u>매우 딱딱한 나무로 만들어졌어요.</u>

I am _____.

(3) <u>설상가상으로,</u> 초가 꺼지고 아버지와 아들은 어둠 속에 남게 되었다.

_____, the candle went out and
father and son were left in the dark.

A. (1) 나무로 된 꼭두각시를 보자, 불쌍한 남자는 자신이 꿈을 꾸고 있는 거라고 생각했고 입을 크게 벌
리고 눈이 튀어나올 듯 한 상태로 그 곳에 주저앉았다. (2) 매우 착하고 친절하게도 당신은 내가 최대한 적
게 고통받길 원했고 난 당신을 영원히 기억하겠어요. (3) 그가 볼 수 있던 것은 바닷물의 푸른 표면에서 빠

(4) 다른 일은 내가 알아서 할게요.

I'll _____.

C. 다음 주어진 문구가 알맞은 문장이 되도록 순서를 맞춰 보세요.

(1) 내가 그럴 자격이 없는데도, <u>그녀는 내게서 눈을 떼지 않았어요.</u>
   (though / even / I / do not / it / deserve)
   → She never loses sight of me, _____.

(2) 나는 물고기랑 아무 관계가 없어.
   (what / to you / said / a week / I / You / ago / remember)
   →

(3) <u>너는 꼭두각시가 나를 어깨에 메고 수영할 만한 힘을 가지는 게 가능하다고</u>
   <u>생각하니?</u>
   (think / possible / to have / Do you / a Marionette / it / the
   strength / for)
   → _____

   to carry me on his shoulders and swim?

(4) 우리가 탈출해야 할 때가 왔어요.
   (has come / us / for / to escape / The time)
   →

D. 다음 단어에 대한 맞는 설명과 연결해 보세요.

(1) totter ▶   ◀ ① twist and turn with quick
                            movement

(2) wriggle ▶   ◀ ② have difficulty speaking

(3) stutter ▶   ◀ ③ walk in an unsteady way

(4) unceremoniously ▶   ◀ ④ done in a sudden or rude way

르게 움직이는 매우 작은 검은 점이 다였다. (4) 그녀의 외투(염소의 털)는 다른 염소처럼 흰색도 검은색
도 아닌, 사랑스런 소녀의 머리카락을 떠올리게 하는 짙은 하늘색이었다. | B. (1) to find myself changed
into a donkey, (2) made of very hard wood, (3) To make matters worse (4) take care of everything
else, | C. (1) even though I do not deserve it, (2) I have nothing to do with fishes, (3) Do you think
it possible for a Marionette to have the strength (4) The time has come for us to escape. | D. (1) ③
(2) ① (3) ② (4) ④

21

Pinocchio finally / ceases to be a Marionette / and
피노키오는 마침내　　　더 이상 꼭두각시가 아니라

becomes a boy.
아이가 된다.

"My dear Father, / we are saved!" / cried the Marionette.
"사랑하는 아빠,　　　우린 살았어요!"　　　꼭두각시는 외쳤다.

"All we have to do now / is to get / to the shore, / and
"이제 우리가 할 일은　　　도착하는 것 뿐이에요　바닷가로,

that is easy."
그리고 그건 쉬워요."

Without another word, / he swam swiftly away / in an
아무 말 없이,　　　그는 빨리 헤엄쳐갔다

effort to reach land / as soon as possible. All at once / he
육지에 도착하려고　　　가능한 한 빨리.　　　갑자기

noticed / that Geppetto was shivering and shaking / as if
깨달았다　　제페토가 떨고 있다는 것을

with a high fever.
열병 걸린 사람처럼.

Was he shivering / from fear / or from cold? Who
떨고 있는 걸까?　　두려워서　　아니면 추워서?　　누가 알겠는가?

knows? Perhaps a little of both. But Pinocchio, / thinking
아마도 둘 다일지도.　　　하지만 피노키오는,

his father was frightened, / tried to comfort him / by
아빠가 겁을 내고 있다고 생각해서,　　　그를 위로하려 했다

saying:
말하면서:

"Courage, Father! In a few moments / we shall be safe /
"용기를 내세요, 아빠!　몇 분 후면　　　우린 안전해 질 거예요

on land."
육지에서."

pierce (어둠·적막 등을) 가르다[찢다] | contented (특히 자기 삶에) 만족[자족]해 하는

"But / where is that blessed shore?" / asked the little old
"하지만   그 축복받은 육지가 어디 있나?"   노인이 물었다.

man, / more and more worried / as he tried to pierce / the
         점점 더 걱정하며   그는 뚫어져라 보았다

faraway shadows. "Here I am searching / on all sides / and
멀리 어둠 속을.   "여기에서 둘러보아도   온 사방을

I see nothing / but sea and sky."
하지만 아무것도 안 보이는 구나 바다와 하늘 밖에."

"I see the shore," / said the Marionette. "Remember, Father,
"저는 해변이 보여요."   꼭두각시가 말했다.   "기억하세요, 아빠,

/ that I am like a cat. I see better / at night / than by day."
 저는 고양이와 같다는 것을.   저는 더 잘 보여요   밤에   낮보다."

Poor Pinocchio pretended to be peaceful / and contented,
불쌍한 피노키오는 침착한 척 했지만   그리고 만족하는 척,

/ but he was far from that. He was beginning to feel
  전혀 그렇지 않았다.   그는 용기를 잃기 시작했다.

discouraged, / his strength was leaving him, / and his
              힘이 빠져버렸고,

breathing was becoming / more and more labored. He felt /
호흡은 변했다   점점 힘들게.   그는 생각했다

he could not go on much longer, / and the shore was still far
얼마 못 갈 것이라고,   그런데 해변은 여전히 멀리 있었다.

away.

Key Expression ✿

as soon as possible : 가능한 한 빨리
'as+형용사/부사+as possible'은 '가능한 ~한(하게)'라는 의미를 가진 구문
입니다. 이때 possible 대신 '주어+can'을 쓸 수도 있습니다.
as soon as possible은 '가능한 한 빨리'라는 의미를 가지고 있으며 흔히
ASAP라고 줄여서 쓰기도 합니다.

ex) He swam swiftly away in an effort to reach land as soon as possible.
    그는 가능한 한 빨리 육지에 닿기 위해 빠르게 헤엄쳐 갔다.
    Pinocchio ran as fast as he could.
    피노키오는 가능한 한 빨리 달렸다.
    That was very good and kind of you to want me to suffer as little as possible.
    친절하게도 너는 내가 가능한 한 적게 고통받기를 원했다.

193

He swam a few more strokes. Then / he turned to
그는 몇 번 더 팔을 저었다.   잠시 뒤   제페토를 돌아보며

Geppetto / and cried out weakly:
                약하게 외쳤다:

"Help me, Father! Help, / for I am dying!"
"도와주세요, 아빠!   도와주세요, 저 죽어요!"

Father and son / were really about to drown / when they
아빠와 아들은   정말 물에 빠질 것 같았다

heard a voice / like a guitar / out of tune / call from the
목소리를 들었을 때   기타 소리 같은   음정이 안 맞는   바다에서부터:

sea:

"What is the trouble?"
"무슨 일이야?"

"It is I and my poor father."
"나와 불쌍한 우리 아빠가."

"I know the voice. You are Pinocchio."
"누구 목소리인지 알겠다.   피노키오구나."

"Exactly. And you?"
"맞아.   넌?"

"I am the Tunny, / your companion / in the Shark's
"난 다랑어야.   네 친구   상어 뱃속에 있던."

stomach."

"And how did you escape?"
"그럼 어떻게 탈출했어?"

"I imitated your example. You are the one / who showed
"너처럼 했지.   바로 너야   내게 방법을 알려 준 건

me the way / and after you went, / I followed."
            네가 간 뒤,   내가 따라갔어."

"Tunny, / you arrived at the right moment! I implore you, /
"다랑어야,   적절한 때에 왔구나!   제발 부탁이야,

for the love / you bear your children, / the little Tunnies, /
사랑으로   네가 네 새끼에게 갖는,   다랑어 새끼들에게,

to help us, / or we are lost!"
우리를 도와줘,   안 그러면 우린 죽어!"

"With great pleasure / indeed. Hang onto my tail, / both
"기꺼이   정말로.   내 꼬리에 매달려,

of you, / and let me lead you. In a twinkling / you will be
둘 다,   내가 너희를 이끌고 갈게.   곧

safe on land."
안전하게 육지에 닿을 거야."

Geppetto and Pinocchio, / as you can easily imagine, / did
제페토와 피노키오는,   여러분이 예상하듯이,

not refuse the invitation; / indeed, / instead of hanging
그 호의를 거절하지 않았다;   실제로는   꼬리에 매달리는 것보다,

onto the tail, / they thought / it better / to climb on the
                  생각하기도 했다   더 낫겠다고   다랑어 등 위에 올라타는 게.

Tunny's back.

"Are we too heavy?" / asked Pinocchio.
"우리가 너무 무겁니?"   피노키오가 물었다.

"Heavy? Not in the least. You are as light / as sea-shells,"
"무거우냐고? 전혀 아니야.   가벼워   조개껍데기처럼,"

/ answered the Tunny, / who was as large / as a two-year-
   다랑어가 말했다,   커다란   2살 된 말만큼.

old horse.

Key Expression ♥

you are the one who~ : ~한 사람은 바로 너야
you are the one who~는 '네가 바로 ~한 사람이야', 즉 '~한 사람은 바로 너
야'라는 의미를 가진 구문입니다. 관계대명사 who를 사용한 관용 표현으로 who
대신에 that을 쓸 수도 있습니다.

ex) You are the one who showed me the way.
내게 길을 가르쳐 준 사람은 바로 너야.
He was the one who gave me the five gold pieces for you.
그가 바로 네게 금화 다섯 닢을 준 사람이야.

---

stroke (수영·조정에서 팔·노를) 젓기 | imitate 모방하다 | implore 애원하다, 간청하다 | bear 갖다[품다]

As soon as they reached the shore, / Pinocchio was the first
해변에 도착하자마자, 피노키오가 먼저 뛰어내렸다

to jump / to the ground / to help his old father. Then / he
땅으로 늙은 아빠를 도와주려고. 그리고

turned to the fish / and said to him:
물고기를 쳐다보며 말했다:

"Dear friend, / you have saved my father, / and I have not
"친구야, 네가 우리 아빠를 살렸어, 말을 찾을 수가 없구나

enough words / with which to thank you! Allow me / to
감사하는 마음을 표할! 허락해 주렴

embrace you / as a sign of my eternal gratitude."
널 안을 수 있게 영원한 감사의 표시로."

The Tunny stuck his nose / out of the water / and Pinocchio
다랑어는 코를 내밀었고 물 밖으로 피노키오는 무릎을 꿇고

knelt / on the sand / and kissed him / most affectionately
모래 위에 입을 맞추었다 너무나 다정하게

/ on his cheek. At this warm greeting, / the poor Tunny, /
그의 뺨에. 따뜻한 인사를 받자, 불쌍한 다랑어는,

who was not used to such tenderness, / wept like a child.
그러한 다정함에 익숙치 않았기에, 아이처럼 울었다.

He felt so embarrassed / and ashamed / that he turned /
그는 너무나 당황스러웠고 창피해서 재빨리 몸을 돌리고는,

quickly, / plunged into the sea, / and disappeared.
바다로 뛰어들어 사라졌다.

In the meantime / day had dawned.
그러는 동안 날이 밝아왔다.

Pinocchio offered his arm / to Geppetto, / who was so
피노키오는 팔을 내주었다 제페토에게, 너무 약해서

weak / he could hardly stand, / and said to him:
서 있을 수 조차 없었던, 그리고 말했다:

"Lean on my arm, dear Father, / and let us go. We will
"내 팔에 기대세요, 아빠, 같이 가요. 걸을 거에요

walk / very, very slowly, / and if we feel tired / we can rest
아주, 아주 천천히, 그리고 만약 지치면, 우리는 쉴 수 있어요

by the wayside."
길가에서 쉬어요."

"And where are we going?" / asked Geppetto.
"이제 어디로 가는 거냐?" 제페토가 물었다.

"To look for a house or a hut, / where they will be kind
"집이나 오두막을 찾으려고요, 친절한 사람이 있을

enough / to give us a bite of bread / and a bit of straw / to
우리에게 빵을 줄 정도로 약간의 짚과

sleep on."
잠을 잘 수 있는."

They had not taken a hundred steps / when they saw / two
백 걸음도 못 가서 그들은 보았다

rough-looking individuals / sitting on a stone / begging for
찌들어 보이는 두 거지들을 돌 위에 앉아서 구걸하고 있는.
alms.

It was the Fox and the Cat, / but one could hardly
그건 여우와 고양이였다. 하지만 좀처럼 그들을 알아볼 수 없었다.

recognize them, / they looked so miserable. The Cat, /
너무 비참해 보여서. 고양이는,

after pretending to be blind / for so many years / had really
장님 행세를 하다가 너무 오랫동안 정말로 잃었다

lost / the sight of both eyes. And the Fox, / old, thin, and
두 눈의 시력을. 여우는, 늙고, 마르고, 털이 거의

almost hairless, / had even lost his tail. That sly thief had
빠졌는데, 꼬리마저 없었다. 그 교활한 도둑은 빠져버려서

fallen / into deepest poverty, / and one day / he had been
극심한 가난에, 어느 날 팔 수밖에 없었다

forced / to sell his beautiful tail / for a bite to eat.
아름다운 꼬리를 먹을 것을 구하기 위해.

"Oh, Pinocchio," / he cried / in a tearful voice. "Give us
"오, 피노키오," 그가 외쳤다 눈물 어린 목소리로. "구호품을 좀 주렴,

some alms, / we beg of you! We are old, / tired, / and sick."
부탁할게! 우린 늙었고, 지쳤고, 병들었어."

"Sick!" / repeated the Cat.
"병들었어!" 고양이가 반복했다.

eternal 영원한 | knelt kneel 의 과거, 과거분사 | affectionately 애정을 담아 | tenderness 다정, 애정 | plunge
(물 속으로) 뛰어들다 | alms 구호금[품] | sly 교활한, 음흉한

197

"Addio, false friends!" / answered the Marionette. "You
"잘 가, 나쁜 친구들!"   꼭두각시가 답했다.

cheated me once, / but you will never catch me / again."
"한 번은 속았지만,   절대 잡히지 않아   다시."

"Believe us! Today we are truly poor / and starving."
"우리를 믿어줘!   지금 우린 정말 가난하고   배고파 죽겠어."

"Starving!" / repeated the Cat.
"배고파 죽겠어! /   고양이가 반복했다.

"If you are poor; / you deserve it! Remember the old
"너희가 가난하다면;   그래도 싸지!   속담을 기억해

proverb / which says: / 'Stolen money never bears fruit.'
이렇게 말하는: '훔친 돈으로는 과일을 살 수 없다.'라고.

Addio, false friends."
안녕, 나쁜 친구들아."

"Have mercy on us!"
"우리에게 자비를 베풀어 줘!"

"On us."
"우리에게."

"Addio, false friends. Remember the old proverb / which
"안녕, 나쁜 친구들.   속담을 기억해   이렇게 말

says: / 'Bad wheat always makes poor bread!'"
하는: '나쁜 밀은 항상 맛없는 빵을 만든다!'라고.

"Do not abandon us."
"우리를 버리지 마!"

"Abandon us," / repeated the Cat.
"우리를 버려."   고양이가 반복했다.

"Addio, false friends. Remember the old proverb: /
"잘 가, 나쁜 친구들.   속담을 기억해 :

'Whoever steals his neighbor's shirt, / usually dies /
'이웃의 셔츠를 훔친 사람은,   보통 죽는다

without his own.'"
자신은 벌거벗은 채."라는.

Waving good-by to them, / Pinocchio and Geppetto
그들에게 작별 인사를 하고,   피노키오와 제페토는 조용히 갔다

calmly went / on their way. After a few more steps, /
               가던 길을.   몇 걸음 후,

they saw, / at the end of a long road / near a clump of
그들은 보았다,   긴 길의 끝에서   나무들 옆에,

trees, / a tiny cottage / built of straw.
작은 오두막을   짚으로 지어진.

"Someone must live / in that little hut," / said Pinocchio.
"누군가 살고 있을 거야   저 작은 오두막에."   피노키오가 말했다.

"Let us see for ourselves."
"우리가 가서 봐요."

They went / and knocked at the door.
가서   문을 두드렸다.

"Who is it?" / said a little voice / from within.
"누구세요?"   작은 목소리가 말했다   안에서.

"A poor father / and a poorer son, / without food and /
"불쌍한 아버지와   더 불쌍한 아들이요,   음식도 없고

with no roof to cover them," / answered the Marionette.
집도 없는,"   꼭두각시가 대답했다.

"Turn the key / and the door will open," / said the same
"열쇠를 돌리면   문이 열릴 거야."   똑같은 작은 목소리가

little voice.
말했다.

Pinocchio turned the key / and the door opened. As
피노키오가 열쇠를 돌렸고   문이 열렸다.

soon as they went in, / they looked / here and there / and
들어가자마자,   찾아보았다   여기 저기

everywhere / but saw no one.
모든 곳을   하지만 아무도 보이지 않았다.

"Oh —— ho, where is the owner of the hut?" / cried
"여기요 — , 집주인은 어디 있어요?"   피노키오가 소리쳤다,

Pinocchio, / very much surprised.
너무 놀라서.

"Here I am, / up here!"
"여기 있다,   여기 위에!"

addio 감탄사 안녕히 가시오 | wheat 밀 | clump 무리[무더기] | hut 오두막

Father and son looked up / to the ceiling, / and there on a
아빠와 아들은 올려다 보았다   지붕 쪽을,   거기 기둥 위에

beam / sat the Talking Cricket.
       말하는 귀뚜라미가 앉아 있었다.

"Oh, my dear Cricket," / said Pinocchio, / bowing politely.
"오, 나의 사랑하는 귀뚜라미야."   피노키오가 말했다,   공손하게 인사하며.

Oh, now / you call me / your dear Cricket, / but do you
"오, 지금   네가 날 불렀니   네 사랑하는 귀뚜라미라고,   하지만 기억하니

remember / when you threw your hammer / at me / to kill
           네가 망치를 던졌을 때를   내게

me?"
날 죽이려고?"

"You are right, / dear Cricket. Throw a hammer / at me
"네가 옳아,   사랑하는 귀뚜라미야. 망치를 던지렴   지금 내게.

now. I deserve it! But spare my poor old father."
      난 그래도 싸!   하지만 우리 불쌍하고 나이든 아빠는 살려 줘."

"I am going to spare / both the father and the son. I have
"난 살려 줄 거야   아빠와 아들 둘 다.

only wanted to remind you / of the trick / you long ago
단지 네게 상기시키고 싶었어   그 장난을   네가 오래 전에 했던

played / upon me, / to teach you / that in this world of
내게.   가르쳐 주기 위해   이 세상에서

ours / we must be kind and courteous / to others, / if we
우리는 친절하고 공손해야 한다는 것을   사람들에게,

want to find / kindness and courtesy / in our own days of
찾고 싶다면   친절함과 예의를   우리가 힘든 날을 보낼 때."

trouble."

"You are right, little Cricket, / you are more than right, /
"네가 맞아, 귀여운 귀뚜라미야,   네가 전적으로 옳아,

and I shall remember / the lesson / you have taught me.
기억할게   교훈을   내게 가르쳐 줬던.

But / will you tell / how you succeeded / in buying this
하지만 말해 줄래   어떻게 성공했는지   이렇게 예쁘고 작은 오두막

pretty little cottage?"
을 사는 걸?"

"This cottage was given to me / yesterday / by a little
"이 오두막은 내가 받은 거야   어제

Goat with blue hair."
파란 털의 작은 염소한테."

"And / where did the Goat go?" / asked Pinocchio.
"그럼   그 염소는 어디로 갔니?"   피노키오가 물었다.

"I don't know."
"모르겠어."

"And / when will she come back?"
"그럼   언제 돌아올까?"

"She will never come back. Yesterday / she went away /
"다시 안 올 거야.   어제   떠났어

bleating sadly, / and it seemed / to me / she said: 'Poor
슬프게 울면서,   보였어   내게   말하는 것처럼:

Pinocchio, / I shall never see him again / ··· the Shark
'불쌍한 피노키오,   난 다시는 그 애를 보지 못할 거야   ··· 상어가 그 애를 잡아

must have eaten him / by this time.'"
먹었음이 틀림없어   지금쯤이면.'"

"Were those her real words? Then / it was she / —— it
"그게 정말 염소가 한 말이었어?   그럼   바로 그녀야   — 바로 —

was —— / my dear little Fairy," / cried out Pinocchio, /
                나의 사랑하는 작은 요정,"   피노키오가 소리쳤다,

sobbing bitterly. After he had cried / a long time, / he
펑펑 울면서.   그는 울고 나서   오랫동안,

wiped his eyes / and then he made a bed / of straw / for
눈물을 닦고는   침대를 만들었다   짚으로

old Geppetto. He laid him / on it / and said to the Talking
제페토를 위해.   그를 눕히고   그 위에   말하는 귀뚜라미에게 말했다:

Cricket:

"Tell me, little Cricket, / where shall I find / a glass of
"말해 줘, 귀여운 귀뚜라미야,   어디에서 찾을 수 있을까   우유 한 컵을

milk / for my poor Father?"
우유   우리 불쌍한 아빠를 위한?"

beam 기둥 | spare 할애하다, (불쾌한 일을) 모면하게 하다 | courteous 공손한 | courtesy 공손함

201

"Three fields away from here / lives Farmer John. He has
"밭을 세 개 지나면   농부인 존이 살고 있어.   그는 소를

some cows. Go there / and he will give you / what you
몇 마리 키워.   거기 가면   줄 거야   네가 원하는 걸."

want."

Pinocchio ran / all the way / to Farmer John's house. The
피노키오는 달렸다   내내   농부 존의 집까지.

Farmer said to him:
농부가 말했다:

"How much milk do you want?"
"얼만큼의 우유가 필요하니?"

"I want a full glass."
"한 컵 가득 원해요."

"A full glass costs a penny. First give me the penny."
"한 컵 가득은 1페니다.   먼저 1페니를 내라."

"I have no penny," / answered Pinocchio, / sad and
"돈이 없어요,"   피노키오가 말했다,   슬프고 부끄러워 하는.

ashamed.

"Very bad, my Marionette," / answered the Farmer, /
"아주 안 됐군, 꼭두각시야,"   농부가 대답했다,

"very bad. If you have no penny, / I have no milk."
"아주 안 됐어.   돈이 없으면,   우유도 없다."

"Too bad," / said Pinocchio / and started to go.
"할 수 없죠,"   피노키오가 말하고   가려 했다.

"Wait a moment," / said Farmer John. "Perhaps / we can
"잠깐만,"   농부 존이 말했다.   "아마도   우린 타협을

come to terms. Do you know / how to draw water / from
할 수 있을 거야.   넌 알고 있니   물을 끌어올리는 법을

a well?"
우물에서?"

"I can try."
"해 볼게요."

come to terms (합의·계약 등의) 조건 | well 우물 | yonder 저기 있는[보이는] | bucketfuls 양동이 하나 가득(의 양) | dripping 흠뻑 젖은, 물이 뚝뚝 듣는[떨어지는] | perspiration 땀

"Then / go to that well / you see yonder / and draw one
"그럼   저 우물로 가서   저기 보이는

hundred bucketfuls of water."
물 백 양동이를 끌어 올려라."

"Very well."
"잘 알겠어요."

"After you have finished, / I shall give you / a glass of
"일을 다 마치면,   줄 것이다   우유 한 컵을

warm sweet milk."
따뜻하고 달콤한."

"I am satisfied."
"좋아요."

Farmer John took the Marionette / to the well / and
농부 존이 꼭두각시를 데려가서   우물로

showed him / how to draw the water. Pinocchio set to
그에게 보여 줬다   물을 끌어올리는 법을.   피노키오는 일하기 시작했다

work / as well as he knew how, / but long before he had
방법을 잘 숙지하면서,   하지만 다 끌어올리기 훨씬 전에

pulled up / the one hundred buckets, / he was tired out /
백 개의 양동이를,   지쳐버려서

and dripping with perspiration. He had never worked so
땀을 뚝뚝 흘리고 있었다.   그는 그렇게 열심히 일한 적이 없었다

hard / in his life.
평생 동안.

Key Expression 🎯

only to의 두 가지 해석법
only to는 to 부정사의 목적을 나타내는 부사적 용법으로 '단지 ~하지 위해서',
그리고 결과의 부사적 용법으로 '~했으나 결국 ~하다'라는 두 가지 의미로 해석
될 수 있어요. 어떻게 해석해야 할지는 문맥에서 파악해야 합니다.

ex) I have only wanted to remind you of the trick
나는 단지 네게 그 장난을 상기시키고 싶었을 뿐이야.
I have brought you here only to give you food and drink?
내가 단지 음식과 물을 주기 위해서 너를 여기에 데려왔을까?
He disappeared only to reappear once more.
그는 사라졌지만 결국 다시 한 번 나타났다.

"Until today," / said the Farmer, / "my donkey has drawn
"오늘까지," 농부가 말했다, "내 당나귀가 물을 끌어 올렸지

the water / for me, / but now / that poor animal is dying."
날 위해, 하지만 지금 그 불쌍한 동물은 죽어가고 있단다."

"Will you take me / to see him?" / said Pinocchio.
"데려다 주시겠어요 그를 만나 보도록?" 피노키오가 말했다.

"Gladly."
"기꺼이."

As soon as Pinocchio went / into the stable, / he spied a
피노키오가 가자마자 마구간 안으로, 작은 당나귀를

little Donkey / lying on a bed / of straw / in the corner
보았다 침대에 누워 있는 짚으로 만든 마구간 구석에.

of the stable. He was worn out / from hunger / and too
그는 지쳐 있었다 배고픔과

much work. After looking at him / a long time, / he
너무 고된 노동으로. 그를 살펴본 후 오랫동안,

said to himself: / "I know that Donkey! I have seen him
혼잣말을 했다: "저 당나귀를 알겠어! 전에 본 적 있어."

before."

And bending low over him, / he asked: / "Who are you?"
그리고 그에게 몸을 구부리며, 물었다: "넌 누구니?"

At this question, / the Donkey opened / weary, dying
이 질문에, 당나귀는 떴다 지치고, 죽어가는 눈을

eyes / and answered / in the same tongue: / "I am Lamp-
그리고 대답했다 그와 똑같은 말투로: "난 램프 심지야."

Wick."

Then he closed his eyes / and died.
그러더니 눈을 감고 죽었다.

"Oh, my poor Lamp-Wick," / said Pinocchio / in a faint
"오, 내 가련한 램프 심지," 피노키오가 말했다 희미한 목소리로,

voice, / as he wiped his eyes / with some straw / he had
눈물을 닦으며 짚으로

picked up / from the ground.
그가 집어 든 땅에서.

"Do you feel so sorry / for a little donkey / that has cost
"그렇게 슬프니   작은 당나귀 때문에   넌 대가를 치른 것도

you nothing?" / said the Farmer. "What should I do / ——I,
없으면서?   농부가 말했다.   "난 어떡해야 하니   — 나는,

/ who have paid my good money / for him?"
      큰 돈을 지불했는데   그걸 사려고?"

"But, / you see, he was my friend."
"하지만,   그는 내 친구였어요."

"Your friend?"
"네 친구라고?"

"A classmate of mine."
"학교 친구요."

"What," / shouted Farmer John, / bursting out laughing.
"뭐라고," 농부 존이 소리쳤다, 웃음을 터뜨리며.

"What! You had donkeys / in your school? How you
"맙소사! 당나귀도 있었니 너희 학교에는?

must have studied!"
참으로 열심히 공부했겠구나!"

The Marionette, / ashamed and hurt / by those words, /
꼭두각시는, 창피하고 상처를 받아서 그 말에,

did not answer, / but taking his glass of milk / returned
대답하지 않고, 우유 한 잔을 가지고

to his father.
아빠에게 돌아갔다.

From that day on, / for more than five months, /
그 날부터 쭉, 다섯 달이 넘는 시간 동안,

Pinocchio got up / every morning / just as dawn was
피노키오는 일어나서 매일 아침 막 동이 트자마자

breaking / and went to the farm / to draw water. And
농장에 갔다 물을 긷기 위해.

every day / he was given / a glass of warm milk / for his
그리고 매일 받아왔다 따뜻한 우유 한 컵을 불쌍하고

poor old father, / who grew stronger / and better / day by
나이든 아빠를 위해. 그리고 아빠는 더 튼튼해지고 나아졌다 날이 갈수록.

day. But / he was not satisfied with this. He learned / to
그러나 그는 여기에 만족하지 않았다. 그는 배웠다

make baskets / of reeds / and sold them. With the money
양동이를 만드는 법을 갈대로 그래서 그것들을 팔았다. 돈으로

/ he received, / he and his father were able to keep from
그가 받은, 그와 아빠는 굶지 않을 수 있었다.

starving.

Among other things, / he built a rolling chair, / strong
그 외에도, 그는 휠체어를 만들었다,

and comfortable, / to take his old father out / for an
강하고 편한, 아빠를 밖으로 데리고 나가기 위해 공기를 쐬기 위해

airing / on bright, sunny days.
화창하고, 햇빛 좋은 날에.

In the evening / the Marionette studied / by lamplight.
밤에   꼭두각시는 공부했다   램프 불을 밝혀.

With some of the money / he had earned, / he bought
돈의 일부로   그가 번,   그는 샀다

himself / a secondhand volume / that had a few pages
중고 책을   몇 페이지가 없어진,

missing, / and with that / he learned to read / in a very
그리고 그것을 갖고   읽는 법을 배웠다   아주 짧은 시간에.

short time. As far as writing was concerned, / he used
쓰기에 관해서는,   그는 긴 막대기를

a long stick / at one end / of which he had whittled /
사용했다   그 한쪽 끝에   깎아서 만든

a long, fine point. Ink he had none, / so he used the
길고, 가는 펜촉을.   잉크가 없어서,   과일즙을 사용했다

juice / of blackberries or cherries. Little by little / his
블랙베리나 체리의.   조금씩

diligence was rewarded. He succeeded, / not only in his
그의 근면함은 보상 받았다.   그는 성공했다,   공부뿐 아니라,

studies, / but also in his work, / and a day came / when
일에서도,   그리고 그 날이 왔다

he put enough money together / to keep his old father
충분한 돈을 모은   아빠를 모실 수 있는

/ comfortable and happy. Besides this, / he was able
편안하고 행복하게.   이것 말고도,   저축할 수 있었다

to save / the great amount of fifty pennies. With it / he
50페니의 거금을.   그 돈으로

wanted to buy himself / a new suit.
사고 싶었다   새 옷을.

One day / he said to his father:
어느 날   아빠에게 말했다:

---

burst out 버럭 소리를 지르다, 갑자기 ~하기 시작하다 | reed 갈대 | secondhand 중고의 | whittle (나무 등을)
깎아서 만들다 | diligence 근면, 성실 | reward 보상하다 | besides ~외에

"I am going to the market place / to buy myself a coat, /
"시장에 갈 거예요   내 외투를 사러,

a cap, / and a pair of shoes. When I come back / I'll be so
모자와,   신발 한 켤레도.   돌아올 땐   내가 너무 멋지게

dressed up, / you will think / I am a rich man."
차려 입어서,   생각하게 될 거예요   내가 부자라고."

He ran out of the house / and up the road to the village, /
그는 집을 뛰어나가   마을로 향하는 길로 갔다.

laughing and singing. Suddenly / he heard his name called,
웃으며 노래하며.   갑자기   그의 이름을 부르는 소리를 들었다.

/ and looking around / to see / whence the voice came, / he
주위를 둘러보다가   알아내려고 어디에서 그 목소리가 나는지.

noticed a large snail / crawling / out of some bushes.
커다란 달팽이를 보았다   기어 나오는   덤불에서.

"Don't you recognize me?" / said the Snail.
"날 모르겠니?"   달팽이가 말했다.

"Yes and no."
"알지도 모를지도."

"Do you remember the Snail / that lived / with the Fairy
"달팽이를 기억하니   살았던   하늘색 머리의 요정과?

with Azure Hair? Do you not remember / how she opened
                모르겠니   그녀가 어떻게 문을 열었는지

the door / for you / one night / and gave you something to
널 위해   어느 날 밤   네게 먹을 걸 주었던?"

eat?"

"I remember everything," / cried Pinocchio. "Answer me
"다 기억해,"   피노키오가 외쳤다.   "빨리 대답해 줘,

quickly, / pretty Snail, / where have you left my Fairy?
예쁜 달팽이야,   나의 요정을 어디에 두고 왔니?

What is she doing? Has she forgiven me? Does she
그녀는 뭘 하고 있니?   날 용서했니?   날 기억하니?

remember me? Does she still love me? Is she very far away
            여전히 날 사랑하니?   아주 멀리 있니

/ from here? May I see her?"
여기에서?   그녀를 만날 수 있을까?"

At all these questions, / tumbling out one after another, /
이 모든 질문에,   차례차례 쏟아져 나오는,

the Snail answered, / calm as ever:
달팽이는 대답했다,   조용하게:

"My dear Pinocchio, / the Fairy is lying ill / in a hospital."
"사랑하는 피노키오,   요정은 아파서 누워 있어   병원에."

"In a hospital?"
"병원에?"

"Yes, indeed. She has been stricken / with trouble and
"그래, 정말이야.   그녀는 겪었어   고난과 병마를,

illness, / and she hasn't a penny left / with which to buy a
         그래서 돈 한 푼 남아있지 않아   빵 한 조각 살만한."

bite of bread."

"Really? Oh, how sorry I am! My poor, dear little Fairy!
"정말이야?   오, 너무 안 됐어!   나의 불쌍한, 사랑하는 작은 요정!

If I had a million / I should run to her / with it! But I have
내가 돈이 많다면   그녀에게 달려 갈 텐데   그 돈을 갖고!

only fifty pennies. Here they are. I was just going / to buy
하지만 50페니밖에 없어.   여기 있어.   마침 가는 중이었어

some clothes. Here, take them, little Snail, / and give them
옷을 사러.   이걸 가져가, 작은 달팽이야,   그리고 나의 착한 요정

to my good Fairy."
에게 전해 주렴."

Key Expression 🎵

not only A but also B : A 뿐만 아니라 B도

not only A but also B는 'A 뿐만 아니라 B도'라는 의미를 가진 상관접속사로 also는 종종 생략되기도 합니다. 같은 의미로 as well as가 있는데 이때에는 A와 B의 위치가 반대가 된다는 사실에 유의하세요.

not only A but also B 구문이 주어로 사용될 때뒤에 오는 동사는 B에 인칭이나 수를 일치시켜야 합니다. 또한 이와 같은 상관 접속사에서 A와 B의 자리에는 명사-명사, 형용사-형용사, to 부정사-to 부정사 등과 같이 같은 형식의 말이 와야 합니다.

ex) He succeeded, not only in his studies, but also in his work.
    그는 공부 뿐만 아니라 일에 있어서도 성공했다.

dress up 옷을 갖춰 입다 | whence (~한) 곳에서 | crawl 기어가다 | tumble 쏟아지다

"What about the new clothes?"
"새 옷은 어쩌고?"

"What does that matter? I should like to sell these rags / I
"그게 뭐가 중요해?   난 이 헌 옷들도 팔고 싶어

have on / to help her more. Go, and hurry. Come back here
내가 입고 있는 그녀를 더 돕기 위해.   자, 서둘러.   여기로 다시 와 줘

/ within a couple of days / and I hope to have more money
며칠 내로   돈을 더 모을 수 있을 거야

/ for you! Until today / I have worked / for my father. Now
네게 줄!   오늘까지   난 일했어   우리 아빠를 위해.   이제

/ I shall have to work / for my mother also. Good-by, / and
일할 거야   우리 엄마를 위해서도.   안녕,

I hope to see you soon."
곧 다시 만나길."

The Snail, / much against her usual habit, / began to run /
달팽이는,   평소와 매우 다르게,   달리기 시작했다

like a lizard / under a summer sun.
도마뱀처럼   여름의 햇빛 아래.

When Pinocchio returned home, / his father asked him:
피노키오가 집으로 돌아왔을 때,   아빠가 물었다:

"And where is the new suit?"
"새 옷은 어디 있니?"

"I couldn't find one / to fit me. I shall have to look again /
"옷을 찾을 수 없었어요   나한테 맞는. 다시 찾아봐야겠어요

some other day."
다른 날."

That night, Pinocchio, / instead of going to bed / at ten
그 날 밤, 피노키오는,   잠자리에 들지 않고   열 시에

o'clock / waited until midnight, / and instead of making
자정까지 기다렸다,   그리고 8개의 바구니를 만드는 대신,

eight baskets, / he made sixteen.
그는 16개를 만들었다.

After that / he went to bed / and fell asleep. As he slept, /
그리고 나서   침대로 가서   잠들었다.   잠을 자는 동안,

he dreamed of his Fairy, / beautiful, smiling, and happy,
꿈에서 요정을 보았다,   아름답고, 웃고 있는, 그리고 행복한,

/ who kissed him / and said to him, / "Bravo, Pinocchio!
요정은 그에게 입을 맞추고   말했다,   "잘했어, 피노키오!

In reward for your kind heart, / I forgive you / for all your
네 친절한 마음에 대한 보상으로,   널 용서한다

old mischief. Boys / who love and take good care of their
네 모든 지난 잘못을.   아이들은   부모를 사랑하고 돌보는

parents / when they are old and sick, / deserve praise
부모가 늙고 병들었을 때,   칭찬을 받을 만해

/ even though they may not be held up / as models of
비록 높게 평가되지는 않더라도

obedience and good behavior. Keep on doing so well, / and
말 잘 듣고 착한 아이들의 모범으로.   계속 착하게 살렴,

you will be happy."
그러면 행복해질 거야."

At that very moment, / Pinocchio awoke / and opened
바로 그 순간,   피노키오는 잠에서 깨어   눈을 크게 떴다.

wide his eyes.

Key Expression ♥

even though : 비록 ~라 하더라도

even though는 '비록 ~라 하더라도'라는 의미의 양보구문을 이끄는 접속사입니다. 양보의 의미를 가진 though나 although를 강조하는 표현이지요. 비슷한 의미를 가진 even if와 혼동할 수 있는데 둘 사이에는 차이점이 있습니다. even if는 가정을 나타내는 if에 양보의 의미를 강조한 표현이지요. even though에는 기정 사실을 나타내는 직설법의 문장이, even if에는 사실의 반대를 가정하는 가정법의 문장이 오게 됩니다.

▶ Even if I had a million dollars~ → 조건/가정의 문장
▶ Even though I am a woman~ → 기존 사실인 문장

ex) Boys who love and take good care of their parents when they are old and sick, deserve praise even though they may not be held up as models of obedience and good behavior.
부모가 나이 들거나 아플 때 사랑하고 잘 돌보는 아이들은 말 잘 듣고 착한 아이의 모범으로 평가받지는 못하더라도 칭찬 받을 만하다.
Even if I were to meet them on the road, / what matter?
내가 길에서 그들을 만난다 해도, 뭐가 문제야?

---

lizard 도마뱀 | praise 칭찬 | hold up 추켜세우다

What was his surprise / and his joy / when, on looking
얼마나 놀라웠고   기뻤을까   자신을 보았을 때,

himself over, / he saw / that he was no longer a Marionette,
알았을 때   그는   더 이상 꼭두각시가 아닌 것을,

/ but that he had become a real live boy! He looked all
대신 진짜 살아있는 아이가 된 것을!   그는 주변을 둘러보았다

about him / and instead of the usual walls of straw, / he
짚으로 된 평소의 벽이 아니라,

found himself / in a beautifully furnished little room, / the
그는 있었다   아름답게 가구들로 꾸며진 작은 방에,

prettiest / he had ever seen. In a twinkling, / he jumped
가장 예쁜   지금까지 본 것 중에.   단숨에,   뛰어내려

down / from his bed / to look on the chair / standing near.
침대에서   의자 위를 보았다   근처에 있는.

There, / he found a new suit, / a new hat, / and a pair of
거기에는,   새 옷이 있었다,   새 모자와,   신발 한 켤레도.

shoes.

As soon as he was dressed, / he put his hands in his
옷을 입고 나서,   그는 주머니에 손을 넣어

pockets / and pulled out a little leather purse / on which
작은 가죽지갑을 꺼냈는데

were written the following words:
거기에는 다음과 같이 쓰여 있었다:

The Fairy with Azure Hair returns
하늘색 머리의 요정이 돌려주다

fifty pennies / to her dear Pinocchio
50페니를   그녀의 사랑하는 피노키오에게

with many thanks / for his kind heart.
매우 고마워하며   그의 착한 마음씨에.

The Marionette opened the purse / to find the money, / and
꼭두각시는 지갑을 열고   돈을 발견했다,

behold / — there were fifty gold coins!
그리고 보았다 — 금화 50개가 있었다!

Pinocchio ran / to the mirror. He hardly recognized
피노키오는 달려갔다   거울로.   좀처럼 자신을 알아볼 수 없었다.

himself. The bright face / of a tall boy / looked at him /
              똑똑해 보이는 얼굴이   키가 큰 아이의   그를 쳐다보았다

with wide-awake blue eyes, / dark brown hair / and happy,
완전히 잠에서 깬 파란 눈을 가진,   진한 갈색 머리와   그리고 행복하게,

smiling lips.
웃고 있는 입술을.

Surrounded / by so much splendor, / the Marionette
둘러싸여   엄청난 화려함에,   꼭두각시는 알 수 없었다

hardly knew / what he was doing. He rubbed his eyes /
           무엇을 하고 있는 건지.   그는 눈을 비비고

two or three times, / wondering / if he were still asleep /
두세 번,   의아해 하다가   자신이 여전히 잠자고 있는 건지

or awake / and decided / he must be awake.
깨어 있는 건지를   결론을 내렸다   깨어있는 게 틀림없다고.

Key Expression ✿

not A but B : A가 아니라 B
not A but B는 'A가 아니라 B'라는 의미의 상관접속사입니다. 마찬가지로 A
와 B에는 같은 형태의 단어나 구, 절이 와야 합니다. 이 구문이 주어로 쓰일 경우
에는 뒤에 오는 B에 수와 인칭을 일치시켜야 합니다.
또한 not A but B 구문은 'B~, not A'와 같이 사용되기도 합니다.

ex) He saw that he was no longer a Marionette, but that he had become a real
    live boy.
    그는 자신이 더 이상 꼭두각시가 아니라, 진짜 살아있는 아이가 되었다는 사실
    을 알았다.
    (→ no longer가 not의 의미를 쓰였으며 that절끼리 연결)
    Fancy his surprise when he saw / that it was not a hand, but a cat's paw.
    그것이 손이 아니라 고양이 발이었음을 알았을 때 그의 놀라움을 상상해 보세요.

wide awake 완전히 깨어 있는 | splendor 훌륭함, 화려함

"And where is Father?" / he cried suddenly. He ran / into
"그런데 아빠는 어디 계시지?" 그는 갑자기 외쳤다. 달려갔더니

the next room, / and there stood Geppetto, / grown years
옆 방으로, 제페토가 서 있었다. 몇 년은 젊어진 모습의

younger / overnight, / spick and span in his new clothes
밤새, 새 옷으로 말끔해지고,

/ and gay / as a lark in the morning. He was once more
명랑한 아침의 종달새만큼. 그는 다시 한 번 제페토 노인이 되

Mastro Geppetto, / the wood carver, / hard at work on a
었다. 나무조각가인, 사랑스러운 그림 액자를 열심히

lovely picture frame, / decorating it / with flowers and
만드는, 그것을 장식하면서 꽃과 잎으로,

leaves, / and heads of animals.
그리고 동물들의 머리로.

"Father, Father, / what has happened? Tell me / if you
"아빠, 아빠, 무슨 일이에요? 말해 주세요 할 수 있다면,"

can," / cried Pinocchio, / as he ran / and jumped / on his
피노키오가 외쳤다, 달려가면서 뛰어올라

Father's neck.
아빠의 목에.

"This sudden change / in our house / is all your doing, /
"이렇게 갑작스런 변화는 우리 집에 일어난 모두 네가 한 일이다.

my dear Pinocchio," / answered Geppetto.
사랑하는 피노키오야," 제페토가 말했다.

"What have I to do with it?"
"내가 무슨 일을 했나요?"

"Just this. When bad boys become good and kind, / they
"바로 이거야. 나쁜 아이가 착하고 친절해지면,

have the power / of making their homes / gay and new /
힘을 갖게 된다 집을 만들 수 있는 즐겁고 새롭게

with happiness."
행복으로."

spick and span 아주 깔끔한, 말끔한 | lark 종달새 | carver 조각가 | ridiculous 웃기는, 터무니없는

"I wonder / where the old Pinocchio of wood / has
"궁금해요   나무로 만든 옛날 피노키오는

hidden himself?"
어디에 숨었죠?"

"There he is," / answered Geppetto. And he pointed to a
"저기 있다."   제페토가 대답했다.   그는 커다란 꼭두각시를 가리켰다

large Marionette / leaning against a chair, / head turned
의자에 기대어 있는,   머리는 한쪽으로 돌아

to one side, / arms hanging limp, / and legs twisted /
가고,   팔은 힘없이 축 쳐진 채,   다리가 꼬여 있는

under him.
그 아래.

After a long, long look, / Pinocchio said to himself / with
오래, 오래 쳐다본 후,   피노키오는 중얼거렸다

great content:
크게 만족해 하며:

"How ridiculous / I was as a Marionette! And how happy
"이렇게 우스꽝스러웠구나   내가 꼭두각시였을 때!   그리고 난 너무나도 행복해,

I am, / now that I have become a real boy!"
       진짜 아이가 되었으니!"

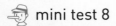 mini test 8

A. 다음 문장을 해석해 보세요.

(1) Poor Pinocchio pretended to be peaceful / and contented, / but he was far from that.
→

(2) The Cat, / after pretending to be blind / for so many years / had really lost / the sight of both eyes.
→

(3) I have only wanted to remind you / of the trick / you long ago played / upon me, / to teach you / that in this world of ours / we must be kind and courteous / to others.
→

(4) Boys / who love and take good care of their parents / when they are old and sick, / deserve praise / even though they may not be held up / as models of obedience and good behavior.
→

B. 다음 주어진 문구가 알맞은 문장이 되도록 순서를 맞춰 보세요.

(1) 이제 우리가 해야할 모든 일은 해변에 도착하는 거예요. 그리고 그건 쉬워요.
(we / do now / to get / have to / is / to the shore / All)
→ _____, and that is easy.

(2) 난 낮보다 밤에 더 잘 봐요.
(at night / see / by day / than / I / better)
→

(3) 네가 바로 내게 길을 가르쳐 준 사람이야.
(the one / are / showed / You / me / who / the way)
→

 Answer

A. (1) 불쌍한 피노키오는 침착하고 만족한 척 했지만, 전혀 그렇지 않았다. (2) 그 고양이는 너무 오랫동안 장님 행세를 한 후 정말로 두 눈의 시력을 잃었다. (3) 나는 단지 네가 오래 전에 내게 했던 그 장난을 상기 시키고 이 세상에서 사람들에게 친절하고 공손해야 한다는 것을 가르치고 싶었을 뿐이야. (4) 부모님이 늙

(4) 아마도 우린 타협을 할 수 있겠구나.
(can / we / to / Perhaps / terms / come)
→

C. 다음 주어진 문장이 본문의 내용과 맞으면 T, 틀리면 F에 동그라미 하세요.

(1) Pinocchio and his father succedded in escaping from the horrible sea monster.
[T / F]

(2) Pinocchio could met his friend Lamp-Wick again, so he was very happy.
[T / F]

(3) Pinocchio succeeded, not only in his studies, but also in his work.
[T / F]

(4) Finally, Pinocchio was forgiven all your old mischief and became a real boy.
[T / F]

D. 의미가 서로 비슷한 말끼리 연결해 보세요.

(1) shiver   ▶   ◀ ① permanent
(2) eternal   ▶   ◀ ② shake
(3) sly   ▶   ◀ ③ fall
(4) tumble   ▶   ◀ ④ cunning

Answer

고 병들었을 때 사랑하고 잘 돌보는 아이들은 비록 말잘듣고 착한 행동의 모범으로써 높이 평가받지는 않을지 몰라고 칭찬 받아 마땅해. | B. (1) All we have to do now is to get to the shore (2) I see better at night than by day (3) You are the one who showed me the way (4) Perhaps we can come to terms. | C. (1) What good times they had, to be sure. (2) I had a little girl once; with eyes like these. (3) I wish someone would write to me so! (4) Please tell the young ladies what I say. | D. (1) ② (2) ① (3) ④ (4) ③

217

The Adventures of Pinocchio를
다시 읽어 보세요.

1

How it happened that Mastro Cherry, carpenter, found a piece of wood that wept
and laughed like a child.

Centuries ago there lived ——

"A king!" my little readers will say immediately. No, children, you are mistaken.
Once upon a time there was a piece of wood. It was not an expensive piece of
wood. Far from it. Just a common block of firewood, one of those thick, solid logs
that are put on the fire in winter to make cold rooms cozy and warm.

I do not know how this really happened, yet the fact remains that one fine day
this piece of wood found itself in the shop of an old carpenter. His real name was
Mastro Antonio, but everyone called him Mastro Cherry, for the tip of his nose
was so round and red and shiny that it looked like a ripe cherry.

As soon as he saw that piece of wood, Mastro Cherry was filled with joy.
Rubbing his hands together happily, he mumbled half to himself:

"This has come in the nick of time. I shall use it to make the leg of a table."

He grasped the hatchet quickly to peel off the bark and shape the wood.

But as he was about to give it the first blow, he stood still with arm uplifted, for he
had heard a wee, little voice say in a beseeching tone:

"Please be careful! Do not hit me so hard!"

What a look of surprise shone on Mastro Cherry's face! His funny face became
still funnier.

He turned frightened eyes about the room to find out where that wee, little voice
had come from and he saw no one! He looked under the bench——no one! He
peeped inside the closet——no one! He searched among the shavings——no one!
He opened the door to look up and down the street——and still no one!

"Oh, I see!" he then said, laughing and scratching his Wig. "It can easily be seen
that I only thought I heard the tiny voice say the words!

Well, well——to work once more."

He struck a most solemn blow upon the piece of wood.

"Oh, oh! You hurt!" cried the same far-away little voice.

Mastro Cherry grew dumb, his eyes popped out of his head, his mouth opened
wide, and his tongue hung down on his chin.

As soon as he regained the use of his senses, he said, trembling and stuttering
from fright:

"Where did that voice come from, when there is no one around? Might it be that
this piece of wood has learned to weep and cry like a child? I can hardly believe
it. Here it is —— a piece of common firewood, good only to burn in the stove, the
same as any other. Yet —— might someone be hidden in it? If so, the worse for
him. I'll fix him!"

With these words, he grabbed the log with both hands and started to knock it about unmercifully. He threw it to the floor, against the walls of the room, and even up to the ceiling.

He listened for the tiny voice to moan and cry. He waited two minutes —— nothing; five minutes —— nothing; ten minutes —— nothing.

"Oh, I see," he said, trying bravely to laugh and ruffling up his wig with his hand. "It can easily be seen I only imagined I heard the tiny voice! Well, well —— to work once more!"

The poor fellow was scared half to death, so he tried to sing a gay song in order to gain courage.

He set aside the hatchet and picked up the plane to make the wood smooth and even, but as he drew it to and fro, he heard the same tiny voice.

This time it giggled as it spoke:

"Stop it! Oh, stop it! Ha, ha, ha! You tickle my stomach."

This time poor Mastro Cherry fell as if shot. When he opened his eyes, he found himself sitting on the floor.

His face had changed; fright had turned even the tip of his nose from red to deepest purple.

2

Mastro Cherry gives the piece of wood to his friend Geppetto, who takes it to make himself a Marionette that will dance, fence, and turn somersaults.

In that very instant, a loud knock sounded on the door. "Come in," said the carpenter, not having an atom of strength left with which to stand up.

At the words, the door opened and a dapper little old man came in.

His name was Geppetto, but to the boys of the neighborhood he was Polendina,*(Cornmeal mush) on account of the wig he always wore which was just the color of yellow corn.

Geppetto had a very bad temper. Woe to the one who called him Polendina! He became as wild as a beast and no one could soothe him.

"Good day, Mastro Antonio," said Geppetto. "What are you doing on the floor?"

"I am teaching the ants their A B C's."

"Good luck to you!"

"What brought you here, friend Geppetto?"

"My legs. And it may flatter you to know, Mastro Antonio, that I have come to you to beg for a favor."

"Here I am, at your service," answered the carpenter, raising himself on to his knees.

"This morning a fine idea came to me."

"Let's hear it."

"I thought of making myself a beautiful wooden Marionette. It must be wonderful, one that will be able to dance, fence, and turn somersaults. With it I intend to go around the world, to earn my crust of bread and cup of wine. What do you think of it?"

"Bravo, Polendina!" cried the same tiny voice which came from no one knew where.

On hearing himself called Polendina, Mastro Geppetto turned the color of a red pepper and, facing the carpenter, said to him angrily:

"Why do you insult me?"

"Who is insulting you?"

"You called me Polendina."

"I did not."

"I suppose you think I did! Yet I KNOW it was you."

"No!"

"Yes!"

"No!"

"Yes!"

And growing angrier each moment, they went from words to blows, and finally began to scratch and bite and slap each other.

When the fight was over, Mastro Antonio had Geppetto's yellow wig in his hands and Geppetto found the carpenter's curly wig in his mouth.

"Give me back my wig!" shouted Mastro Antonio in a surly voice.

"You return mine and we'll be friends."

The two little old men, each with his own wig back on his own head, shook hands and swore to be good friends for the rest of their lives.

"Well then, Mastro Geppetto," said the carpenter, to show he bore him no ill will, "what is it you want?"

"I want a piece of wood to make a Marionette. Will you give it to me?"

Mastro Antonio, very glad indeed, went immediately to his bench to get the piece of wood which had frightened him so much. But as he was about to give it to his friend, with a violent jerk it slipped out of his hands and hit against poor Geppetto's thin legs.

"Ah! Is this the gentle way, Mastro Antonio, in which you make your gifts? You have made me almost lame!"

"I swear to you I did not do it!"

"It was I, of course!"

"It's the fault of this piece of wood."

"You're right; but remember you were the one to throw it at my legs."

"I did not throw it!"

"Liar!"

"Geppetto, do not insult me or I shall call you Polendina."

"Idiot."

"Polendina!"

"Donkey!"

"Polendina!"

"Ugly monkey!"

"Polendina!"

On hearing himself called Polendina for the third time, Geppetto lost his head with rage and threw himself upon the carpenter. Then and there they gave each other a sound thrashing.

After this fight, Mastro Antonio had two more scratches on his nose, and Geppetto had two buttons missing from his coat. Thus having settled their accounts, they shook hands and swore to be good friends for the rest of their lives. Then Geppetto took the fine piece of wood, thanked Mastro Antonio, and limped away toward home.

 3

As soon as he gets home, Geppetto fashions the Marionette and calls it Pinocchio. The first pranks of the Marionette.

Little as Geppetto's house was, it was neat and comfortable. It was a small room on the ground floor, with a tiny window under the stairway.

The furniture could not have been much simpler: a very old chair, a rickety old bed, and a tumble-down table. A fireplace full of burning logs was painted on the wall opposite the door. Over the fire, there was painted a pot full of something which kept boiling happily away and sending up clouds of what looked like real steam.

As soon as he reached home, Geppetto took his tools and began to cut and shape the wood into a Marionette.

"What shall I call him?" he said to himself. "I think I'll call him PINOCCHIO. This name will make his fortune. I knew a whole family of Pinocchi once —— Pinocchio the father, Pinocchia the mother, and Pinocchi the children —— and they were all lucky. The richest of them begged for his living."

After choosing the name for his Marionette, Geppetto set seriously to work to make the hair, the forehead, the eyes. Fancy his surprise when he noticed that these eyes moved and then stared fixedly at him.

Geppetto, seeing this, felt insulted and said in a grieved tone:

"Ugly wooden eyes, why do you stare so?"

There was no answer.

After the eyes, Geppetto made the nose, which began to stretch as soon as finished. It stretched and stretched and stretched till it became so long, it seemed endless.

Poor Geppetto kept cutting it and cutting it, but the more he cut, the longer grew that impertinent nose. In despair he let it alone.

Next he made the mouth.

No sooner was it finished than it began to laugh and poke fun at him.

"Stop laughing!" said Geppetto angrily; but he might as well have spoken to the wall.

"Stop laughing, I say!" he roared in a voice of thunder.

The mouth stopped laughing, but it stuck out a long tongue.

Not wishing to start an argument, Geppetto made believe he saw nothing and went on with his work. After the mouth, he made the chin, then the neck, the shoulders, the stomach, the arms, and the hands.

As he was about to put the last touches on the finger tips, Geppetto felt his wig being pulled off. He glanced up and what did he see? His yellow wig was in the Marionette's hand. "Pinocchio, give me my wig!"

But instead of giving it back, Pinocchio put it on his own head, which was half swallowed up in it.

At that unexpected trick, Geppetto became very sad and downcast, more so than he had ever been before.

"Pinocchio, you wicked boy!" he cried out. "You are not yet finished, and you start out by being impudent to your poor old father. Very bad, my son, very bad!" And he wiped away a tear.

The legs and feet still had to be made. As soon as they were done, Geppetto felt a sharp kick on the tip of his nose.

"I deserve it!" he said to himself. "I should have thought of this before I made him. Now it's too late!"

He took hold of the Marionette under the arms and put him on the floor to teach him to walk.

Pinocchio's legs were so stiff that he could not move them, and Geppetto held his hand and showed him how to put out one foot after the other.

When his legs were limbered up, Pinocchio started walking by himself and ran all around the room. He came to the open door, and with one leap he was out into the street. Away he flew!

Poor Geppetto ran after him but was unable to catch him, for Pinocchio ran in leaps and bounds, his two wooden feet, as they beat on the stones of the street, making as much noise as twenty peasants in wooden shoes.

"Catch him! Catch him!" Geppetto kept shouting. But the people in the street, seeing a wooden Marionette running like the wind, stood still to stare and to laugh until they cried.

At last, by sheer luck, a Carabineer*(A military policeman) happened along, who, hearing all that noise, thought that it might be a runaway colt, and stood bravely in the middle of the street, with legs wide apart, firmly resolved to stop it and prevent any trouble.

Pinocchio saw the Carabineer from afar and tried his best to escape between the legs of the big fellow, but without success.

The Carabineer grabbed him by the nose (it was an extremely long one and seemed made on purpose for that very thing) and returned him to Mastro Geppetto.

The little old man wanted to pull Pinocchio's ears. Think how he felt when, upon searching for them, he discovered that he had forgotten to make them!

All he could do was to seize Pinocchio by the back of the neck and take him home. As he was doing so, he shook him two or three times and said to him angrily:

"We're going home now. When we get home, then we'll settle this matter!"

Pinocchio, on hearing this, threw himself on the ground and refused to take another step. One person after another gathered around the two.

Some said one thing, some another.

"Poor Marionette," called out a man. "I am not surprised he doesn't want to go home. Geppetto, no doubt, will beat him unmercifully, he is so mean and cruel!"

"Geppetto looks like a good man," added another, "but with boys he's a real tyrant. If we leave that poor Marionette in his hands he may tear him to pieces!"

They said so much that, finally, the Carabineer ended matters by setting Pinocchio at liberty and dragging Geppetto to prison. The poor old fellow did not know how to defend himself, but wept and wailed like a child and said between his sobs:

"Ungrateful boy! To think I tried so hard to make you a well-behaved Marionette! I deserve it, however! I should have given the matter more thought."

What happened after this is an almost unbelievable story, but you may read it, dear children, in the chapters that follow.

 4

Pinocchio falls asleep with his feet on a foot warmer, and awakens the next day with his feet all burned off.

Pinocchio hated the dark street, but he was so hungry that, in spite of it, he ran out of the house. The night was pitch black. It thundered, and bright flashes of lightning now and again shot across the sky, turning it into a sea of fire. An angry wind blew cold and raised dense clouds of dust, while the trees shook and moaned in a weird way.

Pinocchio was greatly afraid of thunder and lightning, but the hunger he felt was far greater than his fear. In a dozen leaps and bounds, he came to the village, tired out, puffing like a whale, and with tongue hanging.

The whole village was dark and deserted. The stores were closed, the doors, the windows. In the streets, not even a dog could be seen. It seemed the Village of the Dead.

Pinocchio, in desperation, ran up to a doorway, threw himself upon the bell, and pulled it wildly, saying to himself: "Someone will surely answer that!"

He was right. An old man in a nightcap opened the window and looked out. He called down angrily:

"What do you want at this hour of night?"

"Will you be good enough to give me a bit of bread? I am hungry."

"Wait a minute and I'll come right back," answered the old fellow, thinking he had to deal with one of those boys who love to roam around at night ringing people's bells while they are peacefully asleep.

After a minute or two, the same voice cried:

"Get under the window and hold out your hat!"

Pinocchio had no hat, but he managed to get under the window just in time to feel a shower of ice-cold water pour down on his poor wooden head, his shoulders, and over his whole body.

He returned home as wet as a rag, and tired out from weariness and hunger.

As he no longer had any strength left with which to stand, he sat down on a little stool and put his two feet on the stove to dry them.

There he fell asleep, and while he slept, his wooden feet began to burn.

Slowly, very slowly, they blackened and turned to ashes.

Pinocchio snored away happily as if his feet were not his own. At dawn he opened his eyes just as a loud knocking sounded at the door.

"Who is it?" he called, yawning and rubbing his eyes.

"It is I," answered a voice.

It was the voice of Geppetto.

 5

Geppetto returns home and gives his own breakfast to the Marionette

The poor Marionette, who was still half asleep, had not yet found out that his two feet were burned and gone. As soon as he heard his Father's voice, he jumped up from his seat to open the door, but, as he did so, he staggered and fell headlong to the floor.

In falling, he made as much noise as a sack of wood falling from the fifth story of a house.

"Open the door for me!" Geppetto shouted from the street.

"Father, dear Father, I can't," answered the Marionette in despair, crying and rolling on the floor.

"Why can't you?"

"Because someone has eaten my feet."

"And who has eaten them?"

"The cat," answered Pinocchio, seeing that little animal busily playing with some shavings in the corner of the room.

"Open! I say," repeated Geppetto, "or I'll give you a sound whipping when I get in."

"Father, believe me, I can't stand up. Oh, dear! Oh, dear! I shall have to walk on my knees all my life."

Geppetto, thinking that all these tears and cries were only other pranks of the Marionette, climbed up the side of the house and went in through the window.

At first he was very angry, but on seeing Pinocchio stretched out on the floor and really without feet, he felt very sad and sorrowful. Picking him up from the floor, he fondled and caressed him, talking to him while the tears ran down his cheeks:

"My little Pinocchio, my dear little Pinocchio! How did you burn your feet?"

"I don't know, Father, but believe me, the night has been a terrible one and I shall remember it as long as I live. The thunder was so noisy and the lightning so bright —— and I was hungry. And then the Talking Cricket said to me, 'You deserve it; you were bad;' and I said to him, 'Careful, Cricket;' and he said to me, 'You are a Marionette and you have a wooden head;' and I threw the hammer at him and killed him. It was his own fault, for I didn't want to kill him. And I put the pan on the coals, but the Chick flew away and said, 'I'll see you again! Remember me to the family.' And my hunger grew, and I went out, and the old man with a nightcap looked out of the window and threw water on me, and I came home and put my feet on the stove to dry them because I was still hungry, and I fell asleep and now my feet are gone but my hunger isn't! Oh! —— Oh! —— Oh!" And poor Pinocchio began to scream and cry so loudly that he could be heard for miles around.

Geppetto, who had understood nothing of all that jumbled talk, except that the Marionette was hungry, felt sorry for him, and pulling three pears out of his pocket, offered them to him, saying:

"These three pears were for my breakfast, but I give them to you gladly. Eat them and stop weeping."

"If you want me to eat them, please peel them for me."

"Peel them?" asked Geppetto, very much surprised. "I should never have thought, dear boy of mine, that you were so dainty and fussy about your food. Bad, very bad! In this world, even as children, we must accustom ourselves to eat of everything, for we never know what life may hold in store for us!"

"You may be right," answered Pinocchio, "but I will not eat the pears if they are not peeled. I don't like them."

And good old Geppetto took out a knife, peeled the three pears, and put the skins in a row on the table.

Pinocchio ate one pear in a twinkling and started to throw the core away, but Geppetto held his arm.

"Oh, no, don't throw it away! Everything in this world may be of some use!"

"But the core I will not eat!" cried Pinocchio in an angry tone.

"Who knows?" repeated Geppetto calmly.

And later the three cores were placed on the table next to the skins.

Pinocchio had eaten the three pears, or rather devoured them. Then he yawned deeply, and wailed:

"I'm still hungry."

"But I have no more to give you."

"Really, nothing —— nothing?"

"I have only these three cores and these skins."

"Very well, then," said Pinocchio, "if there is nothing else I'll eat them."

At first he made a wry face, but, one after another, the skins and the cores disappeared.

"Ah! Now I feel fine!" he said after eating the last one.

"You see," observed Geppetto, "that I was right when I told you that one must not be too fussy and too dainty about food. My dear, we never know what life may have in store for us!"

 6

Geppetto makes Pinocchio a new pair of feet, and sells his coat to buy him an A-B-C book.

The Marionette, as soon as his hunger was appeased, started to grumble and cry that he wanted a new pair of feet.

But Mastro Geppetto, in order to punish him for his mischief, let him alone the whole morning. After dinner he said to him:

"Why should I make your feet over again? To see you run away from home once more?"

"I promise you," answered the Marionette, sobbing, "that from now on I'll be good —— "

"Boys always promise that when they want something," said Geppetto.

"I promise to go to school every day, to study, and to succeed —— "

"Boys always sing that song when they want their own will."

"But I am not like other boys! I am better than all of them and I always tell the truth. I promise you, Father, that I'll learn a trade, and I'll be the comfort and staff of your old age."

Geppetto, though trying to look very stern, felt his eyes fill with tears and his heart soften when he saw Pinocchio so unhappy. He said no more, but taking his tools and two pieces of wood, he set to work diligently.

In less than an hour the feet were finished, two slender, nimble little feet, strong and quick, modeled as if by an artist's hands.

"Close your eyes and sleep!" Geppetto then said to the Marionette.

Pinocchio closed his eyes and pretended to be asleep, while Geppetto stuck on the two feet with a bit of glue melted in an eggshell, doing his work so well that the joint could hardly be seen.

As soon as the Marionette felt his new feet, he gave one leap from the table and started to skip and jump around, as if he had lost his head from very joy.

"To show you how grateful I am to you, Father, I'll go to school now. But to go to school I need a suit of clothes."

Geppetto did not have a penny in his pocket, so he made his son a little suit of flowered paper, a pair of shoes from the bark of a tree, and a tiny cap from a bit of dough.

Pinocchio ran to look at himself in a bowl of water, and he felt so happy that he said proudly:

"Now I look like a gentleman."

"Truly," answered Geppetto. "But remember that fine clothes do not make the man unless they be neat and clean."

"Very true," answered Pinocchio, "but, in order to go to school, I still need something very important."

"What is it?"

"An A-B-C book."

"To be sure! But how shall we get it?"

"That's easy. We'll go to a bookstore and buy it."

"And the money?"

"I have none."

"Neither have I," said the old man sadly.

Pinocchio, although a happy boy always, became sad and downcast at these words. When poverty shows itself, even mischievous boys understand what it means.

"What does it matter, after all?" cried Geppetto all at once, as he jumped up from his chair. Putting on his old coat, full of darns and patches, he ran out of the house without another word.

After a while he returned. In his hands he had the A-B-C book for his son, but the old coat was gone. The poor fellow was in his shirt sleeves and the day was cold.

"Where's your coat, Father?"

"I have sold it."

"Why did you sell your coat?"

"It was too warm."

Pinocchio understood the answer in a twinkling, and, unable to restrain his tears, he jumped on his father's neck and kissed him over and over.

7

Pinocchio sells his A-B-C book to pay his way into the Marionette Theater.

See Pinocchio hurrying off to school with his new A-B-C book under his arm! As he walked along, his brain was busy planning hundreds of wonderful things, building hundreds of castles in the air. Talking to himself, he said:

"In school today, I'll learn to read, tomorrow to write, and the day after tomorrow I'll do arithmetic. Then, clever as I am, I can earn a lot of money. With the very first pennies I make, I'll buy Father a new cloth coat. Cloth, did I say? No, it shall be of gold and silver with diamond buttons. That poor man certainly deserves it; for, after all,

isn't he in his shirt sleeves because he was good enough to buy a book for me? On this cold day, too! Fathers are indeed good to their children!"

As he talked to himself, he thought he heard sounds of pipes and drums coming from a distance: pi-pi-pi, pi-pi-pi···zum, zum, zum, zum.

He stopped to listen. Those sounds came from a little street that led to a small village along the shore.

"What can that noise be? What a nuisance that I have to go to school! Otherwise···"

There he stopped, very much puzzled. He felt he had to make up his mind for either one thing or another. Should he go to school, or should he follow the pipes?

"Today I'll follow the pipes, and tomorrow I'll go to school. There's always plenty of time to go to school," decided the little rascal at last, shrugging his shoulders.

No sooner said than done. He started down the street, going like the wind. On he ran, and louder grew the sounds of pipe and drum: pi-pi-pi, pi-pi-pi, pi-pi-pi ··· zum, zum, zum, zum.

Suddenly, he found himself in a large square, full of people standing in front of a little wooden building painted in brilliant colors.

"What is that house?" Pinocchio asked a little boy near him.

"Read the sign and you'll know."

"I'd like to read, but somehow I can't today."

"Oh, really? Then I'll read it to you. Know, then, that written in letters of fire I see the words: GREAT MARIONETTE THEATER.

"When did the show start?"

"It is starting now."

"And how much does one pay to get in?"

"Four pennies."

Pinocchio, who was wild with curiosity to know what was going on inside, lost all his pride and said to the boy shamelessly:

"Will you give me four pennies until tomorrow?"

"I'd give them to you gladly," answered the other, poking fun at him, "but just now I can't give them to you."

"For the price of four pennies, I'll sell you my coat."

"If it rains, what shall I do with a coat of flowered paper? I could not take it off again."

"Do you want to buy my shoes?"

"They are only good enough to light a fire with."

"What about my hat?"

"Fine bargain, indeed! A cap of dough! The mice might come and eat it from my head!"

Pinocchio was almost in tears. He was just about to make one last offer, but he lacked the courage to do so. He hesitated, he wondered, he could not make up his mind. At last he said:

"Will you give me four pennies for the book?"

"I am a boy and I buy nothing from boys," said the little fellow with far more common sense than the Marionette.

"I'll give you four pennies for your A-B-C book," said a ragpicker who stood by. Then and there, the book changed hands. And to think that poor old Geppetto sat at home in his shirt sleeves, shivering with cold, having sold his coat to buy that little book for his son!

 8

The Marionettes recognize their brother Pinocchio, and greet him with loud cheers; but the Director, Fire Eater, happens along and poor Pinocchio almost loses his life.

Quick as a flash, Pinocchio disappeared into the Marionette Theater. And then something happened which almost caused a riot.

The curtain was up and the performance had started.

Harlequin and Pulcinella were reciting on the stage and, as usual, they were threatening each other with sticks and blows.

The theater was full of people, enjoying the spectacle and laughing till they cried at the antics of the two Marionettes.

The play continued for a few minutes, and then suddenly, without any warning, Harlequin stopped talking. Turning toward the audience, he pointed to the rear of the orchestra, yelling wildly at the same time:

"Look, look! Am I asleep or awake? Or do I really see Pinocchio there?"

"Yes, yes! It is Pinocchio!" screamed Pulcinella.

"It is! It is!" shrieked Signora Rosaura, peeking in from the side of the stage.

"It is Pinocchio! It is Pinocchio!" yelled all the Marionettes, pouring out of the wings. "It is Pinocchio. It is our brother Pinocchio! Hurrah for Pinocchio!"

"Pinocchio, come up to me!" shouted Harlequin. "Come to the arms of your wooden brothers!"

At such a loving invitation, Pinocchio, with one leap from the back of the orchestra, found himself in the front rows. With another leap, he was on the orchestra leader's head. With a third, he landed on the stage.

It is impossible to describe the shrieks of joy, the warm embraces, the knocks, and the friendly greetings with which that strange company of dramatic actors and actresses received Pinocchio.

It was a heart-rending spectacle, but the audience, seeing that the play had stopped, became angry and began to yell:

"The play, the play, we want the play!"

The yelling was of no use, for the Marionettes, instead of going on with their act, made twice as much racket as before, and, lifting up Pinocchio on their shoulders, carried him around the stage in triumph.

At that very moment, the Director came out of his room. He had such a fearful appearance that one look at him would fill you with horror. His beard was as black as pitch, and so long that it reached from his chin down to his feet. His mouth was as wide as an oven, his teeth like yellow fangs, and his eyes, two glowing red coals. In his huge, hairy hands, a long whip, made of green snakes and black cats' tails twisted together, swished through the air in a dangerous way.

At the unexpected apparition, no one dared even to breathe. One could almost hear a fly go by. Those poor Marionettes, one and all, trembled like leaves in a storm.

"Why have you brought such excitement into my theater?" the huge fellow asked Pinocchio with the voice of an ogre suffering with a cold.

"Believe me, your Honor, the fault was not mine."

"Enough! Be quiet! I'll take care of you later."

As soon as the play was over, the Director went to the kitchen, where a fine big lamb was slowly turning on the spit. More wood was needed to finish cooking it. He called Harlequin and Pulcinella and said to them:

"Bring that Marionette to me! He looks as if he were made of well-seasoned wood. He'll make a fine fire for this spit."

Harlequin and Pulcinella hesitated a bit. Then, frightened by a look from their master, they left the kitchen to obey him. A few minutes later they returned, carrying poor Pinocchio, who was wriggling and squirming like an eel and crying pitifully:

"Father, save me! I don't want to die! I don't want to die!"

 9

Fire Eater gives Pinocchio five gold pieces for his father, Geppetto; but the Marionette meets a Fox and a Cat and follows them.

The next day Fire Eater called Pinocchio aside and asked him:

"What is your father's name?"

"Geppetto."

"And what is his trade?"

"He's a wood carver."

"Does he earn much?"

"He earns so much that he never has a penny in his pockets. Just think that, in order to buy me an A-B-C book for school, he had to sell the only coat he owned, a coat so full of darns and patches that it was a pity."

"Poor fellow! I feel sorry for him. Here, take these five gold pieces. Go, give them to him with my kindest regards."

Pinocchio, as may easily be imagined, thanked him a thousand times. He kissed each Marionette in turn, even the officers, and, beside himself with joy, set out on his homeward journey.

He had gone barely half a mile when he met a lame Fox and a blind Cat, walking together like two good friends. The lame Fox leaned on the Cat, and the blind Cat let the Fox lead him along.

"Good morning, Pinocchio," said the Fox, greeting him courteously.

"How do you know my name?" asked the Marionette.

"I know your father well."

"Where have you seen him?"

"I saw him yesterday standing at the door of his house."

"And what was he doing?"

"He was in his shirt sleeves trembling with cold."

"Poor Father! But, after today, God willing, he will suffer no longer."

"Why?"

"Because I have become a rich man."

"You, a rich man?" said the Fox, and he began to laugh out loud. The Cat was laughing also, but tried to hide it by stroking his long whiskers.

"There is nothing to laugh at," cried Pinocchio angrily. "I am very sorry to make your mouth water, but these, as you know, are five new gold pieces."

And he pulled out the gold pieces which Fire Eater had given him.

At the cheerful tinkle of the gold, the Fox unconsciously held out his paw that was supposed to be lame, and the Cat opened wide his two eyes till they looked like live coals, but he closed them again so quickly that Pinocchio did not notice.

"And may I ask," inquired the Fox, "what you are going to do with all that money?"

"First of all," answered the Marionette, "I want to buy a fine new coat for my father, a coat of gold and silver with diamond buttons; after that, I'll buy an A-B-C book for myself."

"For yourself?"

"For myself. I want to go to school and study hard."

"Look at me," said the Fox. "For the silly reason of wanting to study, I have lost a paw."

"Look at me," said the Cat. "For the same foolish reason, I have lost the sight of both eyes."

At that moment, a Blackbird, perched on the fence along the road, called out sharp and clear:

"Pinocchio, do not listen to bad advice. If you do, you'll be sorry!"

Poor little Blackbird! If he had only kept his words to himself! In the twinkling of an eyelid, the Cat leaped on him, and ate him, feathers and all.

After eating the bird, he cleaned his whiskers, closed his eyes, and became blind once more.

"Poor Blackbird!" said Pinocchio to the Cat. "Why did you kill him?"

"I killed him to teach him a lesson. He talks too much. Next time he will keep his words to himself."

By this time the three companions had walked a long distance. Suddenly, the Fox stopped in his tracks and, turning to the Marionette, said to him:

"Do you want to double your gold pieces?"

"What do you mean?"

"Do you want one hundred, a thousand, two thousand gold pieces for your miserable five?"

"Yes, but how?"

"The way is very easy. Instead of returning home, come with us."

"And where will you take me?"

"To the City of Simple Simons."

Pinocchio thought a while and then said firmly:

"No, I don't want to go. Home is near, and I'm going where Father is waiting for me. How unhappy he must be that I have not yet returned! I have been a bad son, and the Talking Cricket was right when he said that a disobedient boy cannot be happy in this world. I have learned this at my own expense. Even last night in the theater, when Fire Eater···

Brrrr!!!!! The shivers run up and down my back at the mere thought of it."

"Well, then," said the Fox, "if you really want to go home, go ahead, but you'll be sorry."

"You'll be sorry," repeated the Cat.

"Think well, Pinocchio, you are turning your back on Dame Fortune."

"On Dame Fortune," repeated the Cat.

"Tomorrow your five gold pieces will be two thousand!"

"Two thousand!" repeated the Cat.

"But how can they possibly become so many?" asked Pinocchio wonderingly.

"I'll explain," said the Fox. "You must know that, just outside the City of Simple Simons, there is a blessed field called the Field of Wonders.

In this field you dig a hole and in the hole you bury a gold piece.

After covering up the hole with earth you water it well, sprinkle a bit of salt on it, and go to bed. During the night, the gold piece sprouts, grows, blossoms, and next morning you find a beautiful tree, that is loaded with gold pieces."

"So that if I were to bury my five gold pieces," cried Pinocchio with growing wonder, "next morning I should find —— how many?"

"It is very simple to figure out," answered the Fox. "Why, you can figure it on your fingers! Granted that each piece gives you five hundred, multiply five hundred by five. Next morning you will find twenty-five hundred new, sparkling gold pieces."

"Fine! Fine!" cried Pinocchio, dancing about with joy. "And as soon as I have them, I shall keep two thousand for myself and the other five hundred I'll give to you two."

"A gift for us?" cried the Fox, pretending to be insulted. "Why, of course not!"

"Of course not!" repeated the Cat.

"We do not work for gain," answered the Fox. "We work only to enrich others."

"To enrich others!" repeated the Cat.

"What good people," thought Pinocchio to himself. And forgetting his father, the new coat, the A-B-C book, and all his good resolutions, he said to the Fox and to the Cat:

"Let us go. I am with you."

 10

Pinocchio, not having listened to the good advice of the Talking Cricket, falls into the hands of the Assassins.

"Dear, oh, dear! When I come to think of it," said the Marionette to himself, as he once more set out on his journey, "we boys are really very unlucky. Everybody scolds us, everybody gives us advice, everybody warns us. If we were to allow it, everyone would try to be father and mother to us; everyone, even the Talking Cricket. Take me, for example.

Just because I would not listen to that bothersome Cricket, who knows how many misfortunes may be awaiting me! Assassins indeed! At least I have never believed in them, nor ever will. To speak sensibly, I think assassins have been invented by fathers and mothers to frighten children who want to run away at night. And then, even if I were to meet them on the road, what matter? I'll just run up to them, and say, 'Well, signori, what do you want? Remember that you can't fool with me! Run along and mind your business.' At such a speech, I can almost see those poor fellows running like the wind. But in case they don't run away, I can always run myself···"

Pinocchio was not given time to argue any longer, for he thought he heard a slight rustle among the leaves behind him.

He turned to look and behold, there in the darkness stood two big black shadows, wrapped from head to foot in black sacks. The two figures leaped toward him as softly as if they were ghosts.

"Here they come!" Pinocchio said to himself, and, not knowing where to hide the gold pieces, he stuck all four of them under his tongue.

He tried to run away, but hardly had he taken a step, when he felt his arms grasped and heard two horrible, deep voices say to him: "Your money or your life!"

On account of the gold pieces in his mouth, Pinocchio could not say a word, so he tried with head and hands and body to show, as best he could, that he was only a poor Marionette without a penny in his pocket.

"Come, come, less nonsense, and out with your money!" cried the two thieves in threatening voices.

Once more, Pinocchio's head and hands said, "I haven't a penny."

"Out with that money or you're a dead man," said the taller of the two Assassins.

"Dead man," repeated the other.

"And after having killed you, we will kill your father also."

"Your father also!"

"No, no, no, not my Father!" cried Pinocchio, wild with terror; but as he screamed, the gold pieces tinkled together in his mouth.

"Ah, you rascal! So that's the game! You have the money hidden under your tongue. Out with it!"

But Pinocchio was as stubborn as ever.

"Are you deaf? Wait, young man, we'll get it from you in a twinkling!"

One of them grabbed the Marionette by the nose and the other by the chin, and they pulled him unmercifully from side to side in order to make him open his mouth.

All was of no use. The Marionette's lips might have been nailed together. They would not open.

In desperation the smaller of the two Assassins pulled out a long knife from his pocket, and tried to pry Pinocchio's mouth open with it.

Quick as a flash, the Marionette sank his teeth deep into the Assassin's hand, bit it off and spat it out. Fancy his surprise when he saw that it was not a hand, but a cat's paw.

Encouraged by this first victory, he freed himself from the claws of his assailers and, leaping over the bushes along the road, ran swiftly across the fields. His pursuers were after him at once, like two dogs chasing a hare.

After running seven miles or so, Pinocchio was well-nigh exhausted.

Seeing himself lost, he climbed up a giant pine tree and sat there to see what he could see. The Assassins tried to climb also, but they slipped and fell.

Far from giving up the chase, this only spurred them on. They gathered a bundle of wood, piled it up at the foot of the pine, and set fire to it.

In a twinkling the tree began to sputter and burn like a candle blown by the wind. Pinocchio saw the flames climb higher and higher. Not wishing to end his days as a roasted Marionette, he jumped quickly to the ground and off he went, the Assassins close to him, as before.

Dawn was breaking when, without any warning whatsoever, Pinocchio found his path barred by a deep pool full of water the color of muddy coffee.

What was there to do? With a "One, two, three!" he jumped clear across it. The Assassins jumped also, but not having measured their distance well —— splash!!! —— they fell right into the middle of the pool. Pinocchio who heard the splash and felt it, too, cried out, laughing, but never stopping in his race:

"A pleasant bath to you, signori!"

He thought they must surely be drowned and turned his head to see. But there were the two somber figures still following him, though their black sacks were drenched and dripping with water.

11

The Assassins chase Pinocchio, catch him, and hang him to the branch of a giant oak tree.

As he ran, the Marionette felt more and more certain that he would have to give himself up into the hands of his pursuers. Suddenly he saw a little cottage gleaming white as the snow among the trees of the forest.

"If I have enough breath left with which to reach that little house, I may be saved," he said to himself.

Not waiting another moment, he darted swiftly through the woods, the Assassins still after him.

After a hard race of almost an hour, tired and out of breath, Pinocchio finally reached the door of the cottage and knocked. No one answered.

He knocked again, harder than before, for behind him he heard the steps and the labored breathing of his persecutors. The same silence followed.

As knocking was of no use, Pinocchio, in despair, began to kick and bang against the door, as if he wanted to break it. At the noise, a window opened and a lovely maiden looked out. She had azure hair and a face white as wax. Her eyes were closed and her hands crossed on her breast.

With a voice so weak that it hardly could be heard, she whispered:

"No one lives in this house. Everyone is dead."

"Won't you, at least, open the door for me?" cried Pinocchio in a beseeching voice.

"I also am dead."

"Dead? What are you doing at the window, then?"

"I am waiting for the coffin to take me away."

After these words, the little girl disappeared and the window closed without a sound.

"Oh, Lovely Maiden with Azure Hair," cried Pinocchio, "open, I beg of you. Take pity on a poor boy who is being chased by two Assass —— "

He did not finish, for two powerful hands grasped him by the neck and the same two horrible voices growled threateningly: "Now we have you!"

The Marionette, seeing death dancing before him, trembled so hard that the joints of his legs rattled and the coins tinkled under his tongue.

"Well," the Assassins asked, "will you open your mouth now or not? Ah! You do not answer? Very well, this time you shall open it."

Taking out two long, sharp knives, they struck two heavy blows on the Marionette's back.

Happily for him, Pinocchio was made of very hard wood and the knives broke into a thousand pieces. The Assassins looked at each other in dismay, holding the handles of the knives in their hands.

"I understand," said one of them to the other, "there is nothing left to do now but to hang him."

"To hang him," repeated the other.

They tied Pinocchio's hands behind his shoulders and slipped the noose around his neck. Throwing the rope over the high limb of a giant oak tree, they pulled till the poor Marionette hung far up in space.

Satisfied with their work, they sat on the grass waiting for Pinocchio to give his last gasp. But after three hours the Marionette's eyes were still open, his mouth still shut and his legs kicked harder than ever.

Tired of waiting, the Assassins called to him mockingly: "Good-by till tomorrow. When we return in the morning, we hope you'll be polite enough to let us find you dead and gone and with your mouth wide open." With these words they went.

A few minutes went by and then a wild wind started to blow. As it shrieked and moaned, the poor little sufferer was blown to and fro like the hammer of a bell.

The rocking made him seasick and the noose, becoming tighter and tighter, choked him. Little by little a film covered his eyes.

Death was creeping nearer and nearer, and the Marionette still hoped for some good soul to come to his rescue, but no one appeared. As he was about to die, he thought of his poor old father, and hardly conscious of what he was saying, murmured to himself:

"Oh, Father, dear Father! If you were only here!"

These were his last words. He closed his eyes, opened his mouth, stretched out his legs, and hung there, as if he were dead.

 12

The Lovely Maiden with Azure Hair sends for the poor Marionette, puts him to bed, and calls three Doctors to tell her if Pinocchio is dead or alive.

If the poor Marionette had dangled there much longer, all hope would have been lost. Luckily for him, the Lovely Maiden with Azure Hair once again looked out of her window. Filled with pity at the sight of the poor little fellow being knocked helplessly about by the wind, she clapped her hands sharply together three times. At the signal, a loud whirr of wings in quick flight was heard and a large Falcon came and settled itself on the window ledge.

"What do you command, my charming Fairy?" asked the Falcon, bending his beak in deep reverence (for it must be known that, after all, the Lovely Maiden with Azure Hair was none other than a very kind Fairy who had lived, for more than a thousand years, in the vicinity of the forest).

"Do you see that Marionette hanging from the limb of that giant oak tree?"

"I see him."

"Very well. Fly immediately to him. With your strong beak, break the knot which holds him tied, take him down, and lay him softly on the grass at the foot of the oak."

The Falcon flew away and after two minutes returned, saying, "I have done what you have commanded."

"How did you find him? Alive or dead?"

"At first glance, I thought he was dead. But I found I was wrong, for as soon as I loosened the knot around his neck, he gave a long sigh and mumbled with a faint voice, 'Now I feel better!'"

The Fairy clapped her hands twice. A magnificent Poodle appeared, walking on his hind legs just like a man. He was dressed in court livery. A tricorn trimmed with gold lace was set at a rakish angle over a wig of white curls that dropped down to his waist. He wore a jaunty coat of chocolate-colored velvet, with diamond buttons, and with two huge pockets which were always filled with bones, dropped there at dinner by his loving mistress. Breeches of crimson velvet, silk stockings, and low, silver-buckled slippers completed his costume. His tail was encased in a blue silk covering, which was to protect it from the rain.

"Come, Medoro," said the Fairy to him. "Get my best coach ready and set out toward the forest. On reaching the oak tree, you will find a poor, half-dead Marionette stretched out on the grass. Lift him up tenderly, place him on the silken cushions of the coach, and bring him here to me."

The Poodle, to show that he understood, wagged his silk-covered tail two or three times and set off at a quick pace.

In a few minutes, a lovely little coach, made of glass, with lining as soft as whipped cream and chocolate pudding, and stuffed with canary feathers, pulled out of the stable. It was drawn by one hundred pairs of white mice, and the Poodle sat on the coachman's seat and snapped his whip gayly in the air, as if he were a real coachman in a hurry to get to his destination.

In a quarter of an hour the coach was back. The Fairy, who was waiting at the door of the house, lifted the poor little Marionette in her arms, took him to a dainty room with mother-of-pearl walls, put him to bed, and sent immediately for the most famous doctors of the neighborhood to come to her.

One after another the doctors came, a Crow, and Owl, and a Talking Cricket.

"I should like to know, signori," said the Fairy, turning to the three doctors gathered about Pinocchio's bed, "I should like to know if this poor Marionette is dead or alive."

At this invitation, the Crow stepped out and felt Pinocchio's pulse, his nose, his little toe. Then he solemnly pronounced the following words:

"To my mind this Marionette is dead and gone; but if, by any evil chance, he were not, then that would be a sure sign that he is still alive!"

"I am sorry," said the Owl, "to have to contradict the Crow, my famous friend and colleague. To my mind this Marionette is alive; but if, by any evil chance, he were not, then that would be a sure sign that he is wholly dead!"

"And do you hold any opinion?" the Fairy asked the Talking Cricket.

"I say that a wise doctor, when he does not know what he is talking about, should know enough to keep his mouth shut. However, that Marionette is not a stranger to me. I have known him a long time!"

Pinocchio, who until then had been very quiet, shuddered so hard that the bed shook.

"That Marionette," continued the Talking Cricket, "is a rascal of the worst kind."

Pinocchio opened his eyes and closed them again.

"He is rude, lazy, a runaway."

Pinocchio hid his face under the sheets.

"That Marionette is a disobedient son who is breaking his father's heart!"

Long shuddering sobs were heard, cries, and deep sighs. Think how surprised everyone was when, on raising the sheets, they discovered Pinocchio half melted in tears!

"When the dead weep, they are beginning to recover," said the Crow solemnly.

"I am sorry to contradict my famous friend and colleague," said the Owl, "but as far as I'm concerned, I think that when the dead weep, it means they do not want to die."

Pinocchio eats sugar, but refuses to take medicine. When the undertakers come for him, he drinks the medicine and feels better. Afterwards he tells a lie and, in punishment, his nose grows longer and longer.

As soon as the three doctors had left the room, the Fairy went to Pinocchio's bed and, touching him on the forehead, noticed that he was burning with fever.

She took a glass of water, put a white powder into it, and, handing it to the Marionette, said lovingly to him:

"Drink this, and in a few days you'll be up and well."

Pinocchio looked at the glass, made a wry face, and asked in a whining voice: "Is it sweet or bitter?"

"It is bitter, but it is good for you."

"If it is bitter, I don't want it."

"Drink it!"

"I don't like anything bitter."

"Drink it and I'll give you a lump of sugar to take the bitter taste from your mouth."

"Where's the sugar?"

"Here it is," said the Fairy, taking a lump from a golden sugar bowl.

"I want the sugar first, then I'll drink the bitter water."

"Do you promise?"

"Yes."

The Fairy gave him the sugar and Pinocchio, after chewing and swallowing it in a twinkling, said, smacking his lips:

"If only sugar were medicine! I should take it every day."

"Now keep your promise and drink these few drops of water. They'll be good for you."

Pinocchio took the glass in both hands and stuck his nose into it. He lifted it to his mouth and once more stuck his nose into it.

"It is too bitter, much too bitter! I can't drink it."

"How do you know, when you haven't even tasted it?"

"I can imagine it. I smell it. I want another lump of sugar, then I'll drink it."

The Fairy, with all the patience of a good mother, gave him more sugar and again handed him the glass.

"I can't drink it like that," the Marionette said, making more wry faces.

"Why?"

"Because that feather pillow on my feet bothers me."

The Fairy took away the pillow.

"It's no use. I can't drink it even now."

"What's the matter now?"

"I don't like the way that door looks. It's half open."

The Fairy closed the door.

"I won't drink it," cried Pinocchio, bursting out crying. "I won't drink this awful water. I won't. I won't! No, no, no, no!"

"My boy, you'll be sorry."

"I don't care."

"You are very sick."

"I don't care."

"In a few hours the fever will take you far away to another world."

"I don't care."

"Aren't you afraid of death?"

"Not a bit. I'd rather die than drink that awful medicine."

At that moment, the door of the room flew open and in came four Rabbits as black as ink, carrying a small black coffin on their shoulders.

"What do you want from me?" asked Pinocchio.

"We have come for you," said the largest Rabbit.

"For me? But I'm not dead yet!"

"No, not dead yet; but you will be in a few moments since you have refused to take the medicine which would have made you well."

"Oh, Fairy, my Fairy," the Marionette cried out, "give me that glass! Quick, please! I don't want to die! No, no, not yet —— not yet!"

And holding the glass with his two hands, he swallowed the medicine at one gulp.

"Well," said the four Rabbits, "this time we have made the trip for nothing."

And turning on their heels, they marched solemnly out of the room, carrying their little black coffin and muttering and grumbling between their teeth.

In a twinkling, Pinocchio felt fine. With one leap he was out of bed and into his clothes.

The Fairy, seeing him run and jump around the room gay as a bird on wing, said to him:

"My medicine was good for you, after all, wasn't it?"

"Good indeed! It has given me new life."

"Why, then, did I have to beg you so hard to make you drink it?"

"I'm a boy, you see, and all boys hate medicine more than they do sickness."

"What a shame! Boys ought to know, after all, that medicine, taken in time, can save them from much pain and even from death."

"Next time I won't have to be begged so hard. I'll remember those black Rabbits with the black coffin on their shoulders and I'll take the glass and pouf! —— down it will go!"

"Come here now and tell me how it came about that you found yourself in the hands of the Assassins."

"It happened that Fire Eater gave me five gold pieces to give to my Father, but on the way, I met a Fox and a Cat, who asked me, 'Do you want the five pieces to become two thousand?' And I said, 'Yes.' And they said, 'Come with us to the Field of Wonders.' And I said, 'Let's go.' Then they said, 'Let us stop at the Inn of the Red Lobster for dinner and after midnight we'll set out again.' We ate and went to sleep. When I awoke they were gone and I started out in the darkness all alone. On the road I met two Assassins dressed in black coal sacks, who said to me, 'Your money or your life!' and I said, 'I haven't any money'; for, you see, I had put the money under my tongue. One of them tried to put his hand in my mouth and I bit it off and spat it out; but it wasn't a hand, it was a cat's paw. And they ran after me and I ran and ran, till at last they caught me and tied my neck with a rope and hanged me to a tree, saying, 'Tomorrow we'll come back for you and you'll be dead and your mouth will be open, and then we'll take the gold pieces that you have hidden under your tongue.'"

"Where are the gold pieces now?" the Fairy asked.

"I lost them," answered Pinocchio, but he told a lie, for he had them in his pocket. As he spoke, his nose, long though it was, became at least two inches longer.

"And where did you lose them?"

"In the wood near by."

At this second lie, his nose grew a few more inches.

"If you lost them in the near-by wood," said the Fairy, "we'll look for them and find them, for everything that is lost there is always found."

"Ah, now I remember," replied the Marionette, becoming more and more confused. "I did not lose the gold pieces, but I swallowed them when I drank the medicine."

At this third lie, his nose became longer than ever, so long that he could not even turn around. If he turned to the right, he knocked it against the bed or into the windowpanes; if he turned to the left, he struck the walls or the door; if he raised it a bit, he almost put the Fairy's eyes out.

The Fairy sat looking at him and laughing.

"Why do you laugh?" the Marionette asked her, worried now at the sight of his growing nose.

"I am laughing at your lies."

"How do you know I am lying?"

"Lies, my boy, are known in a moment. There are two kinds of lies, lies with short legs and lies with long noses. Yours, just now, happen to have long noses."
Pinocchio, not knowing where to hide his shame, tried to escape from the room, but his nose had become so long that he could not get it out of the door.

 14

Pinocchio weeps upon learning that the Lovely Maiden with Azure Hair is dead. He meets a Pigeon, who carries him to the seashore. He throws himself into the sea to go to the aid of his father.

As soon as Pinocchio no longer felt the shameful weight of the dog collar around his neck, he started to run across the fields and meadows, and never stopped till he came to the main road that was to take him to the Fairy's house.
When he reached it, he looked into the valley far below him and there he saw the wood where unluckily he had met the Fox and the Cat, and the tall oak tree where he had been hanged; but though he searched far and near, he could not see the house where the Fairy with the Azure Hair lived.
He became terribly frightened and, running as fast as he could, he finally came to the spot where it had once stood. The little house was no longer there. In its place lay a small marble slab, which bore this sad inscription:

> HERE LIES
> THE LOVELY FAIRY WITH AZURE HAIR
> WHO DIED OF GRIEF
> WHEN ABANDONED BY
> HER LITTLE BROTHER PINOCCHIO

The poor Marionette was heartbroken at reading these words. He fell to the ground and, covering the cold marble with kisses, burst into bitter tears. He cried all night, and dawn found him still there, though his tears had dried and only hard, dry sobs shook his wooden frame. But these were so loud that they could be heard by the faraway hills.
As he sobbed he said to himself:
"Oh, my Fairy, my dear, dear Fairy, why did you die? Why did I not die, who am so bad, instead of you, who are so good? And my father —— where can he be? Please dear Fairy, tell me where he is and I shall never, never leave him again! You are not really dead, are you? If you love me, you will come back, alive as before. Don't you feel sorry for me? I'm so lonely. If the two Assassins come, they'll hang me again from the giant oak tree and I will really die, this time. What shall I do alone in the world? Now that you are dead and my father is lost, where shall I eat? Where shall I sleep? Who will make my new clothes? Oh, I want to die! Yes, I want to die! Oh, oh, oh!"

Poor Pinocchio! He even tried to tear his hair, but as it was only painted on his wooden head, he could not even pull it.

Just then a large Pigeon flew far above him. Seeing the Marionette, he cried to him:

"Tell me, little boy, what are you doing there?"

"Can't you see? I'm crying," cried Pinocchio, lifting his head toward the voice and rubbing his eyes with his sleeve.

"Tell me," asked the Pigeon, "do you by chance know of a Marionette, Pinocchio by name?"

"Pinocchio! Did you say Pinocchio?" replied the Marionette, jumping to his feet. "Why, I am Pinocchio!"

At this answer, the Pigeon flew swiftly down to the earth. He was much larger than a turkey.

"Then you know Geppetto also?"

"Do I know him? He's my father, my poor, dear father! Has he, perhaps, spoken to you of me? Will you take me to him? Is he still alive? Answer me, please! Is he still alive?"

"I left him three days ago on the shore of a large sea."

"What was he doing?"

"He was building a little boat with which to cross the ocean. For the last four months, that poor man has been wandering around Europe, looking for you. Not having found you yet, he has made up his mind to look for you in the New World, far across the ocean."

"How far is it from here to the shore?" asked Pinocchio anxiously.

"More than fifty miles."

"Fifty miles? Oh, dear Pigeon, how I wish I had your wings!"

"If you want to come, I'll take you with me."

"How?"

"Astride my back. Are you very heavy?"

"Heavy? Not at all. I'm only a feather."

"Very well."

Saying nothing more, Pinocchio jumped on the Pigeon's back and, as he settled himself, he cried out gayly:

"Gallop on, gallop on, my pretty steed! I'm in a great hurry."

The Pigeon flew away, and in a few minutes he had reached the clouds.

The Marionette looked to see what was below them. His head swam and he was so frightened that he clutched wildly at the Pigeon's neck to keep himself from falling.

They flew all day. Toward evening the Pigeon said:

"I'm very thirsty!"

"And I'm very hungry!" said Pinocchio.

"Let us stop a few minutes at that pigeon coop down there. Then we can go on and be at the seashore in the morning."

They went into the empty coop and there they found nothing but a bowl of water and a small basket filled with chick-peas.

The Marionette had always hated chick-peas. According to him, they had always made him sick; but that night he ate them with a relish. As he finished them, he turned to the Pigeon and said:

"I never should have thought that chick-peas could be so good!"

"You must remember, my boy," answered the Pigeon, "that hunger is the best sauce!"

After resting a few minutes longer, they set out again. The next morning they were at the seashore.

Pinocchio jumped off the Pigeon's back, and the Pigeon, not wanting any thanks for a kind deed, flew away swiftly and disappeared.

The shore was full of people, shrieking and tearing their hair as they looked toward the sea.

"What has happened?" asked Pinocchio of a little old woman.

"A poor old father lost his only son some time ago and today he built a tiny boat for himself in order to go in search of him across the ocean. The water is very rough and we're afraid he will be drowned."

"Where is the little boat?"

"There. Straight down there," answered the little old woman, pointing to a tiny shadow, no bigger than a nutshell, floating on the sea.

Pinocchio looked closely for a few minutes and then gave a sharp cry:

"It's my father! It's my father!"

Meanwhile, the little boat, tossed about by the angry waters, appeared and disappeared in the waves. And Pinocchio, standing on a high rock, tired out with searching, waved to him with hand and cap and even with his nose.

It looked as if Geppetto, though far away from the shore, recognized his son, for he took off his cap and waved also. He seemed to be trying to make everyone understand that he would come back if he were able, but the sea was so heavy that he could do nothing with his oars. Suddenly a huge wave came and the boat disappeared.

They waited and waited for it, but it was gone.

"Poor man!" said the fisher folk on the shore, whispering a prayer as they turned to go home.

Just then a desperate cry was heard. Turning around, the fisher folk saw Pinocchio dive into the sea and heard him cry out:

"I'll save him! I'll save my father!"

The Marionette, being made of wood, floated easily along and swam like a fish in the rough water. Now and again he disappeared only to reappear once more. In a

twinkling, he was far away from land. At last he was completely lost to view.
"Poor boy!" cried the fisher folk on the shore, and again they mumbled a few
prayers, as they returned home.

15

Pinocchio promises the Fairy to be good and to study, as he is growing tired of
being a Marionette, and wishes to become a real boy.

If Pinocchio cried much longer, the little woman thought he would melt away, so
she finally admitted that she was the little Fairy with Azure Hair.
"You rascal of a Marionette! How did you know it was I?" she asked, laughing.
"My love for you told me who you were."
"Do you remember? You left me when I was a little girl and now you find me a
grown woman. I am so old, I could almost be your mother!"
"I am very glad of that, for then I can call you mother instead of sister. For a
long time I have wanted a mother, just like other boys. But how did you grow so
quickly?"
"That's a secret!"
"Tell it to me. I also want to grow a little. Look at me! I have never grown higher
than a penny's worth of cheese."
"But you can't grow," answered the Fairy.
"Why not?"
"Because Marionettes never grow. They are born Marionettes, they live
Marionettes, and they die Marionettes."
"Oh, I'm tired of always being a Marionette!" cried Pinocchio disgustedly. "It's
about time for me to grow into a man as everyone else does."
"And you will if you deserve it —— "
"Really? What can I do to deserve it?"
"It's a very simple matter. Try to act like a well-behaved child."
"Don't you think I do?"
"Far from it! Good boys are obedient, and you, on the contrary —— "
"And I never obey."
"Good boys love study and work, but you —— "
"And I, on the contrary, am a lazy fellow and a tramp all year round."
"Good boys always tell the truth."
"And I always tell lies."
"Good boys go gladly to school."
"And I get sick if I go to school. From now on I'll be different."
"Do you promise?"
"I promise. I want to become a good boy and be a comfort to my father. Where is

my poor father now?"

"I do not know."

"Will I ever be lucky enough to find him and embrace him once more?"

"I think so. Indeed, I am sure of it."

At this answer, Pinocchio's happiness was very great. He grasped the Fairy's hands and kissed them so hard that it looked as if he had lost his head. Then lifting his face, he looked at her lovingly and asked: "Tell me, little Mother, it isn't true that you are dead, is it?"

"It doesn't seem so," answered the Fairy, smiling.

"If you only knew how I suffered and how I wept when I read 'Here lies —— '"

"I know it, and for that I have forgiven you. The depth of your sorrow made me see that you have a kind heart. There is always hope for boys with hearts such as yours, though they may often be very mischievous. This is the reason why I have come so far to look for you. From now on, I'll be your own little mother."

"Oh! How lovely!" cried Pinocchio, jumping with joy.

"You will obey me always and do as I wish?"

"Gladly, very gladly, more than gladly!"

"Beginning tomorrow," said the Fairy, "you'll go to school every day."

Pinocchio's face fell a little.

"Then you will choose the trade you like best."

Pinocchio became more serious.

"What are you mumbling to yourself?" asked the Fairy.

"I was just saying," whined the Marionette in a whisper, "that it seems too late for me to go to school now."

"No, indeed. Remember it is never too late to learn."

"But I don't want either trade or profession."

"Why?"

"Because work wearies me!"

"My dear boy," said the Fairy, "people who speak as you do usually end their days either in a prison or in a hospital. A man, remember, whether rich or poor, should do something in this world. No one can find happiness without work. Woe betide the lazy fellow! Laziness is a serious illness and one must cure it immediately; yes, even from early childhood. If not, it will kill you in the end."

These words touched Pinocchio's heart. He lifted his eyes to his Fairy and said seriously: "I'll work; I'll study; I'll do all you tell me. After all, the life of a Marionette has grown very tiresome to me and I want to become a boy, no matter how hard it is. You promise that, do you not?"

"Yes, I promise, and now it is up to you."

16

Pinocchio, instead of becoming a boy, runs away to the Land of Toys with his friend, Lamp-Wick.

Coming at last out of the surprise into which the Fairy's words had thrown him, Pinocchio asked for permission to give out the invitations.

"Indeed, you may invite your friends to tomorrow's party. Only remember to return home before dark. Do you understand?"

"I'll be back in one hour without fail," answered the Marionette.

"Take care, Pinocchio! Boys give promises very easily, but they as easily forget them."

"But I am not like those others. When I give my word I keep it."

"We shall see. In case you do disobey, you will be the one to suffer, not anyone else."

"Why?"

"Because boys who do not listen to their elders always come to grief."

"I certainly have," said Pinocchio, "but from now on, I obey."

"We shall see if you are telling the truth."

Without adding another word, the Marionette bade the good Fairy good-by, and singing and dancing, he left the house.

In a little more than an hour, all his friends were invited. Some accepted quickly and gladly. Others had to be coaxed, but when they heard that the toast was to be buttered on both sides, they all ended by accepting the invitation with the words, "We'll come to please you."

Now it must be known that, among all his friends, Pinocchio had one whom he loved most of all. The boy's real name was Romeo, but everyone called him Lamp-Wick, for he was long and thin and had a woebegone look about him. Lamp-Wick was the laziest boy in the school and the biggest mischief-maker, but Pinocchio loved him dearly.

That day, he went straight to his friend's house to invite him to the party, but Lamp-Wick was not at home. He went a second time, and again a third, but still without success.

Where could he be? Pinocchio searched here and there and everywhere, and finally discovered him hiding near a farmer's wagon.

"What are you doing there?" asked Pinocchio, running up to him.

"I am waiting for midnight to strike to go —— "

"Where?"

"Far, far away!"

"And I have gone to your house three times to look for you!"

"What did you want from me?"

"Haven't you heard the news? Don't you know what good luck is mine?"

"What is it?"

"Tomorrow I end my days as a Marionette and become a boy, like you and all my other friends."

"May it bring you luck!"

"Shall I see you at my party tomorrow?"

"But I'm telling you that I go tonight."

"At what time?"

"At midnight."

"And where are you going?"

"To a real country —— the best in the world —— a wonderful place!"

"What is it called?"

"It is called the Land of Toys. Why don't you come, too?"

"I? Oh, no!"

"You are making a big mistake, Pinocchio. Believe me, if you don't come, you'll be sorry. Where can you find a place that will agree better with you and me? No schools, no teachers, no books! In that blessed place there is no such thing as study. Here, it is only on Saturdays that we have no school. In the Land of Toys, every day, except Sunday, is a Saturday. Vacation begins on the first of January and ends on the last day of December. That is the place for me! All countries should be like it! How happy we should all be!"

"But how does one spend the day in the Land of Toys?"

"Days are spent in play and enjoyment from morn till night. At night one goes to bed, and next morning, the good times begin all over again. What do you think of it?"

"H'm —— !" said Pinocchio, nodding his wooden head, as if to say, "It's the kind of life which would agree with me perfectly."

"Do you want to go with me, then? Yes or no? You must make up your mind."

"No, no, and again no! I have promised my kind Fairy to become a good boy, and I want to keep my word. Just see: The sun is setting and I must leave you and run. Good-by and good luck to you!"

"Where are you going in such a hurry?"

"Home. My good Fairy wants me to return home before night."

"Wait two minutes more."

"It's too late!"

"Only two minutes."

"And if the Fairy scolds me?"

"Let her scold. After she gets tired, she will stop," said Lamp-Wick.

"Are you going alone or with others?"

"Alone? There will be more than a hundred of us!"

"Will you walk?"

"At midnight the wagon passes here that is to take us within the boundaries of that marvelous country."

"How I wish midnight would strike!"

"Why?"

"To see you all set out together."

"Stay here a while longer and you will see us!"

"No, no. I want to return home."

"Wait two more minutes."

"I have waited too long as it is. The Fairy will be worried."

"Poor Fairy! Is she afraid the bats will eat you up?"

"Listen, Lamp-Wick," said the Marionette, "are you really sure that there are no schools in the Land of Toys?" "Not even the shadow of one."

"Not even one teacher?"

"Not one."

"And one does not have to study?"

"Never, never, never!"

"What a great land!" said Pinocchio, feeling his mouth water. "What a beautiful land! I have never been there, but I can well imagine it."

"Why don't you come, too?"

"It is useless for you to tempt me! I told you I promised my good Fairy to behave myself, and I am going to keep my word."

"Good-by, then, and remember me to the grammar schools, to the high schools, and even to the colleges if you meet them on the way."

"Good-by, Lamp-Wick. Have a pleasant trip, enjoy yourself, and remember your friends once in a while."

With these words, the Marionette started on his way home. Turning once more to his friend, he asked him:

"But are you sure that, in that country, each week is composed of six Saturdays and one Sunday?"

"Very sure!"

"And that vacation begins on the first of January and ends on the thirty-first of December?"

"Very, very sure!"

"What a great country!" repeated Pinocchio, puzzled as to what to do.

Then, in sudden determination, he said hurriedly:

"Good-by for the last time, and good luck."

"Good-by."

"How soon will you go?"

"Within two hours."

"What a pity! If it were only one hour, I might wait for you."

"And the Fairy?"

"By this time I'm late, and one hour more or less makes very little difference."

"Poor Pinocchio! And if the Fairy scolds you?"

"Oh, I'll let her scold. After she gets tired, she will stop."

In the meantime, the night became darker and darker. All at once in the distance a small light flickered. A queer sound could be heard, soft as a little bell, and faint and muffled like the buzz of a far-away mosquito.

"There it is!" cried Lamp-Wick, jumping to his feet.

"What?" whispered Pinocchio.

"The wagon which is coming to get me. For the last time, are you coming or not?"

"But is it really true that in that country boys never have to study?"

"Never, never, never!"

"What a wonderful, beautiful, marvelous country! Oh —— h —— h!!"

 17

Pinocchio's ears become like those of a Donkey. In a little while he changes into a real Donkey and begins to bray.

Everyone, at one time or another, has found some surprise awaiting him. Of the kind which Pinocchio had on that eventful morning of his life, there are but few. What was it? I will tell you, my dear little readers. On awakening, Pinocchio put his hand up to his head and there he found —— Guess!

He found that, during the night, his ears had grown at least ten full inches!

You must know that the Marionette, even from his birth, had very small ears, so small indeed that to the naked eye they could hardly be seen. Fancy how he felt when he noticed that overnight those two dainty organs had become as long as shoe brushes!

He went in search of a mirror, but not finding any, he just filled a basin with water and looked at himself. There he saw what he never could have wished to see. His manly figure was adorned and enriched by a beautiful pair of donkey's ears.

I leave you to think of the terrible grief, the shame, the despair of the poor Marionette.

He began to cry, to scream, to knock his head against the wall, but the more he shrieked, the longer and the more hairy grew his ears.

At those piercing shrieks, a Dormouse came into the room, a fat little Dormouse, who lived upstairs. Seeing Pinocchio so grief-stricken, she asked him anxiously:

"What is the matter, dear little neighbor?"

"I am sick, my little Dormouse, very, very sick —— and from an illness which frightens me! Do you understand how to feel the pulse?"

"A little."

"Feel mine then and tell me if I have a fever."

The Dormouse took Pinocchio's wrist between her paws and, after a few minutes, looked up at him sorrowfully and said: "My friend, I am sorry, but I must give you some very sad news."

"What is it?"

"You have a very bad fever."

"But what fever is it?"

"The donkey fever."

"I don't know anything about that fever," answered the Marionette, beginning to understand even too well what was happening to him.

"Then I will tell you all about it," said the Dormouse. "Know then that, within two or three hours, you will no longer be a Marionette, nor a boy."

"What shall I be?"

"Within two or three hours you will become a real donkey, just like the ones that pull the fruit carts to market."

"Oh, what have I done? What have I done?" cried Pinocchio, grasping his two long ears in his hands and pulling and tugging at them angrily, just as if they belonged to another.

"My dear boy," answered the Dormouse to cheer him up a bit, "why worry now? What is done cannot be undone, you know. Fate has decreed that all lazy boys who come to hate books and schools and teachers and spend all their days with toys and games must sooner or later turn into donkeys."

"But is it really so?" asked the Marionette, sobbing bitterly.

"I am sorry to say it is. And tears now are useless. You should have thought of all this before."

"But the fault is not mine. Believe me, little Dormouse, the fault is all Lamp-Wick's."

"And who is this Lamp-Wick?"

"A classmate of mine. I wanted to return home. I wanted to be obedient. I wanted to study and to succeed in school, but Lamp-Wick said to me, 'Why do you want to waste your time studying? Why do you want to go to school? Come with me to the Land of Toys. There we'll never study again. There we can enjoy ourselves and be happy from morn till night.'"

"And why did you follow the advice of that false friend?"

"Why? Because, my dear little Dormouse, I am a heedless Marionette —— heedless and heartless. Oh! If I had only had a bit of heart, I should never have abandoned that good Fairy, who loved me so well and who has been so kind to me! And by this time, I should no longer be a Marionette. I should have become a real boy, like all these friends of mine! Oh, if I meet Lamp-Wick I am going to tell him what I think of him —— and more, too!"

After this long speech, Pinocchio walked to the door of the room. But when he reached it, remembering his donkey ears, he felt ashamed to show them to the public and turned back. He took a large cotton bag from a shelf, put it on his head, and pulled it far down to his very nose.

Thus adorned, he went out. He looked for Lamp-Wick everywhere, along the streets, in the squares, inside the theatres, everywhere; but he was not to be found. He asked everyone whom he met about him, but no one had seen him. In desperation, he returned home and knocked at the door.

"Who is it?" asked Lamp-Wick from within.

"It is I!" answered the Marionette.

"Wait a minute."

After a full half hour the door opened. Another surprise awaited Pinocchio! There in the room stood his friend, with a large cotton bag on his head, pulled far down to his very nose.

At the sight of that bag, Pinocchio felt slightly happier and thought to himself: "My friend must be suffering from the same sickness that I am! I wonder if he, too, has donkey fever?"

But pretending he had seen nothing, he asked with a smile:

"How are you, my dear Lamp-Wick?"

"Very well. Like a mouse in a Parmesan cheese."

"Is that really true?"

"Why should I lie to you?"

"I beg your pardon, my friend, but why then are you wearing that cotton bag over your ears?"

"The doctor has ordered it because one of my knees hurts. And you, dear Marionette, why are you wearing that cotton bag down to your nose?"

"The doctor has ordered it because I have bruised my foot."

"Oh, my poor Pinocchio!"

"Oh, my poor Lamp-Wick!"

An embarrassingly long silence followed these words, during which time the two friends looked at each other in a mocking way.

Finally the Marionette, in a voice sweet as honey and soft as a flute, said to his companion:

"Tell me, Lamp-Wick, dear friend, have you ever suffered from an earache?"

"Never! And you?"

"Never! Still, since this morning my ear has been torturing me."

"So has mine."

"Yours, too? And which ear is it?"

"Both of them. And yours?"

"Both of them, too. I wonder if it could be the same sickness."

"I'm afraid it is."

"Will you do me a favor, Lamp-Wick?"

"Gladly! With my whole heart."

"Will you let me see your ears?"

"Why not? But before I show you mine, I want to see yours, dear Pinocchio."

"No. You must show yours first."

"No, my dear! Yours first, then mine."

"Well, then," said the Marionette, "let us make a contract."

"Let's hear the contract!"

"Let us take off our caps together. All right?"

"All right."

"Ready then!"

Pinocchio began to count, "One! Two! Three!"

At the word "Three!" the two boys pulled off their caps and threw them high in air.

And then a scene took place which is hard to believe, but it is all too true. The Marionette and his friend, Lamp-Wick, when they saw each other both stricken by the same misfortune, instead of feeling sorrowful and ashamed, began to poke fun at each other, and after much nonsense, they ended by bursting out into hearty laughter.

They laughed and laughed, and laughed again —— laughed till they ached —— laughed till they cried.

But all of a sudden Lamp-Wick stopped laughing. He tottered and almost fell. Pale as a ghost, he turned to Pinocchio and said:

"Help, help, Pinocchio!"

"What is the matter?"

"Oh, help me! I can no longer stand up."

"I can't either," cried Pinocchio; and his laughter turned to tears as he stumbled about helplessly.

They had hardly finished speaking, when both of them fell on all fours and began running and jumping around the room. As they ran, their arms turned into legs, their faces lengthened into snouts and their backs became covered with long gray hairs.

This was humiliation enough, but the most horrible moment was the one in which the two poor creatures felt their tails appear. Overcome with shame and grief, they tried to cry and bemoan their fate.

But what is done can't be undone! Instead of moans and cries, they burst forth into loud donkey brays, which sounded very much like, "Haw! Haw! Haw!"

At that moment, a loud knocking was heard at the door and a voice called to them: "Open! I am the Little Man, the driver of the wagon which brought you here. Open, I say, or beware!"

18

Pinocchio, having become a Donkey, is bought by the owner of a Circus, who wants to teach him to do tricks. The Donkey becomes lame and is sold to a man who wants to use his skin for a drumhead.

Very sad and downcast were the two poor little fellows as they stood and looked at each other. Outside the room, the Little Man grew more and more impatient, and finally gave the door such a violent kick that it flew open. With his usual sweet smile on his lips, he looked at Pinocchio and Lamp-Wick and said to them: "Fine work, boys! You have brayed well, so well that I recognized your voices immediately, and here I am."

On hearing this, the two Donkeys bowed their heads in shame, dropped their ears, and put their tails between their legs.

At first, the Little Man petted and caressed them and smoothed down their hairy coats. Then he took out a currycomb and worked over them till they shone like glass. Satisfied with the looks of the two little animals, he bridled them and took them to a market place far away from the Land of Toys, in the hope of selling them at a good price.

In fact, he did not have to wait very long for an offer. Lamp-Wick was bought by a farmer whose donkey had died the day before. Pinocchio went to the owner of a circus, who wanted to teach him to do tricks for his audiences.

And now do you understand what the Little Man's profession was? This horrid little being, whose face shone with kindness, went about the world looking for boys. Lazy boys, boys who hated books, boys who wanted to run away from home, boys who were tired of school —— all these were his joy and his fortune. He took them with him to the Land of Toys and let them enjoy themselves to their heart's content. When, after months of all play and no work, they became little donkeys, he sold them on the market place. In a few years, he had become a millionaire.

What happened to Lamp-Wick? My dear children, I do not know. Pinocchio, I can tell you, met with great hardships even from the first day.

After putting him in a stable, his new master filled his manger with straw, but Pinocchio, after tasting a mouthful, spat it out.

Then the man filled the manger with hay. But Pinocchio did not like that any better.

"Ah, you don't like hay either?" he cried angrily. "Wait, my pretty Donkey, I'll teach you not to be so particular."

Without more ado, he took a whip and gave the Donkey a hearty blow across the legs.

Pinocchio screamed with pain and as he screamed he brayed:

"Haw! Haw! Haw! I can't digest straw!"

"Then eat the hay!" answered his master, who understood the Donkey perfectly.

"Haw! Haw! Haw! Hay gives me a headache!"

"Do you pretend, by any chance, that I should feed you duck or chicken?" asked the man again, and, angrier than ever, he gave poor Pinocchio another lashing.

At that second beating, Pinocchio became very quiet and said no more.

After that, the door of the stable was closed and he was left alone. It was many hours since he had eaten anything and he started to yawn from hunger. As he yawned, he opened a mouth as big as an oven.

Finally, not finding anything else in the manger, he tasted the hay. After tasting it, he chewed it well, closed his eyes, and swallowed it.

"This hay is not bad," he said to himself. "But how much happier I should be if I had studied! Just now, instead of hay, I should be eating some good bread and butter. Patience!"

Next morning, when he awoke, Pinocchio looked in the manger for more hay, but it was all gone. He had eaten it all during the night.

He tried the straw, but, as he chewed away at it, he noticed to his great disappointment that it tasted neither like rice nor like macaroni.

"Patience!" he repeated as he chewed. "If only my misfortune might serve as a lesson to disobedient boys who refuse to study! Patience! Have patience!"

"Patience indeed!" shouted his master just then, as he came into the stable. "Do you think, perhaps, my little Donkey, that I have brought you here only to give you food and drink? Oh, no! You are to help me earn some fine gold pieces, do you hear? Come along, now. I am going to teach you to jump and bow, to dance a waltz and a polka, and even to stand on your head."

Poor Pinocchio, whether he liked it or not, had to learn all these wonderful things; but it took him three long months and cost him many, many lashings before he was pronounced perfect.

The day came at last when Pinocchio's master was able to announce an extraordinary performance. The announcements, posted all around the town, and written in large letters, read thus:

GREAT SPECTACLE TONIGHT
LEAPS AND EXERCISES BY THE GREAT ARTISTS
AND THE FAMOUS HORSES
of the COMPANY
First Public Appearance of the FAMOUS DONKEY called PINOCCHIO
THE STAR OF THE DANCE
The Theater will be as Light as Day

That night, as you can well imagine, the theater was filled to overflowing one hour before the show was scheduled to start.

Not an orchestra chair could be had, not a balcony seat, nor a gallery seat; not even for their weight in gold.

The place swarmed with boys and girls of all ages and sizes, wriggling and dancing about in a fever of impatience to see the famous Donkey dance.

When the first part of the performance was over, the Owner and Manager of the circus, in a black coat, white knee breeches, and patent leather boots, presented himself to the public and in a loud, pompous voice made the following announcement:

"Most honored friends, Gentlemen and Ladies!

"Your humble servant, the Manager of this theater, presents himself before you tonight in order to introduce to you the greatest, the most famous Donkey in the world, a Donkey that has had the great honor in his short life of performing before the kings and queens and emperors of all the great courts of Europe. We thank you for your attention!"

This speech was greeted by much laughter and applause. And the applause grew to a roar when Pinocchio, the famous Donkey, appeared in the circus ring. He was handsomely arrayed. A new bridle of shining leather with buckles of polished brass was on his back; two white camellias were tied to his ears; ribbons and tassels of red silk adorned his mane, which was divided into many curls. A great sash of gold and silver was fastened around his waist and his tail was decorated with ribbons of many brilliant colors. He was a handsome Donkey indeed!

The Manager, when introducing him to the public, added these words:

"Most honored audience! I shall not take your time tonight to tell you of the great difficulties which I have encountered while trying to tame this animal, since I found him in the wilds of Africa. Observe, I beg of you, the savage look of his eye. All the means used by centuries of civilization in subduing wild beasts failed in this case. I had finally to resort to the gentle language of the whip in order to bring him to my will. With all my kindness, however, I never succeeded in gaining my Donkey's love. He is still today as savage as the day I found him. He still fears and hates me. But I have found in him one great redeeming feature. Do you see this little bump on his forehead? It is this bump which gives him his great talent of dancing and using his feet as nimbly as a human being. Admire him, O signori, and enjoy yourselves. I let you, now, be the judges of my success as a teacher of animals. Before I leave you, I wish to state that there will be another performance tomorrow night. If the weather threatens rain, the great spectacle will take place at eleven o'clock in the morning."

The Manager bowed and then turned to Pinocchio and said: "Ready, Pinocchio! Before starting your performance, salute your audience!"

Pinocchio obediently bent his two knees to the ground and remained kneeling until the Manager, with the crack of the whip, cried sharply: "Walk!"

The Donkey lifted himself on his four feet and walked around the ring. A few minutes passed and again the voice of the Manager called:

"Quickstep!" and Pinocchio obediently changed his step.

"Gallop!" and Pinocchio galloped.

"Full speed!" and Pinocchio ran as fast as he could. As he ran the master raised his arm and a pistol shot rang in the air.

At the shot, the little Donkey fell to the ground as if he were really dead.

A shower of applause greeted the Donkey as he arose to his feet. Cries and shouts and handclappings were heard on all sides.

At all that noise, Pinocchio lifted his head and raised his eyes. There, in front of him, in a box sat a beautiful woman. Around her neck she wore a long gold chain, from which hung a large medallion. On the medallion was painted the picture of a Marionette.

"That picture is of me! That beautiful lady is my Fairy!" said Pinocchio to himself, recognizing her. He felt so happy that he tried his best to cry out: "Oh, my Fairy! My own Fairy!"

But instead of words, a loud braying was heard in the theater, so loud and so long that all the spectators —— men, women, and children, but especially the children —— burst out laughing.

Then, in order to teach the Donkey that it was not good manners to bray before the public, the Manager hit him on the nose with the handle of the whip.

The poor little Donkey stuck out a long tongue and licked his nose for a long time in an effort to take away the pain.

And what was his grief when on looking up toward the boxes, he saw that the Fairy had disappeared!

He felt himself fainting, his eyes filled with tears, and he wept bitterly. No one knew it, however, least of all the Manager, who, cracking his whip, cried out: "Bravo, Pinocchio! Now show us how gracefully you can jump through the rings."

Pinocchio tried two or three times, but each time he came near the ring, he found it more to his taste to go under it. The fourth time, at a look from his master he leaped through it, but as he did so his hind legs caught in the ring and he fell to the floor in a heap.

When he got up, he was lame and could hardly limp as far as the stable.

"Pinocchio! We want Pinocchio! We want the little Donkey!" cried the boys from the orchestra, saddened by the accident.

No one saw Pinocchio again that evening.

The next morning the veterinary —— that is, the animal doctor — declared that he would be lame for the rest of his life.

"What do I want with a lame donkey?" said the Manager to the stableboy. "Take him to the market and sell him."

When they reached the square, a buyer was soon found.

"How much do you ask for that little lame Donkey?" he asked.

"Four dollars."

"I'll give you four cents. Don't think I'm buying him for work. I want only his skin. It looks very tough and I can use it to make myself a drumhead. I belong to a musical band in my village and I need a drum."

I leave it to you, my dear children, to picture to yourself the great pleasure with which Pinocchio heard that he was to become a drumhead!

As soon as the buyer had paid the four cents, the Donkey changed hands. His new owner took him to a high cliff overlooking the sea, put a stone around his neck, tied a rope to one of his hind feet, gave him a push, and threw him into the water.

Pinocchio sank immediately. And his new master sat on the cliff waiting for him to drown, so as to skin him and make himself a drumhead.

 19

Pinocchio is thrown into the sea, eaten by fishes, and becomes a Marionette once more. As he swims to land, he is swallowed by the Terrible Shark.

Down into the sea, deeper and deeper, sank Pinocchio, and finally, after fifty minutes of waiting, the man on the cliff said to himself:

"By this time my poor little lame Donkey must be drowned. Up with him and then I can get to work on my beautiful drum."

He pulled the rope which he had tied to Pinocchio's leg —— pulled and pulled and pulled and, at last, he saw appear on the surface of the water —— Can you guess what? Instead of a dead donkey, he saw a very much alive Marionette, wriggling and squirming like an eel.

Seeing that wooden Marionette, the poor man thought he was dreaming and sat there with his mouth wide open and his eyes popping out of his head.

Gathering his wits together, he said:

"And the Donkey I threw into the sea?"

"I am that Donkey," answered the Marionette laughing.

"You?"

"I."

"Ah, you little cheat! Are you poking fun at me?"

"Poking fun at you? Not at all, dear Master. I am talking seriously."

"But, then, how is it that you, who a few minutes ago were a donkey, are now standing before me a wooden Marionette?"

"It may be the effect of salt water. The sea is fond of playing these tricks."

"Be careful, Marionette, be careful! Don't laugh at me! Woe be to you, if I lose my patience!"

"Well, then, my Master, do you want to know my whole story? Untie my leg and

I can tell it to you better."

The old fellow, curious to know the true story of the Marionette's life, immediately untied the rope which held his foot. Pinocchio, feeling free as a bird of the air, began his tale:

"Know, then, that, once upon a time, I was a wooden Marionette, just as I am today. One day I was about to become a boy, a real boy, but on account of my laziness and my hatred of books, and because I listened to bad companions, I ran away from home. One beautiful morning, I awoke to find myself changed into a donkey —— long ears, gray coat, even a tail! What a shameful day for me! I hope you will never experience one like it, dear Master. I was taken to the fair and sold to a Circus Owner, who tried to make me dance and jump through the rings. One night, during a performance, I had a bad fall and became lame. Not knowing what to do with a lame donkey, the Circus Owner sent me to the market place and you bought me."

"Indeed I did! And I paid four cents for you. Now who will return my money to me?"

"But why did you buy me? You bought me to do me harm —— to kill me — to make a drumhead out of me!"

"Indeed I did! And now where shall I find another skin?"

"Never mind, dear Master. There are so many donkeys in this world."

"Tell me, impudent little rogue, does your story end here?"

"One more word," answered the Marionette, "and I am through. After buying me, you brought me here to kill me. But feeling sorry for me, you tied a stone to my neck and threw me to the bottom of the sea. That was very good and kind of you to want me to suffer as little as possible and I shall remember you always. And now my Fairy will take care of me, even if you —— "

"Your Fairy? Who is she?"

"She is my mother, and, like all other mothers who love their children, she never loses sight of me, even though I do not deserve it. And today this good Fairy of mine, as soon as she saw me in danger of drowning, sent a thousand fishes to the spot where I lay. They thought I was really a dead donkey and began to eat me. What great bites they took! One ate my ears, another my nose, a third my neck and my mane. Some went at my legs and some at my back, and among the others, there was one tiny fish so gentle and polite that he did me the great favor of eating even my tail."

"From now on," said the man, horrified, "I swear I shall never again taste fish. How I should enjoy opening a mullet or a whitefish just to find there the tail of a dead donkey!"

"I think as you do," answered the Marionette, laughing. "Still, you must know that when the fish finished eating my donkey coat, which covered me from head to foot, they naturally came to the bones —— or rather, in my case, to the wood, for as you know, I am made of very hard wood. After the first few bites, those greedy fish found out that the wood was not good for their teeth, and, afraid of indigestion, they turned and ran here and there without saying good-by or even as much as thank you to me. Here, dear Master, you have my story. You know now why you found a Marionette and not a dead donkey when you pulled me out of the water."

"I laugh at your story!" cried the man angrily. "I know that I spent four cents to get you and I want my money back. Do you know what I can do; I am going to take you to the market once more and sell you as dry firewood."

"Very well, sell me. I am satisfied," said Pinocchio. But as he spoke, he gave a quick leap and dived into the sea. Swimming away as fast as he could, he cried out, laughing:

"Good-by, Master. If you ever need a skin for your drum, remember me."

He swam on and on. After a while, he turned around again and called louder than before:

"Good-by, Master. If you ever need a piece of good dry firewood, remember me."

In a few seconds he had gone so far he could hardly be seen. All that could be seen of him was a very small black dot moving swiftly on the blue surface of the water, a little black dot which now and then lifted a leg or an arm in the air. One would have thought that Pinocchio had turned into a porpoise playing in the sun.

After swimming for a long time, Pinocchio saw a large rock in the middle of the sea, a rock as white as marble. High on the rock stood a little Goat bleating and calling and beckoning to the Marionette to come to her.

There was something very strange about that little Goat. Her coat was not white or black or brown as that of any other goat, but azure, a deep brilliant color that reminded one of the hair of the lovely maiden.

Pinocchio's heart beat fast, and then faster and faster. He redoubled his efforts and swam as hard as he could toward the white rock. He was almost halfway over, when suddenly a horrible sea monster stuck its head out of the water, an enormous head with a huge mouth, wide open, showing three rows of gleaming teeth, the mere sight of which would have filled you with fear.

Do you know what it was?

That sea monster was no other than the enormous Shark, which has often been mentioned in this story and which, on account of its cruelty, had been nicknamed "The Attila of the Sea" by both fish and fishermen.

Poor Pinocchio! The sight of that monster frightened him almost to death! He tried to swim away from him, to change his path, to escape, but that immense mouth kept coming nearer and nearer.

"Hasten, Pinocchio, I beg you!" bleated the little Goat on the high rock.

And Pinocchio swam desperately with his arms, his body, his legs, his feet.

"Quick, Pinocchio, the monster is coming nearer!"

Pinocchio swam faster and faster, and harder and harder.

"Faster, Pinocchio! The monster will get you! There he is! There he is! Quick, quick, or you are lost!"

Pinocchio went through the water like a shot —— swifter and swifter. He came close to the rock. The Goat leaned over and gave him one of her hoofs to help him up out of the water.

Alas! It was too late. The monster overtook him and the Marionette found himself in between the rows of gleaming white teeth. Only for a moment, however, for the Shark took a deep breath and, as he breathed, he drank in the Marionette as easily as he would have sucked an egg. Then he swallowed him so fast that Pinocchio, falling down into the body of the fish, lay stunned for a half hour.

When he recovered his senses the Marionette could not remember where he was. Around him all was darkness, a darkness so deep and so black that for a moment he thought he had put his head into an inkwell. He listened for a few moments and heard nothing. Once in a while a cold wind blew on his face. At first he could not understand where that wind was coming from, but after a while he understood that it came from the lungs of the monster. I forgot to tell you that the Shark was suffering from asthma, so that whenever he breathed a storm seemed to blow.

Pinocchio at first tried to be brave, but as soon as he became convinced that he was really and truly in the Shark's stomach, he burst into sobs and tears. "Help! Help!" he cried. "Oh, poor me! Won't someone come to save me?"

"Who is there to help you, unhappy boy?" said a rough voice, like a guitar out of tune.

"Who is talking?" asked Pinocchio, frozen with terror.

"It is I, a poor Tunny swallowed by the Shark at the same time as you. And what kind of a fish are you?"

"I have nothing to do with fishes. I am a Marionette."

"If you are not a fish, why did you let this monster swallow you?"

"I didn't let him. He chased me and swallowed me without even a 'by your leave'! And now what are we to do here in the dark?"

"Wait until the Shark has digested us both, I suppose."

"But I don't want to be digested," shouted Pinocchio, starting to sob.

"Neither do I," said the Tunny, "but I am wise enough to think that if one is born a fish, it is more dignified to die under the water than in the frying pan."

"What nonsense!" cried Pinocchio.

"Mine is an opinion," replied the Tunny, "and opinions should be respected."

"But I want to get out of this place. I want to escape."

"Go, if you can!"

"Is this Shark that has swallowed us very long?" asked the Marionette.

"His body, not counting the tail, is almost a mile long."

While talking in the darkness, Pinocchio thought he saw a faint light in the distance.

"What can that be?" he said to the Tunny.

"Some other poor fish, waiting as patiently as we to be digested by the Shark."

"I want to see him. He may be an old fish and may know some way of escape."

"I wish you all good luck, dear Marionette."

"Good-by, Tunny."

"Good-by, Marionette, and good luck."

"When shall I see you again?"

"Who knows? It is better not to think about it."

20

In the Shark's body Pinocchio finds whom? Read this chapter, my children, and you will know.

Pinocchio, as soon as he had said good-by to his good friend, the Tunny, tottered away in the darkness and began to walk as well as he could toward the faint light which glowed in the distance.

As he walked his feet splashed in a pool of greasy and slippery water, which had such a heavy smell of fish fried in oil that Pinocchio thought it was Lent.

The farther on he went, the brighter and clearer grew the tiny light. On and on he walked till finally he found —— I give you a thousand guesses, my dear children! He found a little table set for dinner and lighted by a candle stuck in a glass bottle; and near the table sat a little old man, white as the snow, eating live fish. They wriggled so that, now and again, one of them slipped out of the old man's mouth and escaped into the darkness under the table.

At this sight, the poor Marionette was filled with such great and sudden happiness that he almost dropped in a faint. He wanted to laugh, he wanted to cry, he wanted to say a thousand and one things, but all he could do was to stand still, stuttering and stammering brokenly. At last, with a great effort, he was able to let out a scream of joy and, opening wide his arms he threw them around the old man's neck.

"Oh, Father, dear Father! Have I found you at last? Now I shall never, never leave you again!"

"Are my eyes really telling me the truth?" answered the old man, rubbing his eyes. "Are you really my own dear Pinocchio?"

"Yes, yes, yes! It is I! Look at me! And you have forgiven me, haven't you? Oh, my dear Father, how good you are! And to think that I —— Oh, but if you only knew how many misfortunes have fallen on my head and how many troubles I have had! Just think that on the day you sold your old coat to buy me my A-B-C book so that I could go to school, I ran away to the Marionette Theater and the proprietor caught me and wanted to burn me to cook his roast lamb! He was the one who gave me the five gold pieces for you, but I met the Fox and the Cat, who took me to the Inn of the Red Lobster. There they ate like wolves and I left the Inn alone and I met the Assassins in the wood. I ran and they ran after me, always after me, till they hanged me to the branch of a giant oak tree. Then the Fairy of the Azure Hair sent the coach to rescue me and the doctors, after looking at me, said, 'If he is not dead, then he is surely alive,' and then I told a lie and my nose began to grow. It grew and it grew, till I couldn't get it through the door of the room. And then I went with the Fox and the Cat to the Field of Wonders to bury the gold pieces. The Parrot laughed at me and, instead of two thousand gold pieces, I found none. When the Judge heard I had been robbed, he sent me to jail to make the thieves happy; and when I came away I saw a fine bunch of grapes hanging on a vine. The trap caught me and the Farmer put a collar on me and made me a watchdog. He found out I was innocent when I caught the Weasels and he let me go. The Serpent with the tail that smoked started to laugh and a vein in his chest broke and so I went back to the Fairy's house. She was dead, and the Pigeon, seeing me crying, said to me, 'I have seen your father building a boat to look for you in America,' and I said to him, 'Oh, if I only had wings!' and he said to me, 'Do you want to go to your father?' and I said, 'Perhaps, but how?' and he said, 'Get on my back. I'll take you there.' We flew all night long, and next morning the fishermen were looking toward the sea, crying, 'There is a poor little man drowning,' and I knew it was you, because my heart told me so and I waved to you from the shore —— "

"I knew you also," put in Geppetto, "and I wanted to go to you; but how could I? The sea was rough and the whitecaps overturned the boat. Then a Terrible Shark came up out of the sea and, as soon as he saw me in the water, swam quickly toward me, put out his tongue, and swallowed me as easily as if I had been a chocolate peppermint."

"And how long have you been shut away in here?"

"From that day to this, two long weary years —— two years, my Pinocchio, which have been like two centuries."

"And how have you lived? Where did you find the candle? And the matches with which to light it —— where did you get them?"

"You must know that, in the storm which swamped my boat, a large ship also suffered the same fate. The sailors were all saved, but the ship went right to the bottom of the sea, and the same Terrible Shark that swallowed me, swallowed most of it."

"What! Swallowed a ship?" asked Pinocchio in astonishment.

"At one gulp. The only thing he spat out was the main-mast, for it stuck in his teeth. To my own good luck, that ship was loaded with meat, preserved foods, crackers, bread, bottles of wine, raisins, cheese, coffee, sugar, wax candles, and boxes of matches. With all these blessings, I have been able to live happily on for two whole years, but now I am at the very last crumbs. Today there is nothing left in the cupboard, and this candle you see here is the last one I have."

"And then?"

"And then, my dear, we'll find ourselves in darkness."

"Then, my dear Father," said Pinocchio, "there is no time to lose. We must try to escape."

"Escape! How?"

"We can run out of the Shark's mouth and dive into the sea."

"You speak well, but I cannot swim, my dear Pinocchio."

"Why should that matter? You can climb on my shoulders and I, who am a fine swimmer, will carry you safely to the shore."

"Dreams, my boy!" answered Geppetto, shaking his head and smiling sadly. "Do you think it possible for a Marionette, a yard high, to have the strength to carry me on his shoulders and swim?"

"Try it and see! And in any case, if it is written that we must die, we shall at least die together."

Not adding another word, Pinocchio took the candle in his hand and going ahead to light the way, he said to his father:

"Follow me and have no fear."

They walked a long distance through the stomach and the whole body of the Shark. When they reached the throat of the monster, they stopped for a while to wait for the right moment in which to make their escape.

I want you to know that the Shark, being very old and suffering from asthma and heart trouble, was obliged to sleep with his mouth open. Because of this, Pinocchio was able to catch a glimpse of the sky filled with stars, as he looked up through the open jaws of his new home.

"The time has come for us to escape," he whispered, turning to his father. "The Shark is fast asleep. The sea is calm and the night is as bright as day. Follow me closely, dear Father, and we shall soon be saved."

No sooner said than done. They climbed up the throat of the monster till they came to that immense open mouth. There they had to walk on tiptoes, for if they tickled the Shark's long tongue he might awaken —— and where would they be then? The tongue was so wide and so long that it looked like a country road. The two fugitives were just about to dive into the sea when the Shark sneezed very suddenly and, as he sneezed, he gave Pinocchio and Geppetto such a jolt that they found themselves thrown on their backs and dashed once more and very unceremoniously into the stomach of the monster.

To make matters worse, the candle went out and father and son were left in the dark.

"And now?" asked Pinocchio with a serious face.

"Now we are lost."

"Why lost? Give me your hand, dear Father, and be careful not to slip!"

"Where will you take me?"

"We must try again. Come with me and don't be afraid."

With these words Pinocchio took his father by the hand and, always walking on tiptoes, they climbed up the monster's throat for a second time. They then crossed the whole tongue and jumped over three rows of teeth. But before they took the last great leap, the Marionette said to his father: "Climb on my back and hold on tightly to my neck. I'll take care of everything else."

As soon as Geppetto was comfortably seated on his shoulders, Pinocchio, very sure of what he was doing, dived into the water and started to swim. The sea was like oil, the moon shone in all splendor, and the Shark continued to sleep so soundly that not even a cannon shot would have awakened him.

 21

Pinocchio finally ceases to be a Marionette and becomes a boy

"My dear Father, we are saved!" cried the Marionette. "All we have to do now is to get to the shore, and that is easy."

Without another word, he swam swiftly away in an effort to reach land as soon as possible. All at once he noticed that Geppetto was shivering and shaking as if with a high fever.

Was he shivering from fear or from cold? Who knows? Perhaps a little of both. But Pinocchio, thinking his father was frightened, tried to comfort him by saying: "Courage, Father! In a few moments we shall be safe on land."

"But where is that blessed shore?" asked the little old man, more andmore worried as he tried to pierce the faraway shadows. "Here I am searching on all sides and I see nothing but sea and sky."

"I see the shore," said the Marionette. "Remember, Father, that I am like a cat. I see better at night than by day."

Poor Pinocchio pretended to be peaceful and contented, but he was far from that. He was beginning to feel discouraged, his strength was leaving him, and his breathing was becoming more and more labored. He felt he could not go on much longer, and the shore was still far away.

He swam a few more strokes. Then he turned to Geppetto and cried out weakly: "Help me, Father! Help, for I am dying!"

Father and son were really about to drown when they heard a voice like a guitar
out of tune call from the sea:

"What is the trouble?"

"It is I and my poor father."

"I know the voice. You are Pinocchio."

"Exactly. And you?"

"I am the Tunny, your companion in the Shark's stomach."

"And how did you escape?"

"I imitated your example. You are the one who showed me the way and after you
went, I followed."

"Tunny, you arrived at the right moment! I implore you, for the love you bear your
children, the little Tunnies, to help us, or we are lost!"

"With great pleasure indeed. Hang onto my tail, both of you, and let me lead you.
In a twinkling you will be safe on land."

Geppetto and Pinocchio, as you can easily imagine, did not refuse the invitation;
indeed, instead of hanging onto the tail, they thought it better to climb on the
Tunny's back.

"Are we too heavy?" asked Pinocchio.

"Heavy? Not in the least. You are as light as sea-shells," answered the Tunny, who
was as large as a two-year-old horse.

As soon as they reached the shore, Pinocchio was the first to jump to the ground
to help his old father. Then he turned to the fish and said to him:

"Dear friend, you have saved my father, and I have not enough words with which
to thank you! Allow me to embrace you as a sign of my eternal gratitude."

The Tunny stuck his nose out of the water and Pinocchio knelt on the sand
and kissed him most affectionately on his cheek. At this warm greeting, the
poor Tunny, who was not used to such tenderness, wept like a child. He felt
so embarrassed and ashamed that he turned quickly, plunged into the sea, and
disappeared.

In the meantime day had dawned.

Pinocchio offered his arm to Geppetto, who was so weak he could hardly stand,
and said to him:

"Lean on my arm, dear Father, and let us go. We will walk very, very slowly, and
if we feel tired we can rest by the wayside."

"And where are we going?" asked Geppetto.

"To look for a house or a hut, where they will be kind enough to give us a bite of
bread and a bit of straw to sleep on."

They had not taken a hundred steps when they saw two rough-looking individuals
sitting on a stone begging for alms.

It was the Fox and the Cat, but one could hardly recognize them, they looked so
miserable. The Cat, after pretending to be blind for so many years had really lost

the sight of both eyes. And the Fox, old, thin, and almost hairless, had even lost his tail. That sly thief had fallen into deepest poverty, and one day he had been forced to sell his beautiful tail for a bite to eat.

"Oh, Pinocchio," he cried in a tearful voice. "Give us some alms, we beg of you! We are old, tired, and sick."

"Sick!" repeated the Cat.

"Addio, false friends!" answered the Marionette. "You cheated me once, but you will never catch me again."

"Believe us! Today we are truly poor and starving."

"Starving!" repeated the Cat.

"If you are poor; you deserve it! Remember the old proverb which says: 'Stolen money never bears fruit.' Addio, false friends."

"Have mercy on us!"

"On us."

"Addio, false friends. Remember the old proverb which says: 'Bad wheat always makes poor bread!'"

"Do not abandon us."

"Abandon us," repeated the Cat.

"Addio, false friends. Remember the old proverb: 'Whoever steals his neighbor's shirt, usually dies without his own.'"

Waving good-by to them, Pinocchio and Geppetto calmly went on their way.

After a few more steps, they saw, at the end of a long road near a clump of trees, a tiny cottage built of straw.

"Someone must live in that little hut," said Pinocchio. "Let us see for ourselves." They went and knocked at the door.

"Who is it?" said a little voice from within.

"A poor father and a poorer son, without food and with no roof to cover them," answered the Marionette.

"Turn the key and the door will open," said the same little voice.

Pinocchio turned the key and the door opened. As soon as they went in, they looked here and there and everywhere but saw no one.

"Oh —— ho, where is the owner of the hut?" cried Pinocchio, very much surprised.

"Here I am, up here!"

Father and son looked up to the ceiling, and there on a beam sat the Talking Cricket.

"Oh, my dear Cricket," said Pinocchio, bowing politely.

"Oh, now you call me your dear Cricket, but do you remember when you threw your hammer at me to kill me?"

"You are right, dear Cricket. Throw a hammer at me now. I deserve it! But spare my poor old father."

"I am going to spare both the father and the son. I have only wanted to remind you of the trick you long ago played upon me, to teach you that in this world of ours we must be kind and courteous to others, if we want to find kindness and courtesy in our own days of trouble."

"You are right, little Cricket, you are more than right, and I shall remember the lesson you have taught me. But will you tell how you succeeded in buying this pretty little cottage?"

"This cottage was given to me yesterday by a little Goat with blue hair."

"And where did the Goat go?" asked Pinocchio.

"I don't know."

"And when will she come back?"

"She will never come back. Yesterday she went away bleating sadly, and it seemed to me she said: 'Poor Pinocchio, I shall never see him again···the Shark must have eaten him by this time.'"

"Were those her real words? Then it was she —— it was —— my dear little Fairy," cried out Pinocchio, sobbing bitterly. After he had cried a long time, he wiped his eyes and then he made a bed of straw for old Geppetto. He laid him on it and said to the Talking Cricket:

"Tell me, little Cricket, where shall I find a glass of milk for my poor Father?"

"Three fields away from here lives Farmer John. He has some cows. Go there and he will give you what you want."

Pinocchio ran all the way to Farmer John's house. The Farmer said to him:

"How much milk do you want?"

"I want a full glass."

"A full glass costs a penny. First give me the penny."

"I have no penny," answered Pinocchio, sad and ashamed.

"Very bad, my Marionette," answered the Farmer, "very bad. If you have no penny, I have no milk."

"Too bad," said Pinocchio and started to go.

"Wait a moment," said Farmer John. "Perhaps we can come to terms. Do you know how to draw water from a well?"

"I can try."

"Then go to that well you see yonder and draw one hundred bucketfuls of water."

"Very well."

"After you have finished, I shall give you a glass of warm sweet milk."

"I am satisfied."

Farmer John took the Marionette to the well and showed him how to draw the water. Pinocchio set to work as well as he knew how, but long before he had pulled up the one hundred buckets, he was tired out and dripping with perspiration. He had never worked so hard in his life.

"Until today," said the Farmer, "my donkey has drawn the water for me, but now that poor animal is dying."

"Will you take me to see him?" said Pinocchio.

"Gladly."

As soon as Pinocchio went into the stable, he spied a little Donkey lying on a bed of straw in the corner of the stable. He was worn out from hunger and too much work. After looking at him a long time, he said to himself: "I know that Donkey! I have seen him before."

And bending low over him, he asked: "Who are you?"

At this question, the Donkey opened weary, dying eyes and answered in the same tongue: "I am Lamp-Wick."

Then he closed his eyes and died.

"Oh, my poor Lamp-Wick," said Pinocchio in a faint voice, as he wiped his eyes with some straw he had picked up from the ground.

"Do you feel so sorry for a little donkey that has cost you nothing?" said the Farmer. "What should I do —— I, who have paid my good money for him?"

"But, you see, he was my friend."

"Your friend?"

"A classmate of mine."

"What," shouted Farmer John, bursting out laughing. "What! You had donkeys in your school? How you must have studied!"

The Marionette, ashamed and hurt by those words, did not answer, but taking his glass of milk returned to his father.

From that day on, for more than five months, Pinocchio got up every morning just as dawn was breaking and went to the farm to draw water. And every day he was given a glass of warm milk for his poor old father, who grew stronger and better day by day. But he was not satisfied with this. He learned to make baskets of reeds and sold them. With the money he received, he and his father were able to keep from starving.

Among other things, he built a rolling chair, strong and comfortable, to take his old father out for an airing on bright, sunny days.

In the evening the Marionette studied by lamplight. With some of the money he had earned, he bought himself a secondhand volume that had a few pages missing, and with that he learned to read in a very short time. As far as writing was concerned, he used a long stick at one end of which he had whittled a long, fine point. Ink he had none, so he used the juice of blackberries or cherries. Little by little his diligence was rewarded. He succeeded, not only in his studies, but also in his work, and a day came when he put enough money together to keep his old father comfortable and happy. Besides this, he was able to save the great amount of fifty pennies. With it he wanted to buy himself a new suit.

One day he said to his father:

"I am going to the market place to buy myself a coat, a cap, and a pair of shoes.

When I come back I'll be so dressed up, you will think I am a rich man."

He ran out of the house and up the road to the village, laughing and singing. Suddenly he heard his name called, and looking around to see whence the voice came, he noticed a large snail crawling out of some bushes.

"Don't you recognize me?" said the Snail.

"Yes and no."

"Do you remember the Snail that lived with the Fairy with Azure Hair? Do you not remember how she opened the door for you one night and gave you something to eat?"

"I remember everything," cried Pinocchio. "Answer me quickly, pretty Snail, where have you left my Fairy? What is she doing? Has she forgiven me? Does she remember me? Does she still love me? Is she very far away from here? May I see her?"

At all these questions, tumbling out one after another, the Snail answered, calm as ever:

"My dear Pinocchio, the Fairy is lying ill in a hospital."

"In a hospital?"

"Yes, indeed. She has been stricken with trouble and illness, and she hasn't a penny left with which to buy a bite of bread."

"Really? Oh, how sorry I am! My poor, dear little Fairy! If I had a million I should run to her with it! But I have only fifty pennies. Here they are. I was just going to buy some clothes. Here, take them, little Snail, and give them to my good Fairy."

"What about the new clothes?"

"What does that matter? I should like to sell these rags I have on to help her more. Go, and hurry. Come back here within a couple of days and I hope to have more money for you! Until today I have worked for my father. Now I shall have to work for my mother also. Good-by, and I hope to see you soon."

The Snail, much against her usual habit, began to run like a lizard under a summer sun.

When Pinocchio returned home, his father asked him:

"And where is the new suit?"

"I couldn't find one to fit me. I shall have to look again some other day."

That night, Pinocchio, instead of going to bed at ten o'clock waited until midnight, and instead of making eight baskets, he made sixteen.

After that he went to bed and fell asleep. As he slept, he dreamed of his Fairy, beautiful, smiling, and happy, who kissed him and said to him, "Bravo, Pinocchio! In reward for your kind heart, I forgive you for all your old mischief. Boys who love and take good care of their parents when they are old and sick, deserve praise even though they may not be held up as models of obedience and good behavior. Keep on doing so well, and you will be happy."

At that very moment, Pinocchio awoke and opened wide his eyes.

What was his surprise and his joy when, on looking himself over, he saw that he was no longer a Marionette, but that he had become a real live boy! He looked all about him and instead of the usual walls of straw, he found himself in a beautifully furnished little room, the prettiest he had ever seen. In a twinkling, he jumped down from his bed to look on the chair standing near. There, he found a new suit, a new hat, and a pair of shoes.

As soon as he was dressed, he put his hands in his pockets and pulled out a little leather purse on which were written the following words:

The Fairy with Azure Hair returns

fifty pennies to her dear Pinocchio

with many thanks for his kind heart.

The Marionette opened the purse to find the money, and behold — there were fifty gold coins!

Pinocchio ran to the mirror. He hardly recognized himself. The bright face of a tall boy looked at him with wide-awake blue eyes, dark brown hair and happy, smiling lips.

Surrounded by so much splendor, the Marionette hardly knew what he was doing. He rubbed his eyes two or three times, wondering if he were still asleep or awake and decided he must be awake.

"And where is Father?" he cried suddenly. He ran into the next room, and there stood Geppetto, grown years younger overnight, spick and span in his new clothes and gay as a lark in the morning. He was once more Mastro Geppetto, the wood carver, hard at work on a lovely picture frame, decorating it with flowers and leaves, and heads of animals.

"Father, Father, what has happened? Tell me if you can," cried Pinocchio, as he ran and jumped on his Father's neck.

"This sudden change in our house is all your doing, my dear Pinocchio," answered Geppetto.

"What have I to do with it?"

"Just this. When bad boys become good and kind, they have the power of making their homes gay and new with happiness."

"I wonder where the old Pinocchio of wood has hidden himself?"

"There he is," answered Geppetto. And he pointed to a large Marionette leaning against a chair, head turned to one side, arms hanging limp, and legs twisted under him.

After a long, long look, Pinocchio said to himself with great content:

"How ridiculous I was as a Marionette! And how happy I am, now that I have become a real boy!"